Early Evita.

Patti

Lu

CROWN
ARCHETYPE

A Memoir by
Patti LuPone

WITH DIGBY DIEHL

Library of Congress Cataloging-in-Publication Data
LuPone, Patti.
    Patti LuPone: a memoir / Patti LuPone.—1st ed.
    1. LuPone, Patti. 2. Singers—United States—Biography.
    3. Actors—United States—Biography. I. Title.
    ML420.L9355A3   2010
    782.1'4092—dc22
    [B]   2010008965

ISBN 978-0-307-46073-8

Printed in the United States of America

DESIGN BY BARBARA STURMAN

10 9 8 7 6 5 4 3 2 1

First Edition

For

MATT AND JOSH,

my family

contents

*I*t's a curious thing. I suppose most people think of

artists as impatient, but I don't know of any first-rate

artist who hasn't manifested in his career an appalling

patience, a willingness to wait, and to do his best *now*

in the expectation that next year he will do better.

—MARK VAN DOREN
(from *The Dialogues of Archibald MacLeish and Mark Van Doren*)

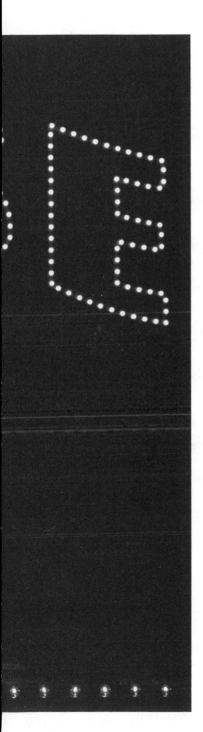

Prologue

Opening Night, *Gypsy*

BROADWAY, 2008

I've opened *Gypsy* four times. The first time, I played Louise (aka Gypsy) in the Patio Players' production of the musical. I was fifteen years old. The Patio Players were a group of kids from Northport, Long Island, who got together in the summer and performed big Broadway musicals on Cathy Sheldon's patio. Cathy was a founding member of the Patio Players as well as our star. In just a few short years these productions, attended by many in the Northport community, began to take their toll on the Sheldons' patio and lawn, so David Babcock, our artistic director, approached the superintendent of Northport Schools. We were miraculously given permission to run amok in the junior high school parking lot, where we built the sets, in the home economics classroom, where we created the costumes (when they weren't being sewn on volunteer mothers' sewing machines), and in the auditorium, where we would now present our musicals. We were a big operation.

All I remember about opening night, at Middleville Junior High School, was that the live lamb freaked out in the spotlight while I was singing Louise's song "Little Lamb." He broke free from me and started clomping and *bah*-ing all over the darkened stage. I learned how to sing through laughter that night. He was fine in the dress rehearsal. Opening night nerves, I guess. You know what they say: "Good dress, bad opening" and vice versa. Most likely he had indigestion from eating my mother's laundry. I was in charge of the sheep for some reason . . . bonding, perhaps? I recall my mother screaming at me on opening day, "Patti Ann! Tie up that damn sheep!"

```
         THE PATIO PLAYERS
              present

         G Y P S Y
          A MUSICAL FABLE
          by Sondheim & Styne
   Directed by            David Babcock
   Music Direction         Jim Kennedy
   Choreography       Patti Ann LuPone
   CAST: In order of appearance
Poster Girls:      Sue Houghton, Jane Shacklett
Uncle Jocko                   Phil Caggiano
George                         Dave Search
Balloon Girl                 Janet Kennard
Baby Louise                   Mary Lavery
Baby June                     Pam Mitchell
Rose                         Cathy Sheldon
Pop                           Curtis Salke
Newsboys: Sean West, John Florence, Walter Gar-
          della, Dana Contino, Jeffrey Shotwell.
Webber                        Phil Caggiano
Herbie                         Lou Trapani
Louise                        Patti LuPone
June                         Nanci Shotwell
Tulsa                          Bo Whitney
Yonkers                       Tom Brennan
Angie                          Dave Search
L.A.                         Peter Contino
Mr. Kringelein                   Rich Rice
Mrs. Goldstone               Kathie Lavery
Miss Cratchitt                Sue Moschini
Hollywood Starlets:
  Agnes-Mary Feeney, Marjorie Maynell Wade,
  Toni Gardella, Wendy Fehse, Barbara Jo Gergle,
  Cathy Trapani
Pasty                         Tom Brennan
Tessie Tura                  Peggy Kennedy
Mazeppa                      Nanci Shotwell
Cigar                         Phil Caggiano
Electra                      Kathie Lavery
Maid                         Connie Fabian
Phil                       Mickey Franklin
Children:  Dana Contino, Wendy Fehse,
           Sidonie Contino
Chowsie                      Babette Kopeck
      by special arrangement with
            TAMS-WITMARK
```

Lambs are born in the spring. We performed in the summer. The lamb was, unfortunately, a sheep. This sheep was going crazy. I was afraid the sheep would fall into the orchestra pit in his desperate attempt to escape. Somehow as I continued singing the tender ballad on a pitch-black stage with only a blue tinted spotlight on me, the frantic sheep was caught before he crapped on every-thing. They put him in the boys' bathroom offstage right, unaware that the tiled bathroom would increase the volume and reverber-ate his *bah*-ing throughout the theatre. At poignant moments in the play, we would hear the plaintive wail of a very unhappy sheep. That's all I remember—except for stripping in front of my biology teacher.

Forty-four years later in August 2006, I opened *Gypsy* for the second time. Only this time I was playing the character of Rose at the Ravinia Festival in Highland Park, Illinois.

The Ravinia Festival, on the grounds of Ravinia Park, is the oldest outdoor music festival in the country. From June till Sep-tember, the festival presents concerts and performances for thou-sands of people who sit in the Pavilion Theatre, or in Martin Hall, or picnic on the lawn. Whenever I walk the grounds, I think what a great way for a kid to grow up—climbing the kid-friendly sculp-tures while Beethoven, played by the Chicago Symphony Orches-tra, is wafting into their tiny subconscious minds. Ravinia has a very large, multigenerational, and loyal audience plus some of the hippest camping equipment I've ever seen. The people with lawn tickets are serious about their concert-going experience. On any given night you can see linen, crystal, and Crock-Pots on Eddie Bauer tables inside L.L. Bean tents.

A musical theatre production presented on the Pavilion stage requires intense preparation and a certain amount of abandon because you have at the most two weeks to put on a Broadway musical. This *Gypsy* was highly anticipated because for half of those forty-four years I had been told by fans, friends, and col-leagues that I should play Rose Hovick, Gypsy and June's mother. When I read the script I did not see the "monster stage mother" that had become the standard description of Rose. I hooked into her love for her children and her desire to do only her best for them, however misguided those intentions were. That's the way I wanted to play her. It was a departure.

My director, Lonny Price, cast a company of extraordinary performers. I was told that some of the "farm boys" flew in from New York City just to audition for it. Lonny somehow convinced the CEO of the festival, Welz Kauffman, that he needed three weeks of rehearsal for this production, which would include our technical week. The technical week is when all the physical elements of the production come together for the first time onstage: sets, lights, props, costumes, staging, and choreography. Everybody involved works ten hours a night trying to coordinate all these elements while also attempting to get the show to under two hours of playing time. It's an exhausting week . . . then we open! Who came up with that schedule, I'd love to know.

The lawn of the Ravinia Festival can accommodate up to 14,000 people. The Pavilion Theatre seats 3,200 people. Most Broadway houses seat half as many as the Pavilion. If a production is successful at Ravinia, we play to over ten thousand people a night. As I understand it, the Pavilion and the lawn were heavily sold for the three nights we performed *Gypsy*. I don't remember much about this opening night. I was too nervous. I don't think I gave anybody an opening night card, which is simply a note of good luck and gratitude: one of the theatre's sweet traditions. I just buried my head, focused, and went out there.

Word of mouth about this *Gypsy* was so good that various producers began vying for the rights to remount this production in London or New York. I waited for word from Lonny Price that Arthur Laurents, who is the show's librettist and controls the rights, would give the consent for the production to proceed. It was a frustrating wait.

Finally I called my longtime friend and press agent, Philip Rinaldi, for his advice. He asked me what my relationship with producer Scott Rudin was. Scott was Arthur Laurents's best friend. Philip suggested that I call Scott. I did but I couldn't get past the receptionist. Philip then called Scott's partner, press agent John Barlow. John paved the way for Scott and me to connect. Scott simply told me to call Arthur Laurents myself. Now, there is a long story here concerning Arthur and me and my banishment from Arthur's work, which included *Gypsy*.

It all started when Arthur offered me his play *Jolson Sings Again*. I didn't do it, but let's save that story for another chapter.

For the moment let's just say Arthur Laurents was really mad at me—really, really mad at me. I now had to call Arthur and plead with him to bring *Gypsy* back to New York only five years after the last revival. I dialed the number. Arthur answered. "Hello, Arthur, it's Patti."

"Yes, I know," he said. I cringed, waiting for the onslaught of five years of Arthur's pent-up anger that was sure to follow. Instead, what I got was a compliment on my performance as Nellie Lovett in *Sweeney Todd.* WHAT?

Then we began to talk about *Gypsy*. He said he wanted to do it, that he would also direct it, and that this production of *Gypsy* would be different. He wanted less bravura and more acting. We talked about casting. We talked about Rose, and I said up front that I couldn't play her as she had been played in the past. There would be no point in bringing *Gypsy* back to Broadway if I couldn't do my interpretation of Rose—under his direction, of course. He agreed.

Arthur mulled over offers from the various producers and settled on Jack Viertel's Encores! Summer Stars series at City Center. The City Center Encores! series brings musicals back to life that would most likely never see another revival. The shows are performed only three times. However, the Encores! Summer Stars series gives these productions a longer run. We had a home in New York. We were off and running. There was never another word about *Jolson Sings Again*.

We went into rehearsal in June 2007. The cast was the best I have ever worked with in my career. Arthur directed me wisely, lovingly, and supportively. We put the past behind us and forged a friendship. I got to work with one of Broadway's best actors, Boyd Gaines, and I discovered that beautiful jewel Laura Benanti.

City Center would not pay for the entire company to rehearse for three weeks, so Arthur wisely asked Jack Viertel if he could have the eleven principals for the first week. Jack agreed. We sat around a table listening to Arthur talk about this musical and what it meant to him while he interjected great, gossipy stories about the original players and a couple of other celebrities he knew. We were spellbound. The room was filled with love and laughter. Boyd, Laura, and I questioned Arthur relentlessly about the meaning of certain scenes. Arthur started to rethink his script as perhaps he had never done before. That one very special week around the table allowed us to explore what I consider to be the best book of a musical ever written.

We opened in July of 2007. I barely remember this opening night, because the pressure was on me. This was not Highland Park, Illinois. This was New York City, New York. I don't think I gave opening night cards to the company on this occasion, either. Maybe I did. All I know is that I loved being in the City Center building again. I consider it one of my theatrical homes in Manhattan. It's where I performed with The Acting Company in the seventies, and where I'd done two very successful performances for Encores! (one of which was my first time back on a New York stage after an unfortunate excursion to London—more about that later). The theatre was not new to me: one important obstacle eliminated.

The audience was rapturous on opening night. Before the show, the producers of City Center and all of the potential Broadway producers came to my dressing room and were over the moon with happiness. We opened gloriously. We just knew we were moving to Broadway. Then Ben Brantley's review came out, followed by Charles Isherwood's review, both in the *New York Times.* They were duly unimpressed with my performance. Regardless, we were sold out for our entire run with near-hysterical audiences. At the end, it appeared I would only play *Gypsy* in three productions and never make it to Broadway. But fate had something else in store. It's absolutely true: If it's meant to be, it will be. Despite tepid reviews from the *Times,* on March 27, 2008, we opened our City Center production at the St. James Theatre on Broadway.

We went through another three-week rehearsal period with Arthur, most of it spent around our beloved table, reading and investigating the play once again. When I revisited Rose, she had sunk further down into my gut and my psyche. I came back to her more centered and calm. The greatest joy I could have gotten was that our entire City Center Company minus one person—Nancy Opel—reprised their roles. It was a reunion of old friends and recognizable characters.

Broadway opening nights are a relief, but that's not what they used to be. They used to be the most hair-raising and nerve-racking performance of the run because it was the night that all of the critics showed up. Today the critics see the play in the last week of previews, so opening night is about family, friends, and the friends of the 25,000 producers. This time I had the presence of mind to be the leading lady and distribute the gifts and good wishes to everybody in the St. James Theatre.

Whenever I return to Broadway, I try to have the same people in my dressing room. It's my insurance that there will be laughter in that room. I had the inimitable Pat White, my very own Thelma Ritter, as my dresser; Vanessa Anderson as my hairdresser; Laura Skolnik of the Ravinia Festival as my personal assistant; and Pam Combs Lyster, one of my oldest friends, to pick up the slack. Angelina Avallone, Broadway's premier makeup artist, was there as well, in and out of the room. I was surrounded by five of the most fantastic women I will ever hope to associate with in the theatre.

I was calm on opening night, knowing that the ladies of the dressing room had distributed my cards and gifts in the morning before I got to the theatre. I arrived in plenty of time to read the cards attached to the flowers my friends had sent me, and to negotiate all of the people coming in and out of my dressing room wishing me luck. Champagne was uncorked. My husband, Matt, and son, Joshua, stayed with me till curtain, the producers came in and out with love and hugs, my longtime friends stopped by for a kiss, cast members threw me luck. Steve Sondheim sat on the couch and chatted with Matt and me about anything and everything. Everybody had a drink in their hand and a huge smile on their face. I was ready, I was in costume, it was fifteen minutes to the places call. Steve wished me luck and left to take his seat. At ten minutes to places, Arthur walked into my dressing room.

The room emptied as if on cue, except for Matt. There was a look in Arthur's eye that totally scared me. I knew he was going to tell me something that I didn't want to hear. He said it, anyway: "I know the review from the *New York Times*." Tears started to well up in his eyes and I said in my mind, *No, no, please, Arthur, no. Don't tell me now! I have to go out and do this show.*

"You got what you deserve. It's a rave," he said. We started crying and hugged each other. It was a rave for all of us. But it was more than that for me; it was vindication. Matt grabbed Arthur and said, "Have you actually seen it?" Matt would not believe it until he saw it with his own eyes.

Places for the company was called. Matt and Arthur left my dressing room. Pat White and I walked to the back of the house, Pat making me laugh as always, and both of us relieved we were finally opening the show. Besides everything else it implied, it meant no more twelve-hour days in technical rehearsals.

The overture began and the audience went nuts. On my cue, I walked down the house right aisle and up onto the stage to an ovation I couldn't see but could certainly hear. I kept my back to the audience and waited to start. I was exhausted from everything—the rehearsals, the previews, the sickness I always get when I walk into a new theatre, the long and fated road to Broadway, finally playing Rose in *Gypsy*. When the ovation died down, I played the show as we had rehearsed it. I went to the opening night party for about an hour, went home with Matt and Joshua, and the next day settled in for the Broadway run of Arthur Laurents's, Jule Styne's, and Stephen Sondheim's *Gypsy*, my fourth production. The following story is about what happened to me from the time I fell in love with the audience at age four, to that crazy sheep in the boys' room at Middleville Junior High School, to my closing night at the St. James Theatre. . . .

Northport, Long Island

1949–1968

Early cheesecake.

I remember the day I fell in love with the stage as if it were yesterday.

When I was four, my father was principal of the Ocean Avenue Elementary School, the only elementary school in my hometown of Northport, Long Island. He started an after-school program, and one item on the curriculum was dance with Miss Marguerite in the school auditorium. I was enrolled. At the end of the school year, we performed a recital called "There's Nothing Like Dancing." It was June 1953. I wore a black Capezio jazz skirt, leotard, and tap shoes. I was downstage right, dancing furiously. I looked out at the audience, and even though it was mostly the parents of the other kids in the recital, I thought that they were all looking at me. *Hey, they're all smiling at me. I can't get in trouble up here. I can do whatever I want, and they'll still smile at me.* I knew from then on that I would spend my life on the stage, because in fact what I really fell in love with was the audience.

The way the family tells it, my brother Bobby saw me in a hula skirt, fell in love with the costume, and followed me into dance. He was seven and I was four. I never looked back. In fact, neither of us did.

My mother and father were first-generation Americans. My grandparents, the maternal Pattis and the paternal LuPones, came over from Sicily and Abruzzo to start a new life in America. They settled in Jamestown and Dunkirk, New York. Neither set of grandparents spoke English, so a lot of Italian was spoken in the houses, but none was spoken to the grandkids. Both families were boisterous and full of laughter, but the Pattis took the prize for the amount of noise

The night I fell in love with the audience at Miss Marguerite's recital.

they could make at a single gathering. There were hints of theatrical blood from a few of the adults, but it was when my mother pulled out the *Encyclopaedia Britannica* and reverently showed me a picture of my great-grandaunt, Adelina Patti, the famous nineteenth-century coloratura, that my voice and my oversized emotional personality started to make sense. *I'm small, but the voice and personality are BIG,* I thought. *Must be in the genes.*

There's a family rumor that Grandma Patti was a bootlegger. They say she hid the liquor under the floorboards of a sewing room and could smell the cops coming a mile away. Grandpa Patti was murdered before I was born, and the other rumor was that Grandma was somehow involved. According to the *Jamestown Evening Journal* of October 10, 1927:

Awakened by two men early Sunday morning, James Patti, 42, was lured from his home on Lakewood Road and shot to death by gunmen who are being sought by the Sheriff's Department. Mystery surrounds the motive for the crime, which baffles authorities. The slaying took place on Howard Avenue, near Patti's home shortly after 5:30 o'clock in a dense fog, which covered the gruesome scene. Patti's son George with Carmelo Calabrese, who was a material witness, found Patti lying in a pool of blood caused by three wounds in his head. . . . [In the past] both Patti and his wife have been arrested on charges of bootlegging. . . . Those who were subjected to the most questioning were Patti's wife, the son George, the daughter Angelina [MY MOTHER!], and Carmelo Calabrese, their neighbor. . . . The widow of the slain man and his daughter [MY MOTHER!] were not locked up, but Calabrese and the Patti youth, George, were kept in jail yesterday but last night all were released except Calabrese.

For two people who couldn't speak a word of English, there was a lot of money in that household. I often wondered just where the money came from. The theory that my grandparents were bootleggers made sense, and personally I loved it. I didn't find any of this out until after my mother's death, when I was researching my family history. I asked one of my cousins about the murder. He turned ashen and said he was sworn to secrecy, but confirmed that yes, somehow Grandma was involved.

It didn't surprise me. My grandmother wasn't a very warm woman. In fact, she was kind of scary. She rarely smiled and had a tough countenance. Not that she didn't love us. She *did* . . . her way. I remember Sunday-morning phone calls between my mother and Grandma—my mother always ending up in tears. I would ask her why she was crying. She said she missed her mother. I wonder if they were discussing Grandpa's murder. I'll never know because they were talking in Italian!

They never did solve Grandpa's murder. When I was fourteen years old, there was an incident where my mother almost let the cat out of the bag. I was standing at the kitchen sink daydreaming. My mother sidled up to me with a small sepia picture of a shirtless man in swimming trunks with his back to the camera. I looked over and asked, "Who's that?"

My mother replied, "Your real grandfather, my father."

"Well, who's the guy I think is my real grandfather?"

Silence.

I waited, then I asked, "Well, what happened to this guy in the picture?"

"I don't know," she responded, then turned and walked away. I was dumbfounded. The Patti household—money and secrets.

My mother and her sisters were fashion plates, beautifully coiffed and dressed, but it was Aunt Tina who wanted to go on the stage. She was the middle sister, dark-haired and beautiful. She took bellydancing lessons and sang whenever she could. With no

From left to right: Tina, Mom, Ann, and Grandma. What a bunch of babes.

solicitation from us she would gyrate and start screeching, most times in an apron with flour on her face. My mother couldn't hold a tune or dance to save her life. She was so devoid of theatrical blood that, later, when Bobby and I were established, she famously said, "I wish you two would stop flitting from job to job!"

"But Ma, the jobs don't last."

My mother was not a stage mother in any respect. She was an American housewife until she and my dad got divorced when I was twelve. My dad had had a dalliance with a substitute teacher. My parents had been married for thirty years, and back then nobody got divorced. The rug was pulled out from under my mother, so she threw her energy into her kids. My twin brothers Billy and Bobby and I were all she had left. She felt ostracized from the community, from the school my dad was principal of, and from the Catholic Church, which frowned on divorce. The humiliation was too much for her to take. Her children became the focus and purpose of her life. The divorce freed me to pursue my dream. Dad wanted all of us to be teachers. Mom's life force was driving us from one lesson to the next. If she was a stage mother, it manifested itself in her pride in her three kids.

I went from dance with Miss Marguerite at the Ocean Avenue Elementary School to the Donald and Rosalie Grant Dance Studio, ending up at the André & Bonnie Dance Studio on Jericho Turnpike in Huntington. André was French, very exotic for Jericho Turnpike, Long Island. He and his wife, Bonnie, created routines for brother-and-sister acts. June and Timmy Gage had a great act. She was a contortionist, so in their routine she was the puppet and Timmy was the puppeteer. Of all the acts that André created, it was my favorite because of June's ability. The positions she could get her body into were amazing. She was a star as far as I was concerned—if she'd just get those buckteeth fixed. There

*Miss
Marguerite's
dance class,
in costume.*

was also Louella and Vincent Milillo. Their name used to make me laugh. They, however, had no sense of humor. Their act was a tango, as I recall.

My twin brothers and I did an adagio waltz to "Belle of the Ball." We were the LuPone Trio. All of us kids were a motley group that performed all over Long Island and Manhattan—Kiwanis clubs, Rotary clubs, the Jones Beach boardwalk, the old Piccadilly Hotel in New York City—and there was Mom, driving Billy, Bobby, and me to our dance recitals. Elaborate costumes were hand sewn, beaded, and sequined if they didn't come out of the trunk from some French revue that André had brought with him from Paris to Jericho Turnpike, Huntington, Long Island. It was the fifties, but it felt like vaudeville. We were troupers on a circuit, albeit the Long Island circuit.

Bobby and Billy had matching outfits with cummerbunds. I was in a white ball gown. I still hadn't grown into my lips. We appeared on Ted Mack's *Original Amateur Hour*. The television show had a live audience, and although it was a family show and many of

The LuPone Trio.

the performers were kids, the audience warm-up guy was a very lowbrow comedian. His jokes were filthy and hysterical. It was my first real introduction to professional show business.

It was also a rude introduction to the world of television. The studio was dirty and the atmosphere was gritty with a no-nonsense "let's get this done" attitude backstage. I was wearing a little tiara, and during the afternoon rehearsal one of the stagehands walked up to me and sprayed something on it—it was a dulling spray because the tiara was too shiny for the TV lights. He then said, "Open your mouth," sprayed the same stuff on my braces and walked away. No introduction, no explanation, no apology. I was thirteen.

But that was nothing compared to what happened next. Bobby and I were hanging underneath a stairwell between the camera rehearsal and the live show when we heard somebody from the program tell one of the contestants with a southern accent and his manager that he would win the contest that night. This was *before* airtime—before we had performed, before *anyone* had performed and the audience had voted. The two of us looked at each other—we couldn't believe what we were hearing. We tried not to believe that Ted Mack's *Original Amateur Hour* was fixed. But what other explanation could there be, especially after the kid from Mississippi, who sang "I Left My Heart in San Francisco," won? Bobby and I ran and told our mother and our dance teachers, but they didn't believe us, or they didn't want to believe us. It was quite an experience. I gave up my junior high school prom for *The Amateur Hour* only to find out that it was fixed. Nothing much changed in my young life, but I added the word "jaded" to my vocabulary . . . that and "dulling spray."

I went back to being a student in Northport. For the most part, school was fun but boring. What inspired me was the Northport school system's incredibly strong music department. I'd started private piano lessons with Miss JoAnn Oberg at seven years old. My mom made me sit up straight and practice one hour every day. I hated practicing, but I loved Miss Oberg. When I turned eight, my third-grade class was led into the Ocean Avenue Elementary School auditorium and told to choose an instrument from the two large posters up on the stage. We were to pick either a band instrument or an orchestra instrument. I said "harp." There was no harp at our elementary school, but my classmate Kathy McCusker whispered the word "cello" to me, so I started playing the cello. I continued to play it until my senior year in high school.

As a junior, I started playing the sousaphone in the Northport High School marching band. Our bandleader, Robert Krueger, was a graduate of Northwestern University and was able to get the most current Northwestern musical arrangements and marching routines. People came to the football games as much to see the band as to see the football team. We had an all-girl sousaphone line. I wanted in because the marching band went to a summer camp with another high school from Nassau County. It was very sexy. (The camp, not the marching band.) We learned routines during the day, and at night there was a whole new crop of boys. One summer, I was quarantined for a week because of extremely bad behavior. When one of my favorite teachers, Esther Scott, came to my room to keep me

company, she laughed her head off because it was full of boys bent on doing the same thing.

In school, what I loved most of all, besides recess, was chorus. I met Esther Scott in junior high. She was the chorus master. When I entered high school, Esther coincidentally made the transition with me. I was incredibly blessed to have her for six years.

When she met my brother Bobby and me, she recognized our talent, supported it, and elevated it. We remain very close friends to this day. While Billy gravitated toward the science department, Bobby and I became her protégés. In addition to nurturing our talent, she also protected us, especially me, because I got into so much trouble in high school. Esther once found me hiding in her office to avoid the assistant principal, who was pacing the hallways of the music department shouting, "Where are you, LuPone? I know you're here somewhere. When I get my hands on you . . . !" Esther laughed when she discovered me under her desk—how unusual for a teacher. There was an irreverence about her that was deeply

Esther and me on the football field at Northport High School.

appreciated by all of her students. Oh, and the trouble I would get into as a child and a teenager is the same trouble I get into now as an adult approaching senior status. I rarely turn down a dare. I want to laugh and have fun, however dangerous or rude. "The

My brother, Bobby, in Jardin aux Lilas, *Juilliard Dance Division.*

© ELIZABETH SAWYER

edge" has always been extremely seductive. All of this equals trouble in my world, but what fun I've had.

I only wanted to listen to Esther. I had no interest in math, science, history, or English. My heart belonged to the music department. It was the only place that I truly studied anything, and it was there that I learned to continue pursuing what I knew was my calling.

Esther helped me expand my horizons far beyond Northport. I attended All-County, All-State, and All-Eastern in chorus. Each of these events made up a single band, orchestra, and chorus. All-County was selected musicians and singers from the high schools in Suffolk County; All-State was again a select few from the high schools in New York State. All-Eastern was the culmination of all of these efforts. We were the best music students from the high schools on the eastern seaboard. You had to audition to participate, and luckily I made it into all three choruses. When I was in the All-Eastern chorus, I was struck by how much talent was out there. During one rehearsal, as I sat in the soprano section, I was humbled and stunned. I stopped singing and started listening. I started asking myself questions: What is this desire I have? What do I need to do to be as good as these people behind me, in front of me, all around me? I went back to Mrs. Scott and talked about my experience.

"You've been bit," she told me. "The rest of your life will be about this investigation."

I remember that my junior high school guidance counselor asked me what I wanted my high school major to be. I told him music. He told me that was not possible, that I had to major in something academic.

"Then why did you ask me?" I said. "I want to major in music."

"You can't do that," he insisted.

I solved the problem my own way. I don't know how I graduated from high school. The only classes I remember showing up for were music. To my mind, the department was filled with the most interesting kids—the misfits, the musical geniuses, the math whizzes, and just a few greasers because music was fun. Our teachers loved what they were teaching, and I loved those teachers because of that. How could you not learn? The music department was alive, inspired, and passionate. I was never out of the vicinity of the department. I attended my other classes, but ultimately the only lessons that stuck were coming out of the music department or out of Mrs. Scott's heart and soul.

Under her guidance, our chorus was selected to sing for NYSSMA, the New York State School Music Association, which was a very prestigious honor. Mrs. Scott was thrilled that our chorus had been selected. She chose an original piece, Arthur Fracken-pohl's *Te Deum,* and she chose me to sing the soprano solo. The convention was held at the Concord Hotel in the Catskill Mountains. It was December. We drove up from Northport the day before and stayed overnight. The morning of the performance I woke up with a fever. I couldn't swallow—it hurt so badly every time I did. I didn't know what was wrong with me and I was too scared to tell anybody except my closest friends. I had several hours before the concert and I continued to get sicker. I was terrified that I wouldn't be able to sing, let alone stand through the performance. It was my first test. Would I be able to overcome this illness and sing the solo? Was this just a case of stage fright? Did I have the inner strength to endure whatever lay ahead for me in this business? There was somebody else who could have sung the part if I was too sick, but this was my first big solo. My name was in the program. I couldn't let myself down. I couldn't let Mrs. Scott down. I had to tell her that I was sick. To this day I can see Esther standing in front of me. She asked me whether I could do it, and I said, "I think I can."

"Then do it," she said.

Before we took the stage, she told us about her son, Gary, who was severely handicapped.

"Would you sing this for Gary?" she asked us. "Music is his joy and the only thing he responds to." Esther didn't cry as she spoke about him, but we did because of her simple request and her moving words. That night she instilled something in us greater than our teenage self-absorption. Whenever Esther spoke, everyone sat up straight and listened. Her compassion and wisdom were uplifting and helped us all transcend the petty disputes and mundane occurrences that were part of our daily school lives. She changed us with the music she chose for us, with the experiences she shared with us, and with the experiences she created for us. After everybody stopped crying, the chorus walked out on that stage with a different physicality, a different posture. We simply carried ourselves taller. There was pride, seriousness, focus—something that removed our egos from the equation and let the music soar.

Swallowing was so painful that I didn't sing a note until I got to my solo. Then I did what I've done all my life. I opened up my mouth and sang . . . "Vouchsafe, O Lord, to keep us this day" . . . the opening words. My voice cracked coming off the F above middle C, but I didn't let it sink me. I did it. We all did it—for Esther and for Gary. At the end of the concert, Esther did something I've never forgotten. She acknowledged the applause but for only a brief second. She turned back and gave us the ovation. The pride and the accomplishment we felt was so heady and like nothing I'd ever felt before. It wasn't the applause as much as it was the feeling of achievement and success. It was an incredible experience and a huge life lesson for all of us.

From that point on, I've never backed down from any test or any challenge. But it took everything I had to get through the performance. As soon as I came offstage, a doctor was on hand, and I was diagnosed with a 105-degree fever and the worst case of tonsillitis the doctor had ever seen. They put me in a car with the assistant principal (the one always chasing me down corridors) for the ride back to Northport. I was lying down in the backseat with a paper bag nearby in case I got sick to my stomach, but the irony did not escape me. The biggest success of my life was being shared with the man who didn't give a shit about our music department and who would've expelled me if he could've. No Esther Scott, no Philip Caggiano or Suzi Walzer, close classmates, no Bo Whitney, my best friend, who held my hand and supported me all through the concert. Just the assistant principal!

And though I was on the verge of wretching in the backseat and isolated from the celebration on the bus, I realized this achievement marked the beginning of the ownership of my talent, the responsibility to it and to the path that chose me at four years old.

The Audition

2

The Juilliard School of Music.

SAMUEL H. GOTTSCHO

May 6, 1968

Dear Miss LuPone:

The scholarship committee of the Drama Division has considered your application for financial aid and will award you a scholarship of $1,200 for the year 1968–69, to be applied against tuition costs. I hope this award will make your attending Juilliard practicable. . . .

Huh? What? No way . . . really? Okay, I guess.

In truth I didn't want to go to Juilliard. I didn't want to go to college at all. I'd known since I was four years old what I was going to do with my life, but my mother wanted me to finish my education, which meant college. Bobby, who had attended the Dance Division at Juilliard, told me the school was starting a drama division, so I auditioned to please my mother and brother. The audition took place a year after my graduation from high school. I honestly didn't care if I got in or not.

During my senior year of high school, singing had become my main focus. My private voice teacher suggested that I audition for Juilliard's Preparatory Division, which was designed to train students ages six through eighteen in the various disciplines of music. I auditioned and was accepted. I studied classical singing, technique, and music theory.

Every Saturday morning I took the Long Island Rail Road from Northport to New York City and then by subway on to Juilliard, which at the time was on West 122nd Street in Harlem. I spent my Saturdays smoking cigarettes on the train. (Remember when you could smoke on trains? Remember when you could smoke?) I then took a voice lesson with a bejangled, bejeweled Marian Mandarin. I didn't learn anything, but that wasn't entirely her fault. She was a good teacher, but I didn't *understand* her teaching methods. She was one of many singing teachers I didn't understand. All I did was imitate her vocal quality and technique, never knowing whether the imitation was correct or whether it suited my voice. Her appearance distracted me as well. She was quite a sight for a seventeen-year-old. Her arms were covered in bangles. Her ten fingers had rings on eight of them. Her hair was clipped and pinned on top of her head in a state of confusion, the clips perilously on the verge of flying into my face when she gesticulated. She would look at me confused. I looked back at her even more confused. Clearly, nothing I did captured her imagination, so in my lesson I just imitated her and snuck peeks at the clock, waiting for the hour to end. Juilliard Preparatory got me nowhere except out of Northport on a Saturday. I take that back. I *loved* music theory and my teacher. However, I wasn't planning on becoming an opera singer.

At the end of the year I had to sing in a recital, knowing that my voice wasn't in the best shape. I truly didn't realize how poorly I sang until I looked at my mother's and my brother's faces afterward. They were embarrassed for me. Then I was embarrassed for me. Still, I didn't care because I didn't want to be an opera singer. The Broadway lights were beckoning. However uninspired the preparatory experience was, I let Marian Mandarin convince me to audition for Juilliard's Opera Department. As far as auditions go, this one was classic. One judge was reading a book, the second judge was filing her nails, the last judge held his head in his hands as he stared at the table. I sang the aria as I watched the totally disinterested panel. I knew my fate, but I didn't care. I lie. I cared a little because I realized I failed in the audition. No one wants to fail in an audition regardless of whether you want the part or not.

A year later, auditions for the newly formed Drama Division were being held at the school on 122nd Street—Juilliard was expanding, and a new building at Lincoln Center was under construction. I arrived pretty much hoping for the same fate, which was no admittance to the prestigious school, but I was eager to impress them, anyway. My classical speech was Kate's epilogue from *The Taming of the Shrew*. My contemporary monologue was Dolly Levi's money speech from *The Matchmaker*. When I finished the classical speech, an older man with a red face and white hair and beard came to the foot of the stage. "I don't think that's what Shakespeare had in mind," he said. It was John Houseman, one half of the artistic directorship of the Drama Division at the Juilliard School. The other half was Michel Saint-Denis, an actor, director, and drama theorist. Among his long list of credits, he co-directed the Royal Shakespeare Company. John Houseman was a prominent producer known most notably for his collaboration with Orson Welles and would become even better known for his Oscar-winning portrayal of Professor Kingsfield in both the movie and television series of *The Paper Chase*. These men created the Drama Division of the Juilliard School—pretty impressive lineage. However, on that particular day, John Houseman wasn't quite the intimidating figure he would later come to epitomize. I wasn't intimidated because I was sure I didn't care whether I got in or not.

After I finished my contemporary speech, the Drama Division panel asked me to do an improvisation. From the darkened theatre where they sat, there was a pause . . . a longish pause. Then someone said, "You've just received a rejection letter from the Drama Division of the Juilliard School." Without thought or preparation I played the scene thus—I walked stage right from where I was standing to an imaginary mailbox. I opened the mailbox with a key, pulled out my mail, flipped through it until I came to "the letter." I saw the address on the envelope, ripped it open in excitement, and read it . . . pause . . . then tossed it over my shoulder and walked away. Big laugh. *I got them*, I thought. They asked me if I could sing. I ran through a mental list of the songs I knew. Inspiration struck with Comden and Green's "You Mustn't Be Discouraged" from *Fade Out, Fade In,* a humorous salute to the idea that however bad things are, they could always get worse. I opened my mouth and out it came. That was the key that unlocked my admission to the school. They called me off the stage into the house, where they surrounded me. They asked me a lot of questions. The one I remember was, Did I play an instrument? I told them the tuba, which was true, but also funny. I left the audition happy because I didn't fail . . . and realized, yes, in fact, I do care whether I got in or not.

One of the reasons I didn't want to go to Juilliard was that I was enjoying my newly independent life in New York City.

Right after graduation from Northport High School, I moved into Manhattan, where I shared a hundred-dollar-a-month sixth-floor walk-up railroad flat with my friend Pam Combs. I found a job right away working at Civic & Co. selling button-down shirts. The owner, Norman Civic, let me take time off for auditions. I was making money. I had a roof over my head. I was auditioning. I'd known pretty much all my life where I would end up—the Broadway Musical Stage—and I was determined to pursue it.

The Making of an Actor

3

Catherine in A View from the Bridge, *1970.*

ESTATE OF DIANE GORODNITZKI

_S_o in May 1968, despite my flippant audition, Juilliard admitted me and even gave me a scholarship—$1,200 for the first year against tuition costs. The remaining tuition was $350. On the acceptance letter is a handwritten note from John Houseman: "That was a very interesting audition."

You never can tell. The less you care, the freer you are.

That first class of the Drama Division was called Group 1— or as I like to call it, "36 lunatics." I was among the tamer lunatics in the group. It seems my teachers' intentions were to take thirty-six of the craziest people they could find across America and train them to become Juilliard actors—actors who would have a very solid technique in vocal production, diction, and acting, and who could play the classics, whether they were American, English, French, or Russian. _Crazy,_ however, was the operative word for my class—and each of us was crazy in our own unique way. Not that the teachers weren't a little loony themselves. Actually, they were as crazy as we were. We just outnumbered them.

On our first day Mr. Houseman assembled the class and famously said to us, "Look to your right, now look to your left. One of you won't be here next year." And thus we began our training in the Drama Division of the Juilliard School. Scared? Intimidated? Happy as clams to be there? We didn't know what hit us from day one.

We were divided into four sections: A, B, C, and D. There were nine students to a section. I was in Group A. Group D stood for "drugs." Most of the students who didn't return for our second year were in that group. The speech and voice departments were headed by Edith Skinner and Elizabeth Smith, respectively. They didn't much care for me, especially Edith Skinner. She wrote the book *Speak with Distinction,* which acting schools still use today. Edith was as much of a character as my voice teacher from Juilliard Preparatory was. She'd come to class looking like a Hollywood contract player from the 1940s, in little dresses, bleached hair, and a lot of makeup, some of it smeared. She could pinpoint your hometown within forty miles by listening to your accent. It was her goal to rid the students of their regionalisms and teach them to speak with a mid-Atlantic accent. This class was extremely technical, but Edith lost me that first year when she put her hands around my throat, shook me, and said, "I'm going to make a lady out of you yet."

"The bet's on," I said to myself.

In that first year, in one of her classes, she introduced us to the diphthong. After we finished "meeting" the diphthong, she slowly walked to the wall of windows, drew back the curtain, and said, "Well, children, we are freeeeeeee. We are out of the fooorrreeeeessstt. We are saaaaiiilling on the Hudson River. Sis, boooomm, baaahhhhh." I thought she'd lost her mind.

However nuts I thought Edith was, she was a brilliant teacher.

Our teachers were all brilliant in their way, and they included
Michael Kahn, Moni Yakim, Liz Smith, and Marian Seldes. Marian
Seldes was my savior at Juilliard. She directed me several times
and had an unfailing confidence in my ability. She was also my
biggest defender. I was more often than not left off the main stage
production cast list. I would be put in a smaller play in a studio,
and Marian would more often than not direct that particular production. She accepted my quirkiness and knew how to connect
with me so that I would eventually understand her concept and
direction of the play. She knew better than most of my teachers
how to bring the best out of me. Boris Tumarin, a Russian director,
was another teacher able to focus my rambunctious spirit. Both
of these people went to bat for me whenever Mr. Houseman had
reservations about my involvement in the class.

Moni Yakim's class was all about movement, focus, and re-
laxation. We loved him. In that first year, one of my classmates,
Larry Reiman, kind of lost his mind. At the end of class the actors
would run in a circle before we lay down on the floor while Moni
walked around and touched each of our third eyes. One day while
running in the circle, Larry started peeling off his clothes until he
was naked. It was a bit disconcerting to the faculty, but it was considered expression, not unexpected or even shocking . . . except to
us. He eventually did lose his mind and vanished from the school,
from his apartment, from Manhattan, never to be seen or heard
from again, only to appear as a lone figure in a parking lot of a
Holiday Inn in Norman, Oklahoma, after we students had become
The Acting Company seven years later. We pulled into the Holiday
Inn and Mary Lou Rosato screamed at the top of her lungs, *"Oh
my God!* It's Larry Reiman!" We clambered to the front of the bus,
the door opened, and Larry simply said, "Hi, guys. How ya doing?"
Larry hung around the company while we were there. When we

left he faded back into the void. Years later I ran into a student of Larry's. He had become a teacher in Norman, I believe. She said, "Was Larry as crazy back then as he is now?"

I looked at her and had to laugh. "Yes, he was," I said. Then I asked, "Is he still alive?"

Anna Sokolow was a modern-dance choreographer and her improvisational dance class was my absolute favorite at school. She was strict, with no sense of humor, but she taught me as much about acting as our bona fide acting teachers. She challenged the surface response, mediocrity, and facility. She made us dig deeper into ourselves, own and externalize our passion. It was a heady class. When Anna joined us we were in our second year of school but our first year in the beautiful new building on West Sixty-sixth Street. Juilliard was now officially part of Lincoln Center, and the north side of the school faced the Chinese embassy. They used to watch us jumping around or crouching in corners or running the length of the room in our black leotards and tights while they were in their Mao Tse-tung uniforms standing against huge picture windows. We would wave to these lifeless figures staring out of their windows. They never waved back. I wondered if they were a wee bit jealous of our uninhibited freedom or if they were secretly planning to obliterate Juilliard and New York City while they were at it. The embassy is now gone. We had an odd communication with those Chinese men. I think we were all very curious about one another.

In our first year, because the Juilliard building was too small to accommodate the drama department, our classes were held in International House at 500 Riverside Drive. It was graduate student housing. René Auberjonois was one of our acting teachers. In the vast auditorium of International House, René gave us his philosophy of acting—"Acting is fucking." Right after he said that, he left the school to play Father Mulcahy in the movie *M*A*S*H.* We were a bunch of eighteen- and nineteen-year-old kids—how were we supposed to apply this insight, let alone understand its deepest meaning?

Our teachers leaving us in the middle of our studies happened often. Many were working actors who taught until they were cast in their next role. In the middle of teaching us what their theory of acting was, they would get a job and leave us standing there. Then another teacher would take over and say, "Well, ignore that. *This* is what acting is." Huh? Wha?

Michael Kahn's acting class was the scariest. He was so brilliant and had a razor-edge delivery. He could and invariably did destroy each and every one of the actors that first year. He was as challenging and uncompromising as Anna was. The difference was we were there to learn how to act, not how to dance, so his class was the most intense of all. If he didn't believe the actor or if he felt we weren't committed, there would be a bloody showdown. He was always right, but in my case he was too intimidating for me to hear what he had to say. Sometimes the very brilliant ones are the least accessible. Michael is a staggeringly good director and he was a great acting teacher, but I was totally scared of him and wasted too much energy being scared, so I can't remember what he taught me. I was just so overwhelmed with fear at school.

There was absolutely no consistency of acting training in those first couple of years. By default we were left to our own devices to put the pieces together. I finally realized that there was no one technique to acting—you have to apply what works in whatever situation you're in. Learn the techniques and use them all. Ultimately it was the smartest way to teach a young actor, but they didn't know that because the department was still forming. We were the experiment, and it was, for the most part, a glorious train wreck. It was always interesting, somewhat strange, startling, and combative. The most brilliant of the actors did not make it through the first year. The training and the psychological breaking down of our individualism to form "the Juilliard Actor" was brutal. I was in tears every night. I was not one of the favorites. John Houseman once called me into his office and said, "You and Miss Nichols do more acting in the cafeteria than you do in class." Nancy Nichols got the leads, though. I just got punished. He also humiliated me in an elevator full of people. I got in and Mr. Houseman was already there. "Hi, Mr. Houseman," I said.

"Louise Bernikow says you are the most illiterate person she has ever met," he responded.

She should get out more, I thought. Well, it was probably true, but come on. I was so embarrassed in front of all those mini-geniuses clutching their cellos and oboes. I said nothing, buried my head, and hated him a little.

At one point they wanted to throw me out of the school. They didn't like my personality. But they couldn't throw me out just because they didn't like me, so they threw a lot of different roles in my direction to see if I might fail as an actor. Instead, the Drama Division actually made me a versatile actor. The school pretty much pigeonholed the actors—leading lady, soubrette, ingenue, character woman—but I played such a variety of roles and ages that I was made incredibly strong and pliable over the four years. I became an example at school. If there was a recalcitrant student who showed promise but was on her way out the door, Suria Saint-Denis, Michel's widow, would say, "Remember Patti LuPone."

John Houseman's favorite actresses were the tall women with high cheekbones—these were the actresses who got the leads on the main stage. He actually told me that I was too short to be a leading lady . . . while I was playing one. I did *The Maids* and *Next Time I'll Sing to You*, two of my most successful productions, in Room 306 at the new school. For the most part that studio was my stage for my remaining three years at Juilliard. It always hurt to be left off the cast list of the main stage production. However, I found ways to ease the pain.

In my second year, René Auberjonois came back to teach at Juilliard. Nancy Nichols, who had become one of my dearest friends, and I were moping in his class. "What's the matter with you?" he asked. We told him that we wanted to go see Delaney & Bonnie at the Fillmore East.

"Just go to the stage door," René said, "and ask for John Ford Noonan. Tell him Wimpy sent you." John was a playwright, and his play *How Boston Won the Pennant* had been produced off-Broadway.

Nancy and I went down there, knocked on the door, and a big, burly guy in overalls answered. "We're looking for John Ford Noonan," we told him. "Wimpy sent us."

"You found him," Noonan answered, and let us in. Nancy and I sat backstage at the Fillmore East every Friday night for the entire year. We saw every great rock-and-roll band. I had so much fun and did everything I could to forget the tormented hell days at school.

Our class would lose actors every year. They would be "eliminated" by the faculty. The end of the year was always filled with tension, anger, and tears. Some kids would be eliminated because they stunk, others left because they couldn't take the insanity anymore. David Schramm was John Houseman's favorite male actor. David didn't much care for Brian Bedford, a new acting teacher. I can't remember exactly what happened, but there were words between David and Brian, and a dramatic exit from the class by

Lizzie in Next Time I'll Sing to You, *1973.*

David. The entire Group 1 was called into Mr. Houseman's office. He was appalled by our ungratefulness, our lack of respect for Brian Bedford. The lecture and rant went on for about a half hour. At the end of it Mr. Houseman said, "I'm eliminating Group 1. That's all. Fuck you. Good-bye."

It was shocking and funny all at the same time. I realized that it was nothing more than an empty threat. At the time the Drama

Division consisted of just us, Group 1, and Group 2, the class behind us. Surely Mr. Houseman would never throw us out, leaving
himself only that class in the school. Group 2 was a knee-jerk reaction to the lunatics in my class. Most of Group 2 was as gray and
mundane as we were off the wall.

In that second year, we started a singing class with Roland
Gagnon, who was the choral master of the American Opera Center (AOC, the Opera Division) at Juilliard. He was another one
of my favorite teachers. Roland was an ex-priest, a deeply intel-
lectual man with a spectacular wine cellar in his apartment hall
closet. He would invite my classmate/boyfriend Kevin Kline and
me to dinner. We would eat and drink a gourmet experience that
he would prepare, then sit in his living room and have philosophi-
cal discussions—well, he and Kevin would have them. I always
felt stupid next to those two, but Roland and I communicated on
another level. We would make each other laugh.

Being invited into his life was so enriching. His singing classes
and the dissertations at the end of them lifted me up and deep-
ened my commitment to this thing I was doing with my life, which,
of course, included singing. Early in our second year, Roland asked
whether any of us wanted to sing in an opera with the American
Opera Center after school. Three students did. I didn't because we
were already at school for thirteen hours a day. I had to get out
of that building and remember who I was. The opera was Save-
rio Mercadante's *Il Giuramento*. At the end of the school year the
AOC's production of the opera and the Juilliard Orchestra were
chosen by Gian Carlo Menotti and Thomas Schippers to represent
America at the Festival of Two Worlds in Spoleto, Italy. I begged
Roland to let me go.

He did, so two other classmates, Sam Tsoutsouvas and Norman Snow, and I joined the Juilliard Orchestra, the American

Opera Center, and the principal soloists from the New York City Opera for the trip to Italy. At the airport, we were well taken care of. All we had to do was show up at the assigned terminal and all of our needs were met. Our sponsor saw to every last detail. The Texas man was a lover of the arts, extremely rich, and a drinker. We were all herded onto the private Pan Am charter, and once we were airborne, the flight attendants broke out the alcohol. As we were approaching the Rome airport, they attempted to auction off the rest of the booze. Pan Am still hadn't unloaded all of it by the time we got off the plane. Bleary-eyed, drunk, and jet-lagged, I arrived in Europe, the place I had longed to be since I was sixteen years old.

We boarded several buses for the journey to Spoleto in the Umbria region. We were assigned guest quarters in homes all over the town. When I was finally settled in my host home on a beautiful street in beautiful Spoleto, a cellist from the orchestra and I went to the local market. We bought the local salami, bread, cheese, olives, and wine, and went to a hillside to eat, drink, and revel in the good fortune bestowed upon us. We got happily shitfaced all over again. It was the beginning of the most glorious month of my young life. *Il Giuramento* was only performed every two and a half days, so my classmate Sam and I had several days free to hitchhike all over Italy, which we did. One night we left after the performance crazily thinking we'd get a ride somewhere. We ended up sleeping in a field while I fended off the advances of Angelo, a cute Spoleto boy we befriended who thought I was a cute, loose American girl, which I was. Sometimes we'd leave at dawn not knowing where we were going but always getting someplace by train or car, having had the best time along the way. In fact, the performances of the opera got in the way of our good times. We ever so slightly resented having to come back to Spoleto.

Situated on an Umbrian hilltop, the town itself is quite beautiful and dates from the ninth century B.C. It had the most massive aqueduct, which had become *the* place to commit suicide. These people were indeed committed. Before they jumped, they carved their names into the stone of the aqueduct—not easy to do. The town has cobblestone streets, beautiful churches, several theatres, and a small amphitheatre. Andrei Serban was there, having directed the Public Theater's production of *Arden of Faversham,* acted by East Village hippies and a couple of real actors. It was experimental theatre at its worst. Peter Brook saw it and picked up the majority of the actors and took them to Iran to develop *Convocation of the Birds.* I was incredulous and unbelievably jealous.

In that magical month, I fell in love with a dancer named Charlie Hayward, I learned the Italian *"basta Angelo,"* I ate myself into oblivion, and I had upstaging contests with Sam right behind the principal tenor while he was singing his big aria. I never wanted to go home, back to the place where I was constantly being judged. I was free for the first time in my life—free of emotional bonds, free to be myself without a history. It's one of the most profound experiences I've ever had, one that shaped me artistically, released me emotionally, and because I was an Italian in Italy, assured me I was normal, even beautiful, in my Italian-ism.

I returned for my third year and continued the arduous training Juilliard had become famous for. That summer I made my professional debut at the Young Vic in London. The New York Public Theater mounted an adaptation of Euripedes' *Iphigenia at Aulis* to occupy the vacant Young Vic Theater while their company was touring. Somehow I think Euripides might not have been too happy with what had been done to it. His play had become a rock musical with twelve Iphigenias. I joined the cast after three girls left for Leonard Bernstein's *Mass* at the Kennedy Center. I remember rehearsing at the Public playing catch-up. These women were a tight ensemble and not necessarily thrilled to see a new face. The only thing I was given to do was a lyric at the top of the show: "Grip your oars and pull hard . . . pull hard and grip your oars." This adaptation was a big hot mess, but what was exciting was the fact that we were actually going to be onstage in London. Again, I couldn't believe my luck.

On the day we were flying, I went to the airport and, because I'd never taken an international *commercial* flight before, I didn't check in at the ticket counter. The only other flight I had taken had been my chartered Spoleto excursion. When it came time to board, I didn't have a boarding pass. There was a bit of a flurry, the company manager did his best to get me a seat, but there was a gate attendant who was hell bent on not letting me on that flight. Somehow I was snuck on with the help of the flight attendants, but when the gate attendant patrolled the aisles counting heads, she found me and threw me off the flight. I don't even know how I had the presence of mind to go to the airport and get on a flight the next day, but I did. There must have been a ticket waiting for me. I arrived in London, found the hotel they put us in, and began a wild ride in seventies London. I befriended two girls in the company and the three of us prowled the London streets together.

The company was made up of blacks, Hispanics, and whites, with the whites being in the minority. The best-known cast member was Nell Carter, who had already made her Broadway debut. We all had to dress in a large chorus dressing room. I don't know why, but all twelve of us were in one room amid racks of costumes. Everybody had a dressing table except the white girls, who were standing and making up. One night as we were getting ready to "grip our oars and pull hard," Nell Carter said to her makeup mirror, "Who's got a knife? I wanna stick somebody tonight." The white girls slithered back against the wall. The show went on and nobody got shanked. We did have the best time in London. My two new friends, Pam and Julian, and I hooked up with Roland Joffé, who'd go on to direct *The Killing Fields,* but who at the time was Sir Laurence Olivier's assistant at the Old Vic. The three of us moved in with Roland for our remaining time there. We had an apartment, we had an English friend/lover, and for some inexplicable reason, Harry Nilsson showed up at our show. Pam, Julian, and I went out with Harry. I had been in love with him forever, was such a huge fan, and here I was chatting him up in his hotel room as if we were the best of friends. I couldn't believe it. I can still see the hotel room and his beautiful blondness.

While we were in residence, the Young Vic celebrated its second birthday, and all of English acting royalty showed up at the party. Among the crowd I spotted Sir Laurence Olivier and Joan Plowright. It took every ounce of courage I had to approach Laurence Olivier, but when we were face-to-face, I was so intimidated I couldn't even speak. He did shake my hand, but I got so depressed at my lack of composure that I fled the party.

Our show stunk, but we were a rock musical cult hit in London. Go figure. We finished our run, I came home to return to school, but I wanted so badly to stay in swinging London.

The workload shifted in our third and fourth years at Juilliard. We spent less time in the classroom and a lot more time performing both at Juilliard and around the state of New York under the aegis of Lincoln Center. For our first Lincoln Center tour, the class was split in half, and my half performed a version of *The Foibles of Scapin* by Molière. There were seven of us touring in a station wagon with a white prop box on the roof of the car. We traveled all of New York State performing this truncated version of *Scapin* in elementary, junior high, and high schools. Our version of the

Scapin, *the Drama Division's first road show, 1971.*

ESTATE OF DIANE CORODNITZKI

play was basically this: All the actors came onstage at the top of the show, introduced their character to the audience, told the audience what Acts I and II were about, and then acted an abbreviated version of Act III. This wonderful play lasted one class period.

We would more often than not perform in the morning, and on one particular occasion we were at a Catholic girls' school. As we were describing our characters to a rapt audience, Sam Tsoutsouvas started laughing out loud, which sent ripples of laughter through the rest of us. When we finished the introduction and left the stage, the stage manager came backstage yelling, "What's so goddamn funny?" Sam, still laughing with tears in his eyes, said, "I listened to the prologue for the first time today, and even I don't understand it." It was true. We'd never bothered listening to the prologue. After the show, we stood around and said it out loud again, making a conscious effort to comprehend it. It didn't make sense. Every time we listened to it after that, no one could keep a straight face.

We played *Scapin* for two years. Something happened to me while I was in rehearsal for it. I was cast as Zerbinette, a character required to enter laughing, then sustain and build the laughter into hysterics through the entire speech she gives to Scapin. It requires substantial comedic technique. Rehearsal was going well—so well, in fact, that I was chosen to represent the new Juilliard actor at the TCG (Theatre Communication Group) yearly gathering of regional theatre artistic directors. I nailed the speech at a performance level, but when I went back into rehearsal, I couldn't find the character again, couldn't maintain the laughter, and I couldn't figure out why or how I had lost it. I'd basically been pushed into performance too soon while I was still discovering the character, a very dangerous thing to do to a young, inexperienced actor. I didn't know how to get back into rehearsal mode. The performance was so successful that I tried to re-create it, but I didn't know *why* it had been successful. I didn't know the character yet. I lost confidence and eventually I was taken out of the part. The director gave me the ingenue role, which didn't suit me. I was taken out of that part and given the smallest role, the messenger. The humiliation was deep, but it taught me a very valuable lesson. Rehearsal is for discovery and development of character. It can't be rushed, because it's all so tenuous. Patience, time, accrued knowledge, and careful preparation will ensure a consistent performance. The experience scared the bejesus out of me, but failure teaches.

Boris Tumarin, the Russian director whom we all adored, then cast me as Catherine in *A View from the Bridge*. This production on

the main stage in our third year was a huge success. Mr. Houseman's dream of a repertory ensemble was taking shape. We grew
up and found our trust and support in one another. We became an
ensemble of actors. We were all in the same play using the same
technique and trusting one another on stage as we had never done
before. I'll never forget Boris's dramatic curtain call and the ovation we received. I don't think anyone expected this level of pro-
fessionalism from us. I was again reminded of my responsibility
to my craft as I had been with Esther Scott and the success we
achieved at the NYSSMA convention in high school.

I was now becoming one of the school's leading ladies, and
the next part I was cast in was Lady Teazle in the Restoration play
The School for Scandal. Gerald Freedman was the director. Ultimately I succeeded in the role and even became the poster girl for
The Acting Company—my face as Lady Teazle adorned The Acting Company posters and press releases for three years—but getting there was a trial because I was crippled with fear. I lacked the
courage to admit I didn't know anything about Restoration and
its very particular language. I'd never said so many words in one
sentence before. It was more complicated than Shakespeare. It was
so bad that at the final dress rehearsal, Gerry said to me, "If you're
an actress, act. If not, put a bushel basket on your head and get off
the stage." The final humiliation came at the end of the play on our
opening night. In the blackout, I was supposed to cross stage right
and exit through the set door to prepare for the curtain call. I was
in such a fog through the entire performance that I walked off the
raised platform onto the deck of the stage and didn't know where
I was. It was pitch black. When I realized what had happened,
I started pounding on the set wall, screaming, "Help! Let me in!
Don't let me die out here!" Somehow I was talked back onto the
stage and through the door before the lights came up. After the

David Ogden Stiers as Joseph Surface and me as Lady Teazle in
The School for Scandal, *1972.*

performance, still in costume, in a complete daze, I walked the hallway of the Drama Division's third floor. I saw Marian Seldes, her arms outstretched, beckoning me. We hugged cheek to cheek. She said, "Yes."

I said, "I don't know, Marian, I was so confused."

"I'm sure you were," she responded and sailed away.

On our Easter break, one of my classmates, Gerry Gutierrez, suggested he direct three of us—Kevin Kline, Sam Tsoutsouvas, and me—in Act 1 of the musical *The Apple Tree* as a surprise for Mr. Houseman. We were classical actors. We didn't do musicals, but we rehearsed and presented "The Diary of Adam and Eve" to the other classes, to our teachers, and to John. It's based on a Mark Twain short story, adapted by Jerry Bock and Sheldon Harnick. It's so tender and funny and heartbreaking. Kevin and I were a couple, so this play was extremely poignant for me. We were a huge success. Mr. Houseman hadn't considered that some of us could sing, and he was delighted. That was when we started to do musicals, the first being Brendan Behan's *The Hostage*. . . . I was left off the cast list.

However, I wasn't left off the cast list of *The Robber Bridegroom,* a brilliant musical based on a Eudora Welty novella. Once again, Kevin and I played opposite each other. I was entrenched in my love for him onstage and off. It wasn't always easy. We were young. We were playing opposite each other on several occasions. He was so handsome and I was so insecure even when we were a couple. Everybody wanted Kevin. He loved all of the women, sometimes at my expense. But I was addicted to him and always came back—until one day I just couldn't anymore.

Kevin and I had met in my third year of Juilliard. It was his first. John Houseman had brought three new actors into our class. They had already graduated from college and were called "advanced students." ("Advanced in what?" the rest of us demanded.) They were resented and we were threatened. When I finally met Kevin, I thought he was Pinocchio and he thought I was a Long Island cheerleader, which I was. One day in an Art Appreciation class I came in late and took a seat next to Kevin. There was heat, and the next thing I know we couldn't keep our hands off each other. It was the beginning of a seven-year relationship that endured several breakups and left an indelible mark on my life. Kevin was my first great love.

The formation of the Juilliard Acting Company was the prelude to the formation of a repertory company in earnest, which is exactly what happened when we graduated in May of 1972. I ended up with a Bachelor of Fine Arts degree, a seat on a Domenico bus, and four years of employment.

The journey was worth far more than the piece of paper at the end. Juilliard taught me to remain open to everything in my life, to every period of theatre, to every style of acting. That lesson was tremendous. I wish I'd studied better, developed more technique. But I also learned that those skills would never be enough. There would always be something intangible about the connection between the actor and the audience. Some of the actors in my class were technically brilliant. They had beautiful speaking voices, beautiful diction, beautiful projection, but they were not very good actors. You can be taught to act, but you can't be taught the X factor.

School was incredibly hard. We were all psychologically ripped to shreds. We had to rebuild character, confidence, and emotional stamina. Some of us made it and some of us didn't. In my class there were attempted suicides and mental institution lockups. The pressure and the competition were intense, but I grew as an actor because I was tested, not because I was supported. I truly believe you learn more from failure than you do from success. I spent four years there, and it was one of the most painful experiences of my life. I kept saying, "I came here with an open heart and soul. Why am I getting beat up?" I don't think they intended to beat us up. Their intention was to build strong American actors articulate in technique, style, and comprehension. Was it worth it? Absolutely. The craft of acting, the process of learning how to act, is such an investigation of one's soul and being. However painful it was, I wouldn't change a minute of the experience, because it prepared me for everything in this business, including the worst experiences my career and my life would survive. The blows took their toll, no question. But I came out a much stronger person and a much stronger actor.

The Acting Company

4

The full company in 1975, our fourth year. I owe my career to John Houseman.

*T*here were many casualties among the original thirty-six members in Group 1 of the Drama Division. Only seventeen of us lived through all the rigors of Juilliard and graduated—fourteen from the original class plus the three advanced students. We brave warriors were the group that became John Houseman's repertory company. He kept our class together after critic Mel Gussow of the *New York Times* hinted in a review that this company *should* stay together. While we were still under the auspices of the school, we were called the Juilliard Acting Company. After graduation we couldn't use the word *Juilliard* in our title anymore, so we became the City Center Acting Company, and when our affiliation with City Center ended, we became just The Acting Company. In 1972 the name sounded so pretentious and we took a lot of heat from our critics. However, The Acting Company is in its thirty-seventh year, still touring classical theatre, and the only repertory company of its kind in America.

The transition from performing at Juilliard to performing as a national repertory company was to a certain extent seamless. Once we graduated, we took select plays from our third- and fourth-year repertoire and spent the entire month of July in performance at the Saratoga Performing Arts Center in Saratoga Springs, New York. This was the best job a young actor could have. We were plying our craft while we were in residence with the New York City Ballet. We would walk across the lawn from our theatre to theirs and watch them rehearse. We all hung out at the same pool on our breaks and days off. It was summer, always a sexy time to me. The grounds of the Performing Arts Center were gorgeous. The swimming pool was part of the Gideon Putnam Hotel, located behind our theatre just beyond the tennis courts. It was a huge pool, with a Grecian theme, and to see the glorious bodies of the New York City Ballet just lolling around in their string bikinis and thongs was almost too much to take. We didn't necessarily become friends with them, but in the four years I spent at Saratoga, I came to idolize the artistry of Gelsey Kirkland, Suzanne Farrell, and Allegra Kent. George Balanchine and Jerome Robbins were the artistic directors, and a few of us turned into hushed and excited fans when we'd see them wandering the grounds. I remember them coming to see Anton Chekhov's *The Three Sisters* our second year and hearing Balanchine exclaiming to Robbins when the play was over and they were heading back to the amphitheatre, "RUSSIANS DON'T TALK LIKE THAT! WHAT A BUNCH OF CRAP THESE ACTORS ARE!" He gesticulated wildly all the way back across the lawn. I was thrilled he even noticed what a bunch of crap we were.

That first summer was quite successful for our newly professional acting company. We received great reviews and we started to develop an audience in Saratoga. It was also the summer that the boys came out . . . as if we didn't *know*. There was such an emotional release one night when, in the dorm we were all living in, one, then another, and then another screamed, "I'm gay!" "I'm gay, too!" "I've always been gay!" "Not as gay as me!" and celebrated their freedom at LAST! We confirmed our love for them, celebrated with them, and deeper bonds were formed.

After Saratoga we returned to New York and made our off-Broadway debut September 27, 1972. We performed at the Good Shepherd Faith Church on West Sixty-sixth Street. For all intents

My first head shot.

and purposes, we were back at Juilliard, because the church is located practically next door. We spent late September and most of October in the church performing our Saratoga repertoire, Gorky's *The Lower Depths,* Brendan Behan's *The Hostage,* Thomas Middleton's *Women Beware Women,* and Richard Brinsley Sheridan's *The School for Scandal.* Our reception was very good, so we were off

to a great start. Then we hit the road—theatre vagabonds working fifty weeks out of the year. The touring aspect, being on the road for months at a time, was totally new to us and we were in for some big lessons. We lost several bookings our first year because our training at school only prepared us for three performances of the play we'd been rehearsing. That's all we ever did. On the road when we got to the fourth performance of any given show, our performances fell apart. We weren't taught to maintain a characterization or a show. We basically stunk, while we behaved like spoiled brats fresh out of some fancy acting school. I remember Potsdam, New York, one of our first stops. Someone mouthed off about "this shithole of a place" while the presenter was standing right outside the dressing room door. We never saw Potsdam again. We had to learn so much more than maintenance on the road—manners and diplomacy for one thing, adaptability being the biggest challenge, and the most important lesson, how to "ghost" in hotel rooms to save money. We all picked out a seat on a Domenico Line bus, chose friendships that would endure a lifetime, and designated an area in the bus restricted for entertainment, which included smoking, poker, and pot. This lasted four years, with actors coming and going and the entertainment changing as ennui set in.

Our backstage crew that first year consisted of one stage manager who could also hang and focus lights, one prop man, and one wardrobe supervisor/dresser—a three-person crew loading in six classical sets and costumes that were not built to tour. The sets were built for the three performances we did at school. We had a big truck to haul the shows and a driver who looked kind of dangerous. He traveled our sets and costumes with his girlfriend and his dog. This gangster actually had affection for us. He would show up at our motel room parties and find the chair that would make him the center of attention. We all paid our respects to him and a few of the girls dared to sit on his lap. I've forgotten his name, but I can still see his face, those sexy and threatening eyes of his, and his girlfriend's long black hair. He drove The Acting Company truck for three years. We hated to see him leave. We all loved him, even after he pulled up to the loading dock of the theatre we were playing one night and started revving the engine of his eighteen-wheeler while we were performing the third act of *The Three Sisters*. The noise was deafening. When we found out it was our driver, we politely asked him why he did that. "I wanted you to speed it up," he barked. "I got a long way to drive."

Whatever you say, you handsome devil with that dangerous thing you got going, I thought. *Before you go, let me sit on your lap.*

Speaking of speeding it up, our bookers never referred to a road map when they were routing us that first year. There were times when we exceeded the hours of travel Actors' Equity rules permitted. If we obeyed the rules, we'd never make the performance. We would literally arrive just in time to throw up bus sickness, throw on a corset, do the play, check into a motel, and the next morning be back on the road for another long haul. We were doing one-night stands. Our crew had to strike the sets, load them out, and in many cases drive several hours to our next stop. They would load in at seven A.M., work all day, and call the show at night. The whole thing repeated itself day after day. The actors had it easier than the crew. The crew drove themselves. We had the greatest bus driver for the entire four years, Bob Blount. I wonder where he is? We loved him very much, too. He would drive that bus like it was a jet plane, smooth and fast. He never got a ticket, and if there was time between performance dates, he would take us to the Grand Canyon or a ski resort in Colorado. I've thought about him and hope he's well. I truly loved that man.

We took Brendan Behan's play *The Hostage* to Bronx Community College, where this time, as we were preparing for the performance, the stage manager was laughing his head off with tears in his eyes. We asked, "What's so goddamn funny, Tommy?"

"There are more of you than there are of them," he said. We had eleven people in the audience and they alternated between watching us and the basketball game. The basketball game won. We ended up with nine people at the end of the show.

We had no masking (black drapes that delineate onstage from offstage), so when we exited, the audience saw us walking out of doors stage right and stage left into classroom hallways. The ultimate humiliation came at the finale of this deeply political play. The company stood in a V and sang the Irish ballad and IRA favorite "The Patriot Game," written by Dominic Behan, Brendan's brother. The music was recorded and the tape was at the wrong speed, the slowest speed, and stayed on the slowest speed for the entire song. The only person who sang in tempo with the tape was Leah Chandler. The rest of us were laughing—at Leah, and at our pathetic situation.

Our first year was just the beginning of the theatrical and life lessons that would serve us better than we ever imagined. Like the first day of school, we didn't know what hit us. Then again, we were an intrepid group and the stranger the situation, the more fun it was.

We were having the time of our lives because we were doing the thing that we had trained so hard for. We had already gained theatre experience, but there were even bigger lessons ahead. One of the biggest was learning how to adapt to the kinds of stages we found ourselves playing. All of a sudden we weren't in the nurturing womb of our Drama Division theatre. We knew how to project in that space. We knew the sight lines and we knew the comfort level. We had freedom. Now we had new stages, new backstages, and new audiences to understand and conquer in only a couple of hours at best. This was blessedly a time when we weren't encumbered with microphones. However, in one theatre, The Acting Company management had to send for our voice teacher, Liz Smith. No one had ever seen a theatre this big. It was someplace upstate New York on a college campus. I have no idea why it was so big unless it was designed for graduation ceremonies. Liz did her best to save the show. She taught us how to project in the space but also how to measure the volume level to preserve the language and the comedy. I mean, this was a *barn*—big! We did our best but I don't think we succeeded that night. The play was Sheridan's *The School for Scandal*. There I was in pink silk and lace sitting on

David Schramm's lap shouting down his ear, "SIR PETER, SIR PETER! YOU MAY BEAR IT OR NOT, AS YOU PLEASE; BUT I OUGHT TO HAVE MY OWN WAY IN EVERYTHING, AND WHAT'S MORE, I WILL, TOO!"

We performed on every possible configuration of a stage. We played Baptist altars, black boxes, gymnasiums, jewel boxes that were on the verge of abandonment, and we played nonexistent stages. We also played some of America's most beautiful theatres, the Fulton Street Opera House in Lancaster, Pennsylvania, and Ford's Theatre in Washington, D.C., to name two. Our experiences were different at each stop. We often encountered miscommunication between the theatre's technical director and our technical director. In one particular case when we came to the theatre, we saw that our set didn't fit on the stage—another adjustment. Where and how do we make entrances and exits in *Measure for Measure* with the set falling off the stage? I mean *literally* falling off the stage. This time they could hear us but they couldn't see us. We abandoned the downstage right and left entrances. That part of the set was floating midair. All those years adjusting to stages ultimately gave me the ability to walk onto any stage and know how to play it in about ten minutes.

Things improved over the following years, though in our second year at Saratoga we were faced with what seemed like an insurmountable dilemma. We toured fifty out of fifty-two weeks of the year. When and where would we be in one place long enough to rehearse a new season? Saratoga, of course! In order to go back on the road for a third year, we would have to perform our existing repertoire at night and rehearse four new plays simultaneously during the day. We had enough plays from school to get though the first two years but now we faced this enormous test. We were never out of rehearsal that month. I remember being pulled out of rehearsal for Jean Anouilh's *The Orchestra* to rehearse my scenes in Christopher Marlowe's *Edward the Second*. There was an overall sense of panic: Could we accomplish this? We could rehearse one play in a month's time, but four?

An interesting thing happened to me while I was juggling these roles. It turned into a great advantage. I'll put an enormous weight in the development of the character—psychological, emotional, whatever. But in this instance, as I left one character midstream, mid-scene even, and went across the hall to rehearse the next one, when I returned to the first one, a bubble had burst. There was an ease and enhanced depth in the characterization. It was as if the pressure was taken off one character and placed on the next one. And so it went for all four characters. It was almost easier to develop four at once than to develop just one. I don't recommend it, but we were forced into that situation. It was a great lesson.

I was capable of multitasking with a sense of relaxed comprehension. It was actually fun to do. It became easy because it was fun. Acting has to be joyful. It can't thrive in an overwrought state. The audience absolutely knows when an actor is uncomfortable, and they can't be taken on the journey of the story if the actor is internalized—meaning too much in their head. And truly, the actor's only responsibility is the telling of the story. We have to enter the stage confident and with a certain command in order to relax an audience and gain their trust to follow us. It was a revelation. I suppose the lessons were flying fast and furious because I was doing so much acting. It was also the year that I learned to leave the character and the play onstage. I got sick of acting. I wanted my life back. I worked hard to leave the theatre each night as me, not as the remnants of the character I had just played. Doing this allowed me to observe all kinds of very interesting things. I'm so curious, anyway, but it's a hard lesson for any twenty-year-old to learn: to get out of the way of their self. I guess I was able to get out of the way of myself because acting was being shoved down my throat. To this day I'm one of the first people out of the stage door at night. Leave it onstage, and carry on with your life.

It was also in that second year that two momentous events occurred. John Houseman saw a "Naked Run for God" and the entire company got crabs—the common term for "pubic lice." "The Naked Run for God" was the equivalent of "streaking." It came about on the road because three of my classmates needed something to do in the off-hours. Cynthia Herman, Jed Sakren, and Sam Tsoutsouvas were the principal players. John had heard about the Naked Run and wanted to see one. We were living in a soon-to-be-abandoned Skidmore College dorm in Saratoga. John also lived there to prove a point: If he could live there, so could we. It was a hellhole. It looked, felt, and smelled like a prison, which we also played that summer—Comstock Maximum Security Prison. We brought *The Hostage* to the prisoners. Now, *that* was live theatre! The prisoners had an attention span of about two minutes. Then they started to get disruptive until the guards shouted for quiet. All was silent until they lost interest again. Eventually they got involved with the story and started shouting at the characters onstage. It was frightening and exciting. The actors playing the male prostitutes had the most to worry about. At the end of our play, we went into the auditorium and mingled with the lifers. I found myself staring at a beautiful blond boy who was in turn staring at the striking of the set, totally mesmerized. His face was angelic, like an awestruck child. I felt as if he wanted to be up there, that he'd never seen anything like this before. That somehow it was magical and he wanted to step into it. I wanted so badly to talk to him and ask him why he was in a maximum-security prison. I didn't because I was scared but mostly because I didn't want to break the spell he was under. As I stared, I wondered what would have happened to this guy if he had discovered the theatre when he was younger. Would he be involved now? Would he be a tech director, a lighting or set designer, or would he have ended up in jail, anyway?

Anyway, back to the "Naked Run." Cynthia, Sam, and Jed arranged it on this one particular night after a show. We all assembled in the common room and waited for the runners. Here they came running naked, nothing unusual, until Cynthia knocked on Mr. Houseman's door. He came out of his room in a knee-length bathrobe. She dis-robed him, knelt down, and with her lily-white hands, cupped his soft penis and kissed it.

AAAAAAAAGGGGGGGGHHHHHH!!!!!!

The company went running—back to their rooms, under stairwells, out of the door—laughing and crying and in shock. John loved it. I can still see the entire scene and his penis. There was not a mention of the event until days later when John was giving us a lecture on something. He stopped midsentence and said, "I'm surprised to see you all wearing clothes."

Momentous event #2. The crabs . . . someone in the company got crabs. We never found out who the culprit was. Well, who's going to fess up to that? All of our costumes hung on racks. The crabs infiltrated the costumes and stayed in "residence" with us for the entire month. They wouldn't leave. They just loved the smell and sweat of Shakespearean and Chekhovian costumes. No matter how much we washed with the goo they put in all of the showers with instructions and warnings, we couldn't get rid of the crabs. The crabs were a communal problem. We all got closer.

This was also the year that I was given the name Flannel Mouth. It was the final dress rehearsal on our opening night of *The Three Sisters*. We were rehearsing the third act and I played Irina.

The Acting Company in Chekhov's The Three Sisters, *1973.*
ESTATE OF DIANE GORODNITZKI

I was crying in my speech. During the rehearsal, I saw John pacing at the back of the house, with Margot Harley, our co-producer, and Liz Smith, our voice teacher, trying to pacify him. A few hours later, places for the company was called. I began to walk to the stage in my virginal white costume. On the way out of the dressing room I said, "Hello, Mr. Houseman." He grabbed me by the throat, started shaking me furiously, and said, "I want to beat you black and blue until you are bloody with bandages all over your face." *What the hell?* It turned out that in rehearsal he couldn't understand what I was saying through my crying, and Margot and Liz wouldn't let him speak to me. All he could do was unleash his frustration on me at the places call, anointing me Flannel Mouth. Apparently my teachers enjoyed choking me. First Edith Skinner, now John. What a bunch of sadists. I started to take my diction problem somewhat seriously before they killed me.

The second season at Saratoga was successful. Then we hit the road, but built into our touring schedule was our return to New York City and our official Broadway debut in December/January 1974 at the Billy Rose Theatre. The plays for our Saratoga and Broadway seasons were Shakespeare's *Measure for Measure, The Three Sisters,* John Gay's *The Beggar's Opera,* and James Saunders's *Next Time I'll Sing to You.* I received good notices. Douglas Watt of the *Daily News* called my comedy "smart." Those words were music to my ears. A New York critic thought I was smart! We finished our Broadway season and hit the road again.

The Acting Company was funded by the National Endowment for the Arts and we played mostly universities. The NEA gave money to the schools and the schools would choose their desired art form. In our second year, our tour expanded throughout the Midwest. On the bus for hours and after long stretches of highway with nothing but fields and cows and flat, flat land, we would stop at these super-sized Holiday Inns, the likes of which I had never seen before. The lobbies resembled the deck of a ship. You could shop for anything—food, clothes, tires, and diesel oil all in one store just left of the front desk. There might be a shuffleboard court or an Olympic-size swimming pool in the lobby. These places were gigantic and so much fun. I remember two of the Holiday Inns—one where we adopted a dog who was stranded on the meridian of the highway. We named him Scapin. Kevin and I brought him to our room and bathed him. We took him to the vet and gave him a start in life. We cared for him for a week but then had to let him go. It broke my heart. We left him in the hotel kennel and told the front desk about him, but I'll never know if Scapin enjoyed a long and happy life. Our company manager wouldn't let us keep him, the bitch (the company manager, not the dog). We sought revenge. The bitch stood four foot seven inches in high heels. Our fantasy was to lengthen her clothes and put oversized furniture in her motel room. We never did get our revenge. She left us, and our next company manager's last name sounded like a sexual disease. Our company managers remained unpopular.

The other Holiday Inn was in North Platte, Nebraska. We were traveling to a theatre in Alliance, Nebraska. It was winter and a snow shower was threatening to turn into a blizzard. The state troopers stopped our bus at the Holiday Inn. We would have to stay the night, but not before someone on the bus came up with the brainstorm of "ghosting." One person checked in and three others snuck into the room. We could cheat the hotel and save a lot of money was the thinking. The rooms had double beds, so we all slept together. No big deal. We took "group grope" at Juilliard. We were very lucky at this Holiday Inn because we were one of the first arrivals. By the end of the night there were no more rooms left and people had to sleep on the floor of the lobby. We were there for three days and the inn ran out of everything, but we had so much fun—snowball fights during the blizzard, swimming in the pool again during the blizzard, watching TV, shopping in the anything-you-can-buy store just left of the lobby (we spent hours in there). It was first-class entertainment for endless hours. The downside was the loss of the date. If we didn't play, we didn't get paid. We didn't play. Oh, well. When you're young, things like not getting paid don't seem to matter as much as they do now. Much like manners and diplomacy.

In our third year we didn't come into New York, I don't know why, but we continued expanding our tours to now include the South and the West. We passed through Toad Suck Ferry to get to

Kevin and me as Macheath and Lucy Lockit in
The Beggar's Opera, *1973.*

Conway, Arkansas, where we played *The Three Sisters*. I remember thinking, *Why do we play* Chekhov *in these Podunk towns?* But that night the audience knew the play as well if not better than we did. This audience had such a keen desire to see the play that they prepared for it. I underestimated their longing for Anton Chekhov. Another lesson: Never underestimate your audience.

Kevin took a year off from the company. I was alone on the road. One night in Akron, Ohio, over the phone, he told me he loved me. I felt dizzy and asked him to repeat what he said. He did. I thought we were in love, but they were words he had never spoken before. It was almost too late for me. I had gone through so much with him and this love was deeply painful as well as ecstatic. . . . I had been trying to wean myself off of Kevin, but I dug in and gave us another try.

In our fourth year we, as an ensemble, started to meditate. A new face joined the company, Jack O'Brien, who would later go on to win multiple Tony Awards for directing, among other things, *Hairspray* and *The Coast of Utopia*. He came on the bus, gave a bit of a speech, and then wrapped it up by declaring, "I'm just a Broadway baby!" We really didn't know what to make of that comment or him.

Jack felt that to keep the ensemble tuned up and tuned in, we should meditate. We all went to the Transcendental Meditation Center in New York, paid our hundred dollars, got a lecture about meditation and its sixteen thousand mantras, instructions on how to meditate, and an individual mantra—or so we thought. Back on the road we were in L.A. at an amusement park on a day off. Sam and Ben Hendrickson were on the loop de loop. Sam said, "I think I'm going to throw up."

Ben freaked and said, "No, no, don't throw up in this little car, all over me. Think of your mantra! 'Shering, shering.'"

Kitty Duval in The Time of Your Life, *1974.*

ESTATE OF DIANE
GORODNITZKI

Sam stared at him in disbelief. "Shering? That's MY man-traaAAAAAHHH," and spewed all over Ben.

We found out that the center had given us only two mantras for twenty-one actors. That was officially the end of the bus rides where we all had to shut up because *one* of us thought it was time for *all* of us to meditate.

Jack directed some of our most successful productions. *The Time of Your Life* was one of them. We were in St. Joe, Missouri, performing the play when we started to get heckled by some kids sitting in the first couple of rows. The gay boys were targeted, but it seemed more like there was nothing better to do on a Saturday night in St. Joe, Missouri. These kids bought tickets to taunt the actors. I thought a couple of our men were going to jump off the stage and a fight would ensue, but the hecklers were moved to the back of the theatre by the theatre management. They continued to heckle and no one in the audience could do anything about it. It was bizarre—a group of kids terrorizing the theatre audience and the audience being held hostage. We got on the bus after the show, depressed and asking the question, *Where are we and why?* The road was wearing us down.

We did return to New York City in October/November of 1975 and played our last season together at the Harkness Theatre. The

Kevin and me again as Jamie Lockhart and Rosamund Musgrove in The Robber Bridegroom, *1975.*

ESTATE OF DIANE GORODNITZKI

fourth-year repertoire was William Saroyan's *The Time of Your Life,* *The Three Sisters,* Christopher Marlowe's *Edward the Second,* and Alfred Uhry and Robert Waldman's musical *The Robber Bridegroom.* It was a typical season for The Acting Company—you either loved us or you hated us. *The Robber Bridegroom* gave me some of the sweetest moments I've ever spent on a stage, while the three actresses playing the three sisters, Olga, Masha, and Irina, were booed in one of our curtain calls. As Irina, I was one of the actresses, but I'm positive it was Masha who was getting booed! After our Broadway run, we once again went back out on the road, and as it would turn out, it was the last time. The New York stops were just that—stops on a long tour that took us all over the country. New York City was where we lived and paid taxes, but as members of this company, the bus and motel rooms had become home.

One night in Omaha I got a telephone call from Margot Harley. I had just received my first Tony nomination for Best Featured Actress in a Musical, as did Alfred Uhry for Book and Lyrics for *The Robber Bridegroom.* I was rooming with Mary Lou Rosato. Kevin and I had broken up again (so much for love). I fell backward on the bed and stared at the ceiling. My head was spinning. It was surreal. I was in Omaha, Nebraska, and New York was beckoning. It was a crappy motel room, not an agent's office or a luxurious hotel. It didn't make sense and then I wondered how the rest of the company would react. I can't remember how they reacted. We just continued touring. And that was that. (P.S., I didn't win the Tony. Kelly Bishop did for *A Chorus Line.*)

The 1975–76 season was the last year of my association with The Acting Company. When eleven of us quit, the company as I knew it disintegrated. Kevin and I were leaving anyway, but others quit because we had a new associate artistic director who joined us in Lexington, Kentucky, to tell the company that some of them would not be enjoying leading parts anymore. One actor quit. Then another, then three, then five, then eleven said enough is enough. Half of the company walked, some in anger, some in solidarity. After eight years with the same actors, I felt both relief and deep emptiness. Kevin and I returned to New York (we were back together again, oy vey!). I thought about the people I would miss, the parts I wouldn't play, the plays I would never do, the great summers in Saratoga, the lessons I learned, the laughter . . . the great peals of belly-shaking laughter. It was finished and I had to start over again.

We were tired of the road, sick of one another, and this experience was truly over. It was eight years later, four years in the Drama Division at Juilliard and four years on the road with The Acting Company. We loved and hated one another. There are actors from those eight years together I don't ever want to see again. There are people who have stopped talking to me. There are blood friendships. There's no denying that we all learned monumental lessons. As far as the acting was concerned, we were armed with fifteen years' experience from four years on the road. We trained daily, and we grew. Some of us have had long careers. Some never went beyond the company. Love relationships formed, broke up, left their lifelong mark. Again, I wouldn't change one minute of it. When the company dissolved in Lexington, Kentucky, it was traumatic and liberating. That's where I met David Mamet, who became such an important person in my life that he gets his own chapter. But the next thing that happened was a dream come true with a hefty price tag.

The Baker's Wife, or *Hitler's Road Show*

1976

"Meadowlark."

*T*here's a saying in the theatre that if Hitler were alive today, his punishment should be to send him out on the road with a musical in trouble. *The Baker's Wife* would have been the perfect sentence for Adolf. For me personally, it was a devastating experience from the minute I started rehearsals.

The idea came from a 1930s French movie, Marcel Pagnol's *La Femme du Boulanger*. In 1976 producer David Merrick was mounting the musical version for Broadway and had lined up some major talent. Because he wanted the same kind of success producer Hal Prince had with *Fiddler on the Roof*, Merrick hired Joe Stein, who had written the book for *Fiddler*, to write *The Baker's Wife*. Composer Stephen Schwartz was writing the score. Joe Hardy was the director. Jo Mielziner, in what would be his last work before he died, was the set designer. Jennifer Tipton was the lighting designer, and our costumes were designed by Theoni Aldredge. Rumor had it Merrick wanted Zero Mostel to star as Aimable the baker. Zero didn't do it—maybe he knew something the rest of us didn't. Our producer got what he thought was the next best thing, Chaim Topol, who had played Tevye in the 1971 film version of *Fiddler on the Roof.* In this particular case, the space between the best thing and the next best thing could have filled the Grand Canyon.

The Baker's Wife was my first theatrical venture after I left The Acting Company. It wasn't the show I thought I was going to do. At the time, John Houseman was getting ready to take *The Robber Bridegroom* back to Broadway for an extended run. We heard this rumor on the road and wondered if we would be going with it. Our company had already made *The Robber Bridegroom* a hit during a limited Broadway engagement in October of 1975, and we had been playing it to great success on the road for eight months. It was the most popular show of our 1975–76 season.

In March, months after The Acting Company Broadway run, I was thrilled to be recognized for my work with a Featured Actress Tony nod after we'd done only fourteen performances as part of our repertoire. It was an honor, and in a Broadway first, two siblings were nominated in the same year; my brother Bobby received a Best Featured Actor in a Musical nomination for his portrayal of Zach in *A Chorus Line.*

Despite the nomination, Mr. Houseman asked me to *audition* for the second Broadway run. I refused. *There's no way I'm auditioning for a role I was just nominated for,* I thought. Moreover, Kevin and I were the only cast members from The Acting Company who were even asked to audition. Everyone else was shut out. I couldn't believe that our company wasn't going back to Broadway. However, Kevin swallowed his pride and actually consented to read. Another lesson I learned was that when you swallow your pride, you often choke on it. Kevin didn't get the part.

The whole thing seemed highly disloyal. Not only were they

Backstage with Kevin at the Harkness Theatre during The Robber Bridegroom's *run in New York, 1975.*

our producers, they had been our teachers at Juilliard. Now they were turning their backs on the very actors who were in part responsible for this production—and they were negating their training of us. Obviously they didn't trust us. It was a real slap in the face and a wake-up call. For the new production they had cast Barry Bostwick in Kevin's part, the robber bridegroom, and now they wanted me to audition with him. I remember that the only thing I *would* do was stand next to him onstage. What did those geniuses expect to learn? I'm short? He's tall?

Months earlier I had auditioned for *The Baker's Wife* on one of The Acting Company's breaks from touring. I wanted the part of Genevieve, the title role, because of the beautiful song,

"Meadowlark." It was a coveted part, but I didn't get it—at first. Even though I didn't get the part, an awareness of the play somehow stayed in the back of my mind. The Acting Company was in residence in Ann Arbor, Michigan, for a month. While we were there, Kevin and I were in our hotel room, watching TV, waiting for the evening show, when in my stream of consciousness I thought, *Oh,* The Baker's Wife *went into rehearsal today.* Little did I know that before long The Acting Company would no longer exist as the company I knew and that I would soon be joining the company of *The Baker's Wife.*

I had a scheduled meeting with Mr. Houseman—it was always "Mr. Houseman," I never called him John; he was just too intimidating. A day or two before our meeting, I got a call from Helen Nickerson, the general manager of David Merrick's production office. "Can you fly out to Los Angeles?" she asked me. "We want you to replace Carole Demas in *The Baker's Wife.*"

"Yes," I told her, "but first I have to cancel an appointment." I called Mr. Houseman to tell him that I couldn't make our meeting because I was being flown out to L.A.

"Don't make any decisions until you talk to me," he said. *Oh, now I'm hot to you because somebody else wants me,* I said in my mind. Eventually he did offer me Rosamund, but I didn't take it. I took the role of Genevieve instead. I made the choice on my agent's advice. "You've already done this," he said of *Bridegroom.* "Do something new."

In the simplest possible terms, the plot of *The Baker's Wife* revolves around a young woman named Genevieve and her husband, Aimable the baker. He is older, not sexy, not handsome. She falls for Dominique, a virile young chauffeur, and runs off with him, breaking her husband's heart so badly that he stops baking bread. Aimable's melancholy affects the entire town, now breadless. After spending several days with her lover in a hotel, Genevieve begins to understand that she may have made a mistake. The townspeople plead with her to return to her husband. She does. *La Femme du Boulanger* is a great movie. I wish I could say the same of the musical, *The Baker's Wife*.

I arrived in Los Angeles in May of 1976. I walked into a situation I knew nothing about. All I knew was that Carole Demas had been fired, not that the show was in trouble. The situation was not as dysfunctional as it would become, but there was already discomfort because they'd gone through a long rehearsal period, they'd opened to tepid reviews, and the leading lady had been fired. That's not a good sign.

I joined the cast at the beginning of a very long pre-Broadway run that would go from Los Angeles to San Francisco to St. Louis to Boston to Washington, D.C., before heading to New York. They had just opened in L.A., and the show was sold out for its entire six-week run there—and the Dorothy Chandler is a big house. We had a Civic Light Opera subscription audience, we had Stephen Schwartz, and we had Topol—all of which assured us a sellout.

It didn't take much to see that the show had problems. Signs of trouble were everywhere, even this early in the run. Carole Demas wasn't the biggest problem in the show, but of course they shot the messenger. "We'll fire the leading lady, and everything will be fine." That was the logic at first.

But things were not fine. There were sparks of tension between David Merrick and Stephen Schwartz about what should be done to make the show better, sparks that regularly detonated in serial dismissals. Heads continued to roll in L.A., the first stop on our tour. In addition to the leading lady, we also lost the orchestrator and the conductor.

The Baker's Wife was a musical that just didn't work. Even though we had some of Broadway's most successful talent, nobody could define what was wrong, and nobody knew how to fix it. We already knew how bad it was in L.A., but that was as good as it would ever get. After that, from one revision to another, from one city to another, it just went downhill. Several actors, sure that the show was doomed, tried to jump ship. Keene Curtis was seen in a phone booth crying, begging Helen Nickerson to release him from his contract, to no avail. We were all trapped in this turkey and we knew it. The fact that we were all trapped in it for six months on the road wore us down.

The book was a problem, but so was everything else. The sets were a problem. The lights were a problem. The costumes were a problem. The orchestrations were a problem. The choreography was a problem. The relationship between Stephen Schwartz and David Merrick was a problem. One constant problem was a song called "Bread," the big Act I chorus number, which became the Waterloo of the show. Because the cast kept rehearsing different versions of it day after day after day, it became a running joke. Every day, there would be a rehearsal of "Bread." Every night, the new version would go into the show. The next day, they would change it again. That night that version would go in, and the next day they would change it again, and on and on and on.

We were never *out* of rehearsal. The show kept deteriorating, and everything they did to change it just made it worse. From the Dorothy Chandler in L.A., we went to the Curran in San Francisco, where we opened to eleven of the most devastating notices I've ever seen in my life. No surprise there—we followed *A Chorus Line* into the Curran Theatre. The Curran was also the first theatre where the ushers took pity on us. They sent us candy backstage; they invited us to go out for drinks. They did anything they could to make us feel better. After that, ushers continued to take pity on us at every stop on our tour. It was as if there was an underground usher gossip mill—each theatre prepared the next for the disaster heading their way.

We played to subscription audiences, so despite the reputation that preceded us, they showed up anyway. Poor suckers. At the curtain call they were kind to the performers, yet baffled at the mess they had just witnessed.

Early in the San Francisco run, our second stop, the cast was told to wait in our dressing rooms after the performance, because David Merrick himself was coming to talk to us. He kept us waiting for almost an hour after the curtain. I had a childhood friend in my dressing room and we had planned to go out for supper. He sat on the floor for two hours, waiting for the meeting to be over. When Mr. Merrick arrived, we were called over the intercom to a darkened stage with just one ghost light illuminated. We huddled together, waiting for the man. As if by magic, he appeared in front of the ghost light, so that he was entirely backlit. All I could see was the dome of his bowler hat atop his blackened silhouette.

He started to talk in gentle, hushed tones, thanking us for all of our hard work on this musical that he was so proud to be producing. He then started to lay out what needed to be done to ensure its Broadway success. He handed out four proposals, A, B, C, and D. I can't remember what A, B, and C were, but D's proposal was to continue rehearsing with the following conditions: Drop a city from the tour, return to New York City, and go back into rehearsal for nine weeks with a negotiated salary. Here's where it gets a little squirrely. If the performance salary for the actor was more than five hundred dollars a week, there would be no rehearsal pay. If the actor made under five hundred a week in performance, the rehearsal pay would be negotiated with the Merrick office. In other words, the star and the principals, who clearly

Kurt Peterson as Dominique and me as Genevieve.

made more than five hundred dollars a week, would go back into rehearsal for nothing; no performance fee and no rehearsal fee. The chorus, you can bet, would make a pittance. Ultimately, Equity gave him two weeks' rehearsal.

Because the scene onstage that night was so dramatic, and because we were a bit daunted by the fact that Broadway's Greatest Living Showman had come to address the company in person, we were all in awe of his persuasive oratory. *Anything for you,* we thought at first, but in the light of day we said, *"Whaaaat?!"* We realized what David Merrick was asking us to do. We all voted no, which made the entire company shake in fear—the actors said no to the producer. This was only our second stop and we were already outraged and exhausted. As it turned out, for the entire six months of the tour we never stopped rehearsing during the day and performing at night.

Our director, Joe Hardy, got the axe as well. In San Francisco we were director-less, but rehearsals continued. Each day the creators would present changes that were worse than the day before, but they would go in the show that night, anyway. The next day, those changes came out and that night we played the new changes. It was simply a retreading and reshuffling of the existing material. What had been in the second act went into the first act. What had been in the first act went into the second act. Lines that had been spoken by one person were now spoken by a different person. What this person had been singing, now somebody else was singing, or it was cut altogether but then would go back in the next day, with yet somebody else singing it or saying it or moving it. Nothing really significantly changed. And the company was still rehearsing "Bread." Blessedly I was not in that number.

It seemed that nothing was going right, including the scenery. Jo Mielziner had put our sets on a pair of turntables. On stage left we had the café exterior. When you rotated it, there was the set for the inside of the café. On stage right was the facade of the bakery. After it rotated, the other side came into view, the bakery interior and the bedroom interior upstairs. At the beginning of one performance in San Francisco, I was singing "Gifts of Love" up in the bedroom. I looked to my left to see the entire café spinning like a top. *Oh God,* I thought to myself, *even the scenery has lost its mind.* Small wonder I started popping Valium, ten milligrams at a time. What had happened was that the stagehands had wound the turntable too many times in one direction. In order to make it rotate at all, they had to unwind it during the song. It looked as if the café had decided to sing along with me.

Not that there weren't good times. There were. I was on the

road with great people, and we had as much fun as we could under the circumstances. I started hanging out with two guys in the cast, Timmy Jerome and Pierre Epstein, back when we were still in L.A. We'd go to the beach together, have dinner together. They would come to my sweet little apartment in Westwood and I would make them breakfast. They became my protectors, my big brothers. We were the Three Musketeers.

During the run at the Curran, Timmy and Pierre said, "Come and live with us." I slept on a cot in their condo in Sausalito—and partied. There was a lot of partying at the pool with company members, with rock-and-roll guitarists, with John Lithgow, who was at the theatre next to ours, doing *Same Time Next Year,* and with Kevin, who had come out to visit me.

On one day off, Timmy, Pierre, and I went to Yosemite with some other friends. We were all sleeping in the same tent—two to a sleeping bag. None of us thought anything of it—this company had become blood because we were all in this together. Nobody could be more temperamental than the next person because we were all being beat up on a daily basis. So when I had to sleep in the same sleeping bag as Timmy, that was no big deal. He was my friend, my buddy. When we woke up, Timmy nuzzled up to me and whispered in my ear, "Hey, Patti, you wanna get up—or get down?" I laughed and got out of the bag.

I had the best time with those two guys. I remember one time driving over the Golden Gate Bridge on my way downtown to the theatre. The fog was rolling in. The city lights were twinkling. It was gorgeous. I thought to myself, *I'm working in a big Broadway-bound musical. I don't particularly care how bad the show is. This is* great. *How lucky am I?* Not very, it would turn out.

I may have thought I was having a great time, but we were still caught in the power struggle between David Merrick on one

"Meadowlark."

side and Stephen Schwartz on the other. One particular bone of contention—besides "Bread"—was a solo of mine, "Meadowlark." It's a beautiful soaring ballad, but at seven minutes plus, it was way too long, David insisted, yet Stephen refused to cut it. Needless to say, I was on Stephen's side—in my opinion, those seven minutes flew by. Take the time out of "Bread" if you want to cut something. Finally, while we were running in Boston, our fourth stop, David Merrick was overheard in a bar vowing, "I'll get that song out of the show if I have to poison the birdseed."

He then took matters into his own hands to solve the problem. The next day, we had both a matinee and an evening performance. In the morning David went into the orchestra pit, pulled all the charts for "Meadowlark" off the music stands, locked them in his attaché case, and returned to Manhattan. Before the matinee, Bobby Borad, our stage manager, came to my dressing room and broke the bad news to me that "Meadowlark" had been cut from the show. But David's victory was short-lived. When Stephen found out what had happened, he took countermeasures. The charts magically rematerialized. By the evening performance, the song was back in.

After that, "Meadowlark" became a test of wills between them—it's in, it's out/in/out/in/out. In hindsight, and even at the time, I knew Stephen was right. "Meadowlark" is a haunting, beautiful song. Director Trevor Nunn was so taken by it—he kept hearing women sing it in auditions—that he mounted a London version of *The Baker's Wife* in 1989. That production was not a success, either. The problem then was the same as it had been in 1976, and nothing has changed since. *The Baker's Wife* has been revived and revived, each time because of Stephen Schwartz's beautiful score. But there's a fine line between a hit and a flop, and *The Baker's Wife* has never made it across that border. "Meadowlark," however, has continued to have a life of its own—and rightfully so. It is one of the most beautiful musical theatre songs ever written, and even though the show never made it to New York, it has become almost as much a signature song of mine as the one about tears and Argentina.

As the show continued to rot, my personal condition deteriorated right along with it. I was falling apart. I couldn't sleep even on the Valium. One morning I looked in the mirror and went, "What happened?" My face was covered in tiny raised white dots. Danny Troob, our rehearsal pianist, just looked at me and said, "You look like Anna Magnani on a bad day." That would've been funny if she wasn't ninety and I wasn't twenty-six.

There were more firings. The choreographer was next. I realized that the creative team was no longer functioning as a team at all. The disagreements between Stephen and David were constant. Even though everyone behind the scenes was individually talented, they were never in sync. Nobody got together on the concept. The set was heavy and the lighting was dark. Even though we were supposed to be in the sunny South of France, it looked like we lived in a Welsh mining camp. Theoni Aldredge had given us gorgeous, flowy, bias-cut costumes that made us look like we belonged on the runways of Paris rather than in a bucolic little village in Provence. And not only were we overdressed, we were over-orchestrated as well. The orchestra in the pit sounded like Broadway—all brass—not anything like the French countryside.

The constant revisions and rehearsals were bad enough, but even worse was the hideous behavior of my costar, the Israeli actor Chaim Topol. Throughout his time as Aimable, he was anything but. It seemed that he hated, well, everything. He didn't like the lyrics, so he refused to sing them. Paying audiences actually heard "Blah, blah, blah, blah, blah" out of his mouth. He was obnoxious, unprofessional, and verbally and physically abusive to the cast. I know there are supposed to be two sides to every story, but believe me, both sides thought he was an asshole.

How bad did it get? Really bad. On my first day of rehearsal he grabbed my breast, "just to see how much meat was on my bones." I let it go because I figured I had to make friends with this guy. That never happened. I had to call him Mr. Topol. He wouldn't acknowledge me onstage, so the loving relationship between Aimable and Genevieve didn't exist.

Timmy Jerome, who played the teacher, had to deliver a character description of Aimable, which Topol was not playing. So Timmy decided to go to his dressing room to discuss the lines

with Topol to see if there could be some resolution. Timmy's lines described Aimable as old, jolly, and in love with Genevieve. Timmy said, "You aren't playing that, so it makes no sense when I say it."

Topol contemplated what Timmy had said and replied, "Yes, I see . . . Mmm. Hmm. Let me think about it." The next day, he put white powder in his hair and went onstage playing jolly like a hillbilly in heat, making goo-goo eyes at me, Genevieve. He was mocking Timmy in front of the rest of the cast and acting like a total idiot in front of a paying audience. He thought of himself as the virile chauffeur, not as the old man. He actually opened his costume shirt to reveal his hairy chest. Ew.

My relationship with Topol deteriorated to the point where he actually announced, "I don't believe a word she says, onstage or off." I don't know why. It was clear I hated him in both places. Eventually seven of us in the cast wrote a letter to Actors' Equity, asking to have his Equity card revoked, because he was so damaging to the production and detrimental to the company's morale.

For all of his bad behavior, he was also taking work away from an American actor.

There were two women in the cast, however, who were vying for the sexual attentions of Topol. They both had minor roles. Topol used those women, or at least one of them, against the rest of the company. He needed allies, and he didn't have any—except for these two women. His dressing room was opposite mine, and on many occasions I would see the younger and sexier girl walk into his dressing room in a short dressing gown, and come out later with it half off. The other one (who was not as young as the sexy chorine), was desperately in love with him. At one point, when she found out about the seven of us who wrote the letter to Equity, she just looked at us with rage and tears pouring out of her eyes, screaming, "You're shits! You're just a bunch of shits!"

Sticks and stones, sister. Here, have a Valium.

We had the Equity-approved two-week break between Boston and Washington, so we all trooped back to New York, where David Merrick came yet again before the company to tell us that now he *really* knew what was wrong with the show—and he was going to fire Topol. I would've jumped up and down if I'd had any energy, but I had to start rehearsal. What a bloody mess this was.

Shortly after we arrived in Washington, D.C., the last stop on our pre-Broadway tour, Topol was gone. While we were in D.C., I was subpoenaed to testify at an arbitration hearing because David had filed a claim against Topol. Actually, we all were subpoenaed—the entire cast. If we weren't rehearsing, we were sitting around an arbitration table at ten o'clock in the morning. On the first day of the arbitration, David said, "The only person who's come out of this ahead is Carole Demas." He'd had to pay off her contract when she was let go back in Los Angeles, so now she wasn't in this shit with the rest of us. It was meant as a joke, but none of us were laughing.

My new Aimable was the American actor Paul Sorvino. Sorvino looked like a husky defensive lineman and sounded like Dennis Day. Although far better known as a television and film actor, he did have some Broadway experience, having appeared in *That Championship Season*. He joined our company all full of bravado, enthusiasm, and superiority. "What's the matter with you?" he said on his first day with the company. "Where's your energy? C'mon! Give it your all! We've got to pull this together!" I hated him on sight.

I wasn't alone. The company looked at him dead in the eyes and filled with venom. A pep talk was not what anyone wanted to hear. Fairly or unfairly, everyone took an instant dislike to him, and his attempts to rally us fell on deaf ears. We were simply too exhausted and too raw. We'd been through enormous pain together, and here he was berating us for not showing him 150 percent support or the desire to give our best. He was also the classic show-off tenor. On that first day before he was officially introduced to us, whenever a new cast member would enter the rehearsal room, he would hit a high C. It was like having Howdy Doody at Auschwitz.

The new director was a guy named John Berry and he joined us in Washington. Berry had virtually no experience with musicals at all. His chief asset was that during his time as an expat in Paris, he'd come to know Marcel Pagnol, the man who wrote the film on which the musical was based. That was not nearly enough to compensate for the fact that he was an obnoxious human being with absolutely revolting personal hygiene. He had dirty fingernails, greasy hair, dandruff on his collar, and a really shoddy personality. One day I sat down near him—who knows why—and he said, "What—did you come over here to suck up to the director?" *In your dreams, douchebag,* I said to myself. *You are* beyond *disgusting.*

And as if his personality wasn't bad enough, he had no idea

what he was doing. As one reviewer put it, "With an awkwardness that is painful, Berry squashes every chance for a build, punctures every potential uplift, stamps out all possibilities for charm, and then shrugs helplessly over the mess he has made." I thought the critic was too kind.

The song "Bread" was still in the show, but our rehearsals were now focused on a boule game that would be the show's new opening. There were endless hours spent throwing balls in a kind of slow motion. *Good one, John. You really saved the show with that one.*

He rubbed everyone the wrong way—literally. He actually came to blows with Pierre Epstein. Pierre and John got into an argument about something. Pierre was so enraged that he lifted a café table over his head and started wielding it like a medieval axe, preparing to smite the evil ogre Berry. Berry came after Pierre with his fists cocked, and there was a moment in time when everything froze, as we waited for one or the other to throw the first blow. That's when some people grabbed Pierre and pulled him away, and others grabbed John and pulled him away.

The rest of us went running out of the rehearsal room—some in tears, some in shock, all of us asking, "Why are we going through this in our lives?" In situations like that—I've lived through them a couple of times in my career—your head is spinning. Your eyes can't focus. You feel inhuman, but you're experiencing supremely human emotions: terror, disorientation, and denial. You begin looking around in a desperate attempt to find something to laugh at, or you will sink into utter despair. I felt like I was in purgatory. Would I go to heaven now because the show would finally close? Or would I continue my descent into hell, where there would be no "Meadowlark," just Sorvino's ear-splitting high C's and endless rehearsals of "Bread"?

Meanwhile, even though November 21, 1976, opening night

at the Martin Beck, was fast approaching, at D.C.'s Kennedy Center Opera House we were still rehearsing by day and performing at night. Bad word of mouth spreads faster than good—our audiences were tiny and getting smaller by the day. The decline in the audiences matched the decline in the show itself—it was a long way down from playing the sold-out Dorothy Chandler in Los Angeles. Finally at a matinee at the Kennedy Center in D.C., we set a house record for the least-attended show in the history of the place: We had 25 people in the 2,700-seat house. These people didn't have the good sense to get into one row. All we saw was a sea of red.

And while I was suffering in *The Baker's Wife,* it never escaped me that *The Robber Bridegroom* had become a success on Broadway. I questioned my decision many times.

After one of our last matinees, John Berry called the company to the stage. He looked at me and said, " 'Meadowlark' is cut tonight, and for good." This reduced my part to, "Hello, Aimable. Good-bye, Aimable. Hello, Aimable." That was my cue. I walked off the stage.

"Where are you going?" he called after me.

"To my dressing room."

"Get back here!" he demanded. "There's notes."

"Go to hell," I replied as I kept on walking.

I went into my dressing room, slammed the door, took a magazine, and threw it at the mirror. It didn't make the right sound, so I picked up my wig block and heaved it at the mirror. Still not right. I grabbed my makeup mirror and hurled it as hard as I could—a resounding crash was followed by the tinkling of shattered glass. Ah, that was the right sound.

I started crying and screaming uncontrollably. I kept screaming, regardless of the effect it would have on my voice for the evening show. I was keening like a banshee—I just couldn't take it anymore.

The company swooped down on my dressing room like a flock of seagulls—a flock of seagulls bearing Valium. They were actually giving me Valium before the evening performance! They opened my mouth, put the Valium on my tongue with a little water, tilted my nose to the ceiling, and rubbed my throat till I swallowed.

When they left, Bobby Borad came into my dressing room, sat me down, and said, "Patti, relax. We're closing." It was just two days shy of our opening at the Martin Beck Theatre. The three-sheets and the posters were up. The marquee was lit. My name was finally in lights on Broadway. And I couldn't wait for them to pull the plug.

Because our closing notice went up right before a Wednesday matinee, we had to be paid our full weekly salary—highly unusual and rarely done. Needless to say, the entire company rejoiced. So did the ushers. At the sight of the notice on the call-board, there were tears of joy, raucous, delirious laughter, hugs and kisses. This was a closing notice!

After our performances that day, we went to an usher's house and had one helluva celebration. Our hosts had actually baked a collection of breads with inscriptions like "So long!" "Good luck!" "We'll miss you!" and "You'll never have to rehearse 'Bread' again!"

This was my first taste of how vicious and emotionally debilitating a musical could be.

My agent had thought *The Baker's Wife* would make me a star. Instead, it put me on the unemployment line. After the show closed, I returned to New York a deeply wounded and emotionally scarred human being. Kevin and I were still together, but he couldn't shake me out of my depression. I was in Valium withdrawal for nine months. I gained forty pounds. I lived in a blue robe and slept fourteen hours a day. I'd wake up, go to the refrigerator, eat, and then go back to sleep. I should have bronzed that blue robe.

David Mamet and Me

6

Peter Weller and me as Nicky and Ruth in The Woods.

*I*n 1976, David Mamet boarded the bus with The Acting Company in Louisville, Kentucky, and rode it to Columbus, Ohio. Unbeknownst to us, John had commissioned him to write a play for the company. In the end, he didn't write the play, but he took that ride with us, sat in a seat right behind me, and watched the loud and nonstop antics of the now eleven liberated actors. He didn't say much but he smiled a lot. I can't remember when David and I became friends. All I remember is that we became fast friends, and when I finally got off the road for good, we started hanging out together in Chelsea, where we all lived—Kevin and I on West Twenty-first Street, and David on West Twentieth. It was a lovely twist of fate. He'd come over to our apartment and I would make us all breakfast. We would spend days together. He always brought me little trinkets, all of which I still have. Somewhere in that burgeoning friendship, David asked Kevin, Sam Tsoutsouvas, and me to act in one of his plays. The play was called *All Men Are Whores*. We did it at the Yale Cabaret in New Haven on November 20,

1976, less than two weeks after *The Baker's Wife* closed in D.C. and before the Valium withdrawal kicked in. I think there were more people in that little cabaret than at the last performance of *The Baker's Wife*!

David directed. It was my first experience with this man whose words, rhythm, and subject matter were curious to me. He was mesmerizing when he talked—about anything—but especially when he talked about acting, and about his plays and about the language of his plays. He was an important teacher in my growth as an actor. I've always believed that my association with David gave my career an added dimension and weight. I have an uncanny ease with his language and characters. He's extremely musical and I guess so am I. It was evident to me in his writing just how musical he was, but it was a complete surprise to see him sit down at the piano and start playing. He's bold and raw and I'm definitely that, if anything. I've always been able to lose myself in David's theatrical world. It's one of my favorite places to be: onstage in a Mamet play under David's direction.

David was just beginning to be recognized as a playwright, and had written and directed *Sexual Perversity in Chicago* in 1974 at Goddard College, his alma mater. The following year, *American Buffalo* was presented at the Goodman Theatre in Chicago. He was on the verge of becoming the fabled David Mamet with the opening of the Broadway production of *American Buffalo,* starring Robert Duvall, Kenneth McMillan, and John Savage. I remember walking down West Forty-seventh Street and both of us looking up at his name in lights on the Barrymore marquee. It didn't sink in with either of us.

While we were at Yale, he asked me to do *The Woods*. He handed me the play in the dormitory we all spent the night in and said, "Read it." David was the first playwright to ask me to originate a role in one of his plays. I read *The Woods,* and I shook—it was such an intense piece. I didn't quite understand it but I liked him so much and I also realized that this young American playwright was asking me to take a risk with him. I decided then and there that I would follow him anywhere. Kevin wanted to play the part of Nicky but David refused. "No," he said, "it will break up your relationship."

Well, Kevin didn't play the part, but it *still* broke up our relationship. The emotions churned up by the play were incredibly powerful. There are just two characters, Nicky and Ruth. David called it "a celebration of heterosexual love." Ruth loves Nicky. Nicky ends up hitting her. The play deals with mixed signals and violence. Peter Weller was cast as my Nicky.

But before we went into rehearsal, I did a winter stock play at the Poinciana Playhouse in Palm Beach, Florida. The play was *A Lion in Winter* with Fritz Weaver and Beatrice Straight. David joined me there and we managed to get into trouble. I remember the two of us walking down the street in broad daylight, scaring the shit out of the old folks passing us. "Young people on these streets? Must be muggers!" "Yeah, kind of . . ." David and I were actually thrown out of the Breakers hotel. We found a golf cart after our ejection from the hotel and started making doughnuts on the golf course. We were bad together. At one point we were in a restaurant, and who knows what happened. It wasn't a pleasant meal. We were paying the bill and complaining to the hostess about our server. Something didn't sit well with David—her answer, most likely. What I saw next was David flick a dollar bill to the floor as if the bill had a weight on it. I mean in one fell swoop that bill dashed to the floor. "There's your money," he told her. "You'll have to pick it up yourself if you want it." I saw David's rage. I was scared and thrilled by it. It's a rage I can translate onstage.

David was one of the founders and artistic directors of the Saint Nicholas Theatre in Chicago. That's where we would premiere *The Woods*. David, Peter, and I left for Chicago. We stayed in the Lincoln Hotel and I entered a period in my life that would drastically change me forever.

David used to live and write in the Lincoln Hotel. Perhaps the place was good discipline for a writer, but it was in fact a flea-bitten dive. There was an all-night restaurant attached to the hotel called Jeff's Laugh In, and that's about all there was to it. I was miserable—back on the road rehearsing a play that was forcing me to look deeply into my heart, and then having to go "home" to a squalid hotel room. I began to fall apart emotionally because of the effect the play was having on me. The story of love and the relationship of these two lovers hit too close to home. My relationship with Kevin was teetering again. I would rehearse scenes that were reminiscent of my life with Kevin and I wouldn't be able to leave those feelings in the rehearsal room. They wouldn't go away, these persistent voices telling me how much I had been lying to myself, lying to Kevin, and how much Kevin had been lying to me. There were also powerful feelings developing that were turning into love for Peter—my Nicky. My world was disintegrating. I couldn't separate the play from my own life and I couldn't find a way out of this depression. No one knew that I was sobbing on the floor in my hotel room every night. Kevin was in New York, David was getting together with Lindsay Crouse, Peter was in a long-standing relationship, and I was lost—alone in that disgusting hotel room and emotionally lost. My best friend, Jeffrey Richman, flew to Chicago to hold my hand a couple of times. My demeanor changed, but I wasn't clear if it was the effect the play was having on me or if I was primed for a life-changing experience. Everything was happening around this devastating play. Some people could see that I was in bad shape—women mostly—and they tried to help as best they could, but I had to make my own admissions and changes. The irony is that all of this angst fed the character.

We opened *The Woods* on November 11, 1977, and the reviews were good. I loved a line one reviewer used: "To congratulate David Mamet on his ear for speech is to miss the main thing about him. He is no ear, but a stethoscope." What fun it is to speak his dialogue and unravel his complex characters. I refuse to let it be said that David cannot write female roles. I've played several of them and they are deep emotional beings. He loves women. He's a great acting teacher as well. When I began working with him, I was struck by how he could reduce the craft of acting to its most fundamental procedure and simplify the task. His directives, such as "Let the script do the work, you have the fun," taught me to focus on the text. "Dare to live in the area where you do not know what is going on" taught me to trust the concept of letting go of control. It was interesting to watch David the director edit David the playwright. He is not so possessive and precious about his writing. It's all in the interest of telling the story. David trusts actors as well. When we were rehearsing a reading of his play *The Blue Hour,* we had a note session. The actors were sitting in the house and David was on the stage. He stopped the note session to say, "Leave actors alone, they'll make the perfect stage picture." If only more directors would trust the actor.

David left Chicago after we opened. I was stuck in a run of this extraordinary, difficult, devastating play, depressed as hell in freezing Chicago—not what I bargained for. I had good times, though, even as I tried to make sense of my miserable life in that disgusting hotel room. I met great people in Chicago. Besides the women, there were two of David's best friends, JP Katz and Rokko Jans, Bill Macy, Colin Stinton, the cast of David's play *The Water*

Engine, and Muhammad Ali. Yes, Ali—go figure. It wasn't a total loss. The ignominious end to the Chicago experience was at the closing night party at the Lincoln Hotel. Kevin came to visit me. In a drunken stupor I declared my love for Peter to Peter with Kevin standing right next to me. Silence. Kevin took me back to my room. We held each other in bed and re-committed ourselves to the relationship—until he slept with a chorus girl in Boston while he was doing *On the Twentieth Century.* We finally broke up for good six months later. I sat in a rocking chair in the middle of my apartment, blared *Also Sprach Zarathustra,* and kept thinking, *I'm alone, I'm alone with me. I have to stop lying and grow up.*

Joe Papp wanted to bring *The Woods* to the Public Theater. He wanted me as Ruth, but he didn't want Peter, and he didn't want David to direct. I was upset because my performance was based on Peter's acting and David's direction, but eventually with David's encouragement I agreed that I would do it. I ended up not doing it and the reason was *Evita.*

David had now found a home in New York City, the Public Theater, so I started working with him there. I joined the Chicago company of *The Water Engine* when, for some reason, two women were fired. I replaced them, completed the run at the Martinson Theatre, and took the play to the Plymouth Theatre on Broadway, opening March 6, 1978.

It's a play about a radio station that puts on the radio play *The Water Engine.* During the course of the evening, the actors switch back and forth between the real characters in *The Water Engine* and the radio station actors. *The Water Engine* play is about a guy who has invented an engine that runs on water. The government does not want these plans patented, so they kill the inventor and his blind sister—but not before he mails the plans to the local drugstore kid.

When I went to see it downtown at the Public, it was great. It was done in a theatre where food and alcohol were served—a kind of cabaret environment. While the houselights were still up, the actors entered the stage, chatted with one another, checked props, etc., then an ON AIR light came on as the houselights dimmed, and one of the actors, Colin Stinton, came down to the microphone at the edge of the stage and welcomed the studio audience and the affiliates to "WCMJ 590 on your radio dial." The audience became very silent—we were "On the Air." (Of course we weren't, but the theatrical device was brilliant and worked.)

When we moved uptown to the Plymouth Theatre on West Forty-fifth Street, some major changes occurred. For one thing, the fourth wall was dropped. The fourth wall is the space between the actor and audience, from the foot of the stage out to the depth of the theatre, and if there's no fourth wall, the actors see and acknowledge the audience. If it's dropped, we are staring into a void even if we make eye contact with the audience. But it's still a black void, a middle distance. Musicals don't have the fourth wall when the character is singing. But the wall is dropped when scenes are played unless the character has an "aside," a line directed to the audience. The fourth wall was not dropped when we played downtown, so we acknowledged the audience, and the audience was in the studio with the radio actors, us.

We didn't know why the director would make such a radical change to the way we had been playing it. With this new direction that the play was taking, Colin Stinton said to Steven Schachter, the director, David, and Joe Papp, "You can only be an audience member once, then you start to second-guess the audience. We start at the beginning of the play every night and you never take our point of view into consideration." I spun around at his words. I hadn't ever thought of it that way. I just blindly trusted my directors, but it's so true. Who knows the audience's temperature better than the actor who is playing to them—the storyteller telling the story from the foot of the stage back out to the house? Producers and directors lose perspective on a play after multiple viewings. They have a tendency to forget that the audience will see it only once. As a result, the creators often second-guess themselves and their audience. They stop trusting their initial instincts. I thought Colin was brave and brilliant to protest this move, but they dropped the fourth wall, anyway. As a result, the play lost that precious intimacy and we only ran for a month. Who knows if it was because of that change. I had such a great time doing it, though. It was a Mamet environment. I got a little scared every night places was called and I entered the playing area. It just smelled of danger: The lighting was dark and shadowy, the set was a 1930s radio station, complete with a sound-effects booth, the story was dangerous and pro- phetic. It was delicious, brilliantly conceived and directed, and the production fit the Plymouth Theatre perfectly. I loved this com- pany of actors. I was so sorry *The Water Engine* closed.

From there I moved on to the ill-fated *Working,* another short- lived Broadway experience. The most wonderful thing to come out of *Working* was meeting author Studs Terkel. He was so enthusias- tic and bright-eyed and always generous with the actors. It was a joy when he unexpectedly showed up. What a pity it wasn't a smash because Studs's book is great. When *Working* closed after disas- trous reviews, running only two weeks, I continued my work with David at the Public, where he directed a reading of *The Blue Hour.*

David taught me that when you "act" upon the words in any play, you make more work for yourself and ultimately defeat the playwright. Under David's tutelage, I also learned why I had a ten- dency to rush through the performance—I was not trusting the playwright. I learned that *I* didn't write the words and my sole responsibility was to deliver the playwright's words without comment, without acting upon them, which is hard to do if you don't trust yourself to start off with.

Working with David reinforced what I learned at Juilliard but had failed to fully realize: Remain open. David's lessons were a tremendous help to me, especially the one about "letting the script do the work"—just speak. That, for me, was a real breakthrough. The easier I played it, the more I comprehended the material. I think it was the ability to trust—my mind, my choices, and truly, my being on the stage to begin with. I also learned to trust the script's silences and pauses. For me they are as intense and as much fun, if not more so, than a Mamet word volley. It was the perfect illustration of "dare to live in the area where you do not know what is going on." That is a hard lesson to grasp but one that ultimately is the most liberating.

In October 1982, I went to the opening of *Edmond* at the Provincetown Playhouse on MacDougal Street and was blown away. I sat there and thought, *I wish I was in this.* Not much later, David and director Gregory Mosher called me on the phone and asked me to replace Linda Kimbrough, who was returning to Chicago. I said yes immediately. My agent berated me for agreeing to replace Linda because it was an off-Broadway contract and if I worked for less money than I commanded on Broadway, it would affect my negotiating status. I told him that everyone who knew me knew I worked with David, but *Edmond* came along not long after my first success on Broadway, *Evita,* and apparently I was supposed to sit and wait for the next great part. How many years later did that happen? If I had heeded the agent's advice, I would've missed an opportunity to be in another scary, wonderfully complex, dark Mamet environment. Colin Stinton headed the cast and I played the smallest female role, his wife. I didn't care. I was working with

The cast and playwright (top row, far right) of Edmond, *1982.*

great actors in one of David's best plays. This cast became my family for as long as we worked together. We had several late nights in
my apartment. And it was the "stoned" company. The boys would
get high in their dressing room before the show and the smoke
wafted into the girls' dressing room. It all worked for the play.

Edmond is about the disintegration of an average white male
as he leaves the comfort of his wife and home and slides inadver-
tently into the depths of New York's underbelly, commits murder,
and comes face-to-face with his prejudice in prison. Colin was brilliant as Edmond, as was Laura Innes as Glenda (and every other
part she's ever played). David brings out the best in actors, I swear.

It would be fifteen years—a total of thirteen plays and musicals
and one four-year television series—before I worked with David
again. But we came together once more on *The Old Neighborhood*

in 1997. I played Jolly opposite Peter Riegert's Bobby. Our scene felt like one sentence in thirty minutes of playing time. David wrote a sonata for two instruments and Peter and I played it with joy every night. We rehearsed in Boston, where David was living with his wife, Rebecca Pidgeon, who was also in the play. It was here that David and I broke the silence concerning my lack of courage in talking to him about my choice of *Evita* over *The Woods* (see "*Evita,* Part 1," page 111). David simply said to me, "I heard you thought I was mad at you. I'm not, never was." He said this as we walked to an antique store on a lunch break.

Boston is also where I had a huge fight with Peter Riegert during rehearsal, stormed out of the room, got to the elevator, then turned around and walked back into the room. Peter was still yelling at me, "Don't leave the room!" I replied, "I'm back," which was a big step for me. Peter and I calmed down, then left rehearsal with the director standing there in a total stupor. We spent the night bonding as friends and finding the brother and sister of the play that allowed us to sing the second act of *The Old Neighborhood* for our entire Broadway run. I couldn't wait to get onstage with him or Jack Willis, my husband in the scene with Peter, a rock of an actor, a great one, and a dear friend who was my Herbie in *Gypsy* at the Ravinia Festival. It is always a blessing when the actors you play opposite become your friends. They become lifelong friends.

David now lives in L.A. with the beautiful and generous Rebecca and their two children. I rarely see them, but I'm waiting for the next play that shakes me to my core and lifts me to another level in heart, soul, mind, and craft. I can't imagine the rest of my career without David in it.

7

Evita, Part 1

AUDITION AND OUT OF TOWN, 1979

"Rainbow High."

*I*t made me a star. It was the most difficult role I had been given to play. It also gave me a reputation and a shadow of controversy that has followed me to this day and took its toll on every aspect of my life. Nothing has ever come easy for me. What many believe must have been a glorious ascent into heady stardom was, for me, a trial by fire, with the constant threat of being burned at the stake. But I did it. I accomplished this part and I wouldn't change any of it. Okay, that's not entirely true—there's a shitload I would've changed. But ultimately it was worth it. Why? Because of the lessons, the lessons, the lessons.

The height of anticipation over the Broadway production of *Evita* was pretty much the first of its kind for a musical. With Hal Prince directing, a score by Andrew Lloyd Webber, and lyrics by Tim Rice, it had received great notices when it opened in London. The hype stateside was unbelievable, and with good reason. Hal's production was extraordinary. There's no question that it was, and is, a benchmark in musical theatre.

The music had been around for a couple of years. In 1976, Tim Rice and Andrew Lloyd Webber put out a concept album of *Evita,* with Julie Covington, David Essex, and Colm Wilkinson singing the leads. As I listened to it, all I could think was that this guy, Andrew Lloyd Webber, hated women. The high notes in the score, which the character of Evita sits on all night long, are placed in the *passaggio,* or the passage. The *passaggio* are the weakest notes to produce as the voice passes from chest to head.

Both Kevin Kline and Paul Gemignani, the legendary Broadway conductor, told me I *had* to audition for *Evita.* There was only one problem: Every actress in the country wanted this part— Barbra Streisand, Ann-Margret, Meryl Streep, Faye Dunaway, even Raquel Welch. Clearly, Patti LuPone, with one pre-Broadway disaster to her credit, was a dark horse. But what they were finding out was almost nobody could sing it. There are still probably only a handful of women who can sing *Evita* in the original keys.

Joanna Merlin was the casting director. She'd seen me onstage at Juilliard and with The Acting Company. She knew I could act, but at that point, nobody knew whether I could sing. After the preliminary audition, Joanna asked me to keep myself free for the final callback. *Okay,* I thought, *maybe the dark horse is actually in the race.*

Meanwhile, in October of 1978, I was doing *Catchpenny Twist* by Stewart Parker at the Hartford Stage when I got an audition for Steven Spielberg's film *1941.* I read the script and thought, *Ooh yeah, I want this part,* but Nancy Allen was already cast in the role. Steven, however, liked my audition so much that he created a small part for me so I could be in the movie. Even though I had to fly myself out to L.A. and put myself up, I was willing to do it because I wanted to work with Steven. Who could blame me? A Steven Spielberg film was a guaranteed blockbuster, right? Yeah, up until *1941.*

I flew out to California a couple of weeks before I was scheduled to shoot. There was nothing to keep me in New York. Kevin and I were no longer together, my run in *Catchpenny* was over, and I was sitting in my apartment waiting, which is what most actors do when they're not acting.

I went to Universal Studios looking for the set of *1941*. I walked a bit, then came around the corner just as they turned on the arc lights. They were so bright that my eyes went into negative. I was looking at the biggest set I'd ever seen, in negative vision. That was my first impression of moviemaking. *This is Hollywood,* I thought. I was dumbstruck and thrilled beyond description at the enormity of Hollywood movies.

To save money, I was staying at my best friend Jeffrey's house. The house itself was lovely, but there was no stove, no shower (just a tub with one of those hoses used to bathe dogs), and one bed, which we shared. It didn't matter. I was with my best friend in sunny California, making a Hollywood movie directed by Steven Spielberg at Universal Studios. I was on my way.

Steven was very nice to me from the minute I arrived. We used to have lunch together. I was quite shy around him, partly because I was in awe of him and partly because I had a crush on him. My part was tiny; I worked in the USO scene with Penny Marshall and Joe Flaherty. For

Steven Spielberg at work.

With Penny Marshall on the set of 1941.

some reason I had billing, and a picture in the end credits. I had one line: "Say, you devil . . . How's about a deviled egg?" I didn't care. I was working on a Steven Spielberg movie. It couldn't miss, right?

It was a great group of people, both cast and crew. Janet Healy was Steven's assistant; Sally Dennison was the casting director; Mary Ellen Trainor, who at the time was engaged to Bob Zemeckis, was associate to the producer, Buzz Feitshans. All three were wonderful, generous women and I became good friends with each of them. To this day I don't know why, but I was introduced to all of the people at the top on this movie. I was kind of dumbfounded, and I thought, *What a very nice place this Hollywood is. This is where I want to stay. I want be a movie star and hang out with nice people and be in big hit movies like* 1941.

That first night I visited the set, I watched Dan Aykroyd work. I knew him from *Saturday Night Live,* but that night, I remember being so taken by his intensity and acting ability. Dan and I became friends on this movie, and I was lucky to work with him again on *Driving Miss Daisy.* Dan is a brilliant actor.

Then finally: the reason I'm here! They scheduled the USO scene. What fun it was getting a call sheet with my call time, showing up at the crack of dawn to get made up for the day's work, and then working fourteen hours. What else did I have to do? I was young. I was in heaven.

A couple of weeks into the shoot, Treat Williams, one of the leads, was not called to the set, so he left town. Then Steven changed the shooting schedule for that day and needed Treat, but Treat was nowhere to be found. Buzz Feitshans and Steven were furious because the day was now wasted due to his absence. As a result, nobody in the cast was allowed to leave Los Angeles for the rest of the filming. Naturally, I then got the call to return to New York for the *Evita* final callback. Oh shit.

I went to Buzz and asked for special permission to go to New York. "No way," he said. Then I went to Janet Healy, who went to Steven, who told Buzz to let me go. He didn't want to do it. "If you're not back on Tuesday morning," Buzz threatened, "your career in Hollywood is over." Really, people talk like that out there. But even that was thrilling to me—I had a career in Hollywood!

I flew to New York on the eighteenth of February 1978. I went home to my apartment, and on the morning of the nineteenth I woke up to a foot of snow on the ground. My heart sank, but I headed for the audition, anyway. When I got out of the subway, I was at the wrong end of Forty-second Street and had to trudge two long blocks to the Shubert Theater. I had my luggage with me because I had a flight back to L.A. when the audition was over. I was in California clothes (sneakers and jeans), and by the time I got to the theatre, I was soaked from the knees down.

I was pissed off because I knew in my heart I wasn't getting out of JFK that night, which meant that I wouldn't be on the set in Los Angeles the next day, which meant that when I finally did get back to Los Angeles, my career in Hollywood really would be over. When I got to the Shubert, my eyes were filled with blood.

I looked at the stage from the wings and I saw a white line

across the floor. *Oh,* I thought, *I guess we're not supposed to cross it.*
What that white line was was the set for *A Chorus Line.*

When my name was called, I walked onstage and took a giant
step in front of the white line, in defiance. I sang "Buenos Aires,"
then "Don't Cry for Me, Argentina," and then "Rainbow High."

John Houseman used to tell me that I perform better when
I'm mad. Well, I was mad that day, so mad that I started crying
during "Argentina." I barreled through the other two numbers. All
I could think about was my dead career in Hollywood. They said
they'd let me know in a few days. *Yeah, who cares?* I thought. I met
up with my brother Billy at the audition and I said, "I'm not getting out of here tonight, am I?" I knew by the look on his face I
was screwed.

I hailed the one cab driving around the city streets, then went
to the airport to find that, yes, indeed, my flight was canceled.
What could I do? I lay down and slept on the airport floor, with my
hair in big rollers for my *1941* hairdo, wearing a sleep mask.

People would go by and laugh at me. Their laughter would
wake me up. The humiliation was palpable. I had forgotten, or
more likely didn't know, to carry phone numbers for the film's
production office to tell them I was stranded. For some reason, I
did have Mary Ellen's number. I called her, cried, and begged for
forgiveness. She was so cool. Everyone was alerted to my plight,
and she kept in touch with me until I was finally able to board a
plane the next day.

That almost didn't happen. I found out the hard way that
when your flight is canceled, the airline does not automatically put
you on the next flight out. You have to rebook. In the morning I
went to the counter expecting to get on the first flight out. "Sorry,"
they told me, "you don't have a seat. This flight is sold out."

Suddenly I saw Christopher Reeve, who also went to Juilliard,

*Opening night in Los Angeles with Robert Stigwood
and Christopher Reeve.*

and who had just become a big star in *Superman*. We said hello, then I instantly burst into tears. Chris tried to comfort me—maybe there was something he could do.

The next thing I knew, they were announcing the boarding for the L.A.-bound flight, and I heard my name called over the loudspeaker. Chris had gotten me on his plane, in first class. He had come in and scooped me up like a real-life Lois Lane—in big rollers. The cabin was filled with actors and agents and Hollywood types grateful to be leaving the blizzard of '78 behind. We had all been stranded, but nobody looked as bad as I did. I have a feeling some of them had a laugh over my ridiculous appearance. I didn't care. I was on my way back to my career in Hollywood.

I made it to the set by eleven o'clock that morning, and when I arrived, I got a round of applause. Nobody had thought I was going to make it. Somebody asked how I got out, and I told them, "Superman."

Two days later, I was having my lunch in the makeup room when I was called to the phone. "Congratulations!" my agent said. I started to cry.

They were not tears of joy. I was very ambivalent about this— even though my friend Jeffrey tells me that when I was rehearsing my audition in his no-stove, one-bed house in L.A. I said to him, quite calmly, "This is the next thing I'm supposed to do." But I really didn't like the music. I wanted to work with Hal Prince, but I did not want to do *Evita.*

I was crying because I wanted to continue working with David Mamet. *The Woods* was being revived at the Public, but I wasn't sure I wanted to do it if David wasn't directing. He said, "Yes, you do. Ulu Grosbard is directing."

Now I had to tell David that I couldn't do *The Woods* because I had to do this musical. I knew how important playing *Evita* would be for my career. I knew it would be historical working with Hal. I knew the dizzying heights I would experience being the chosen leading lady of *Evita* after this much-hyped, Scarlett O'Hara–like search.

I never did call David, my friend and champion. I didn't have the guts to. I ignored my responsibility to him, and then it was too late to call. This was another one of those times in my life when I didn't have courage. Just like the time I was cast as Lady Teazle in *The School for Scandal* at Juilliard, and I wasn't able to admit to the director that I didn't know how to spell *Restoration,* let alone act it. I've never had the courage to speak up in the moment.

On the set of *1941,* while I was crying, everyone else was happy for me. When Steven found out that I got the part, he announced it on the set and said to me, "I know talent." He was proud that he'd cast me in his movie, and proud that I'd landed the role of Evita because *Evita* was everywhere, including Hollywood, three thousand miles away from New York City, six thousand miles away from London.

That evening I drove home to Jeffrey's. "Everybody's been looking for you!" he shouted as I walked in the door. "Earl Wilson has called three times."

"How does Earl Wilson know I'm staying with you?" I said. At that very moment the *New York Post* columnist called again. I still don't know how he got the number. We talked, or rather, he fired off questions and I stammered idiotic answers. My nerves were jangled and I was feeling totally spaced out. *What is happening?* I wondered.

Days later, I was sitting in Jeffrey's living room and thought, *I'm going on a roller-coaster ride.* And then it hit me—that was exactly what Evita had done as well. That's how I was going to play her, I decided, with a big smile on my face as if she were saying, *Look at me. Look what I got away with.* It was truly a revelation. Interpretations don't generally come to me like that, or that fast.

The first day at rehearsal, Hal said to me, "I don't want you to smile," before I even smiled. "And I want gnarled hands."

Uh-oh. That's 180 degrees from the way I wanted to play her. I knew Evita had to have a sense of humor. She had to have a wink in her eye or the audience would not be able to come to her, or me playing her. But Hal Prince was my director, so rehearsals went on and I did what I was told to do. I learned the music, the dances, the scenes, but for the most part it was an out-of-body experience. I began to realize that I didn't know how to sustain the singing of the role. I was scared shitless. One bright spot, however, was the fact that another Juilliard alum, Mandy Patinkin, was cast as Che.

At the beginning of rehearsal I was plagued with people telling me things that Elaine Paige, the original London Evita, did in the part. The producers brought three dancers over from the London production and they'd say, "Patti, now right here Elaine would do this. Here's where Elaine did this." I was polite for about two days. And then a Broadway reputation was born. "Shut up," I said. "I don't want to hear another word about Elaine's performance. If you tell me what she did, then I don't have a chance to discover it for myself. I'm an actor. I'll figure it out."

Well, that made me real popular with the kids in the chorus. I couldn't deal with that; I had no time. But I did, unfortunately, have to deal with the alternate Eva, who played the Wednesday and Saturday matinees. She was nipping at my heels, praying for me to fail or fall so she could have my part. It was a real-life *All About Eva.*

Eva and her alternates have a sordid history. There was the Austrian alternate whose ex-boyfriend pulled a Tonya Harding on the first Eva—two nights before opening night. The ex-boyfriend hired thugs to beat the crap out of Eva, just so the alternate, who was unaware of the plot, could open the show. She did. Critics were impressed, but her run as Eva lasted ten days. The plot was exposed, the boyfriend was arrested and spent two years in jail. The alternate was quoted in the press saying her career was ruined. It probably was. I mean, how do you come back from that? Tonya didn't. Maybe the alternate was a contestant on Viennese Celebrity Boxing. But I digress. . . .

My work was cut out for me. In addition to the difficulty of the singing, I really had to know who this woman was, because she was real. I read every book written about her. Hal gave me a tape of four speeches she had made from the Casa Rosada in a space of two years. She sounds very young in the first two speeches, then she sounds like she's eighty when she gives the speech declining the vice presidency. At that point, she's dying of cancer, and you actually hear the physical disintegration through her voice.

What I gleaned from the books was that Eva Duarte was an opportunist, and a very smart one. After she married Juan Perón and became a powerful woman in her own right, something unheard of then, she continued using the methods of the military but was simply more ruthless and vindictive in her responses. Juan Perón was part of the military establishment, but the books portray him as a slightly complacent, perhaps lazy man. Eva was ambitious, hungry, rich, and powerful, but I don't think she revised the tactics the military government used. The brilliant move she did make was to embrace the lower classes, her people, known as the shirtless ones, the *descamisados.*

And they embraced her back. Because one of their own had risen to this great height, and because she did not forsake them, she became more powerful than the president, her husband. It was an amazing political coup. She eventually fell out of favor with the *descamisados,* though, because her ambition, greed, and vengeance were unbridled.

She discovered that she had cancer during this decline in her popularity. Many of the *descamisados* believed they may have caused her illness by abandoning her. When she died at age thirty-three, they petitioned the Vatican to canonize her: Santa Evita.

The story is truly fantastic. I would have pro-Peronistas and anti-Peronistas come backstage and say the same thing to me: "You have her to a T." I don't think it was my performance they were talking about. It was the memory of Evita and her powerful influence over the people who lived through her regime. One journalist despised her because he lived under house arrest for many years, but his son adored her because he had learned how to write by writing "Evita loves me" over and over at school.

Eva Perón was even more powerful in death than she was in life. She was embalmed and a crypt that would have rivaled the Statue of Liberty was being built for her body when Perón was overthrown and Evita's corpse was stolen. In an effort to obliterate her spiritual hold over the country, the new regime filled up five caskets, four with sand, one with Evita. Each casket was sent to a different part of the world. It was a huge miscalculation. The country rioted and a president was killed—all in the name of recovering their beloved Evita.

Her body disappeared for seventeen years and only one person knew where she was. After Isabelita and Juan Perón married and Perón was again running for office, Isabelita convinced the Peronistas to bring Eva back to Argentina. That one person who knew her whereabouts was still alive and told them where she was buried. Evita was in Italy under the name of María Maggi. When they exhumed her, she was still perfectly preserved, with a scant hair out of place. Scary, huh? That became the political trinity: Evita, Juan, and Isabelita. I think the three of them won the election.

We had four weeks of rehearsal in New York before going to Los Angeles. Unlike *The Baker's Wife, Evita*'s out-of-town run would be short, May through August, just L.A. and San Francisco, before coming to Broadway.

So there I was. I had landed the part, I was in rehearsal, and I was overwhelmed by what I had to accomplish. The blocking I could do; the acting I could do. The singing was frightening. Evita Perón's voice was pitched high and the music reflected that height. The D, E, F, and G an octave above middle C were not intended to sound sweet. Which means there needed to be power behind the voice. The score, for me, was almost impossible to sing because I had no power in the *passaggio*.

As I recall, the day after we completed our New York rehearsals, we flew to L.A. and went straight to a sitzprobe (the company's first sing-through with the orchestra) at the Dorothy Chandler Pavilion. (Yes, I was back at the Dorothy Chandler, scene of my last crime, *The Baker's Wife*.) There were no microphones for the singers in the rehearsal room, and I remember Ruthie Mitchell, Hal's assistant, motioning to me from across the room to go easy with my voice. But it was so exciting. I was singing with the orchestra for the first time. In my ignorance, I ended up singing over both the orchestra and chorus.

By the end of the night, after a flight, a sitzprobe, and a rehearsal onstage where more singing was required, I had lost my voice. There was nothing—no sound, nothing. Panic. The next day I was sent to Dr. Hans von Leden, L.A.'s preeminent throat doctor, who said to me, "Your vocal cords look like raw hamburger meat. You cannot speak for the next five days." It was five days till opening night. I was freaking out. Now, besides not being secure in my vocal ability, I was not able to do the technical rehearsals, which meant I couldn't walk the stage, deal with the sets and props, learn the orchestrations, or master the split-second-quick costume changes, all fourteen of them.

Panic, fear, and failure set in. I was doomed before I began my run. I went to the doctor every day, and on the fourth day, I was healed enough to open the following night. I don't know how I did it—sheer willpower, I guess. I opened the show, sang, acted, changed costumes, danced, and avoided bumping into the scenery the best I could.

I was out the following night. I blew out my voice in one show.

My reviews were bad, my confidence nonexistent. It's pretty much a blur, the following weeks, but I do remember going to a member of the chorus, David Vosburgh, during a performance and asking him what the vowel sound for "glory" was. He told me. Then I asked him if he would help me with the score. He said, "My partner said to me last night, 'Can you help Patti?'" It was divined.

We started to work together, and ended up working on the score and on a vocal technique for most of my run. The producers put a piano in my dressing room and gave David a bonus. David saved my job. He gave me so much more than just the ability to finally sing the role. He gave me inner strength, and the valuable lesson that nothing is impossible—that diligent work, patience, and trust are the only things that will see you through to the very end of any journey.

The run in Los Angeles was very hard on me. There was tension with the stage management and tension with the alternate, who was going on for me more frequently than I ever anticipated. But there was always some manifestation, a sign from God that assured me I would conquer this part and survive. One of the manifestations was the uncanny appearance of the *Evita* groupies, who became known as the *descamisados*. They would sit in the first row and lob pink roses at me during my curtain call. You know when they throw roses at you that they're telling you you're good. Somehow they always showed up when I needed support the most.

I also had a visitation from Evita herself the night before I opened. I couldn't talk about it for years. I thought I was nuts, actually, making up things in my mind to quell my fears, but Evita appeared to me three times during my run. She was there. Los Angeles was the first visitation. My family had flown in for opening night. My brothers went to stay with my cousin, and my mom stayed with me in the Hollywood Hills house I was renting. I was still on vocal silence. For two nights before their arrival, I had nightmares about Evita that would wake me up as only a nightmare can. My eyes would open in fear, and I would see, in the next room, a black rectangular box floating low to the floor. *What am I looking at?* I asked myself. *Oh yes, that's the fireplace in the living room.* Next night: same nightmare, same image upon awakening. *It's only the fireplace. Go back to sleep.*

On the third night, my mom arrived. She and I were sleeping in the same bed. I was on my back to her left, and she had her back to me. I woke up again from the nightmare only to see a female figure standing next to the bed, right next to me. She was wearing a colorless, diaphanous floor-length robe—almost like a shroud. She had shoulder-length hair that flipped up at the ends. She had no face.

I was terrified. I tried to scream but I had no air in my lungs; no sound would come out. I think my mouth was frozen open. I tried to nudge my mom, but there was a weight on my entire body. I felt paralyzed. I stared at this specter, and she didn't move for what seemed like forever. There were no thoughts in my head, just this paralysis.

She finally, and I kid you not, flew out the little window, and as the last bit of her dress disappeared into the night, the weight on my body lifted. I bolted upright and said out loud, "Good-bye, Evita." It shocked me to say those words, but I knew it was true. It was her. What happened next was that my mind, my heart, and my being just started releasing all this pent-up tension. I think she was saying, *You'll be fine because I won't let you stink in this part. I'll be circling.*

I truly believe Eva was manipulating her entire glorious comeback. She had been vilified thirty years earlier, and she would now be glorified. Maybe it was all made up in my head, but what did happen was that my crippling fear started to subside. I slowly began to trust my training, my talent, and I set about conquering the beast. It didn't happen in the nine weeks in Los Angeles; too many things were going on at once. I still had no command of the score, and there was no joy, only fear onstage every night. The bad notices kept coming and coming, and rumors were surfacing about my imminent firing.

Hal called me on the phone a couple of weeks after we opened to tell me he was returning to L.A. I thought, *Oh shit! I'm doing my interpretation of the role, not his.* Richard Allen, my hairdresser, actually thought I would be fired for changing my performance from what we had rehearsed to what I was now performing. Nothing was working; my voice was failing, so my first step in trying to find some comfort level onstage was developing a character I could be comfortable with while remaining true to the play. It was radically different from Hal's interpretation, but after he saw me in the role he said, "That's just what I wanted." Duh, *what?* I counted it as a blessing. But that's not why Hal returned to L.A. He told me that he was going to say something to the company that he and I would laugh about twenty years later. Well, it's been *thirty* years and I'm still not laughing.

He assembled the company after the show and told us that an item would be appearing in Suzy Knickerbocker's column in the *New York Post.* It would say that I was being fired and that Hal was waiting for clearance from Equity for Elaine Paige to take over my part in the American production. He also said that not a word of it was true. I was stunned, which was kind of amusing since I was already in a walking coma and didn't think anything else could surprise me. Wrong again, Patti. "When you think you've hit the bottom, there's always one step further down you can go. . . ."

The truth is that, yes, I was going to be fired. I found out seven years later when Clive Barnes, the New York theatre critic, casually told me that he had been consulted by Robert Stigwood and David Land, the producers, about who should replace me. Clive told me he said, "No one. Let her figure it out." Clive and Hal were the only two people on the creative end who trusted that I would. Thank God I did. I would've hated to let those two men down. No, the joy of being fired from a high-profile role would lie in wait for another fifteen years.

The last and most devastating blow in the L.A. run was my not being able to finish my final performance. Nine weeks after opening night I was still frozen in fear onstage, but at least I was not missing shows. However, Andrew Lloyd Webber wanted to record the album during our final week of performing. He also wanted to start at ten in the morning. I said no. I agreed to record in the afternoon, but I told them that the recording sessions had to be broken up throughout the week. I was recording the album during the day and singing it again at night, not a great idea for someone who was having difficulty singing it once. We completed the recording, and on the Saturday morning of the final performance, I had nothing left. I was once again devastated by my vulnerability, and by the control those two tiny muscles, the vocal cords, had over my life.

The whole world was coming to the final performance in Los Angeles. It was sold out and tickets were being scalped. I started the show, and it was during "Buenos Aires," my first big vocal-cord-busting solo, that I started to talk the song. I was, in a word, fucked.

At the end of the first act I knew I couldn't finish the show. I had gone to a healer in Los Angeles in all sorts of desperation and she was at the show. At intermission, she did her best laying-of-hands on my throat. My doctor, who was also there, looked down my throat. Nothing could be done.

I was shell-shocked. I'd never been knocked off the stage

before. I'd never not finished a performance. My only thought was to get the hell out of the building as fast as I could before I heard the alternate singing "Argentina." In fifteen minutes, I packed up a dressing room that I'd lived in for nine weeks. I did take special care, though, with one of my most prized opening night gifts—a galvanized bucket of snow, from Steven, Buzz, and the company of *1941*.

Jeffrey, my mom, and I went back to my house. I don't know how I got through that night. I seriously doubted my ability to play this part . . . and San Francisco was looming. The next day, as my mom and I drove north up the Pacific Coast Highway, I was once again on vocal silence. We passed what I took to be a very bad sign as we left L.A. On the way out of Malibu, I saw the most horrific car and pickup-truck accident, with several dead bodies covered but sprawled out across the entire highway. The image has never left me, and it is one I still associate with my run in L.A.

We arrived in San Francisco, where we went through another technical rehearsal, and I sang too hard. I blew another opening and I was out again. My notices were equally as bad as they had been in Los Angeles. Despite it all, I settled in for a seven-week run.

The stage of the Orpheum Theatre was where I had the second visitation from Evita. It happened during a preview. At the beginning of the show, as the movie screen was tracking back, a stage light overhead exploded. It shattered and rained down tiny pieces of glass over the center section, right where I was sitting. In my career it is the one and only time that has ever happened to me. The date was July 26, the anniversary of her death.

In San Francisco, the backstabbing within the cast, which had already started in Los Angeles, got a lot more intense. Down in the basement of the Orpheum Theatre, where the chorus and dancers lived, somebody put up the alternate's good notices next to my bad notices. When I found out about these reviews going up on the wall in the basement and nobody having the decency to take them down, it was beyond upsetting. I talked to stage management about the problem before the performance. They just didn't give a flying fuck. They should have controlled it, but they did nothing. I remember crying out loud, "I'm too small for this." It went in one ear and out the other. I had no support backstage.

After the show, Richard Allen, my hairdresser, and Sal Mistretta, a member of the company, took me out to calm me down. I normally never went out after the show because of my voice. They took me to North Beach, the Italian neighborhood. I got drunk and threw up red (tomato sauce) on a pink Cadillac.

It became even crazier when I arrived at the Pacific Heights Victorian mansion that had been rented for me, sight unseen. I didn't actually live there; I just slept there and woke up there. The house may have been gorgeous, but it was infested with mice. To deal with the problem, the owner had put rat poison behind a dresser in my bedroom. Here I was, alone in this mansion, and as soon as the lights went out and I tried to sleep, the mice jumped into the rat poison. If that dresser hadn't been so heavy, I would've moved it and jumped in with them. *It's a test*, I told myself. *All of this is a test.*

One night I came back after the show and looked down the hallway into the kitchen. I saw a mouse sitting up in the middle of the kitchen floor. I walked by it and said, "Hello. I know you, my little friend." Then I got on the phone with David Schramm, my classmate from Juilliard. We talked for about forty-five minutes, and all that time the mouse didn't move.

When I hung up the phone, I realized that the mouse was dying. I got down on my hands and knees to face the critter. I explained, "I didn't put the rat poison down. This isn't my house."

And with that, the mouse sort of reared up with one paw, as if to say, *You killed me.*

Here I was on all fours, in a staring contest with a mouse. Nothing can be more absurd, I realized. It was the staring contest that actually lifted the black cloud over my head. *Fuck it,* I thought. *I'm going to get through this because on top of everything else, I'm conversing with a mouse.* Bing. That was it.

I was still working daily with David Vosburgh. We'd have a voice lesson during the day, and then in the performance I'd try to apply what I'd learned. It was extremely difficult. I'd get the head of the horse right, and the tail would fall off. I'd get the head and the tail, and a leg would fall off. It just never gelled. But at least I was working on it and David was helping me break down the score and develop a vocal technique so that I'd be able to sing it . . . eventually.

Through it all Mandy Patinkin was my ballast, my savior. Whenever I was onstage with him, not only was there great respect and love crossing the boards from one actor to another, one friend to another, he also saved my ass. Whenever he saw that I was tied in a knot, he took me by the shoulders. He said some sage things and kept me onstage. For that I will be forever grateful to him. Beyond grateful. Mandy is an angel for me; he was heaven-sent. I will love him forever.

The wonderful thing about theatre is the lessons one learns, the life experiences that accrue. And because it's such a subjective profession, the lessons, good or bad, are deep. In the case of *The Baker's Wife,* we all put aside any differences we might have had with one another's personalities and bonded because we were in that hellhole together. We shed blood together. Mandy and I had known each other before *Evita,* but now we really became good friends.

It was Mandy who worked with me to make sure the audience understood what was going on. *Evita* is expositional. She was born; then when she was fifteen she hooked up with this guy, then she went here; when she was twenty, she went there. If you don't know the story of her life, it can be very difficult to comprehend what's happening onstage. Mandy and I worked very hard at connecting the dots.

Unfortunately, San Francisco was not an entirely happy experience for him, either. He got German measles from one of the kids. The theatre had to be disinfected. He was out for three weeks. I couldn't wait for him to come back—so much did my performance and well-being depend on Mandy. He is a bright light.

It was also in San Francisco that the "arms in a V" pose at the end of "Don't Cry for Me, Argentina" was born. It happened when famed photographer Martha Swope joined us to shoot the pictures for the front of the theatre and for the program. Martha asked me to lift my arms, elbows slightly bent. That was Elaine Paige's pose, and at that point I really didn't want anyone else telling me to imitate Elaine.

"I don't do that," I told her. "I do this." And then I raised my arms in a V. I did it spontaneously. I don't know what I'd been doing at the end of "Don't Cry for Me, Argentina" before that day. I just know I'd never done the V before. *Well*, I thought, *I guess that's what I do now*. It became my final pose in "Argentina," and I took it with me to New York in September.

I used to have long talks with Peter Marinos, who, besides Mandy, became a close cast mate. He would come to my dressing room an hour before curtain, almost every night. We would talk about how the performances were going. Recently he recounted this story to me:

"High Flying, Adored."

"As I remember it, we were discussing 'Don't Cry for Me, Argentina,' and you said you felt it was cheesy to gesture in rhythm to the underscoring. I disagreed and said, 'To me, looking up at the Casa Rosada, it looks stronger when your gestures are accompanied by the music.' You were setting some of the moves, and after a couple performances, you asked me, 'What does that look like?' I said, 'I think it looks great.' Then we named the gestures you were doing because we had nothing better to do. This is what you did and what we named them: Right arm extended to *descamisados*—'I love you.' Left arm extended to *descamisados*—'I love you.' Both arms up in a V—'I'm fabulous.'"

Peter continued, "Then I suggested that on the final chord, just before the Casa Rosada revolved, you drop your head slightly to the side. I believed, subliminally, the audience would see Christ on the cross, and applaud. At first you said absolutely not. Then you tried it. For the first time, there was a full-on audience ovation mirroring the *descamisados'* cheering. We had a good laugh after the show."

When we did the *Life* magazine shoot for the New York opening, there was a picture of me with my arms outstretched. Below my picture was a picture of the actual Evita with her arms in that exact pose. I had never seen that picture before. She was, indeed, circling.

Evita, Part 2

8

Lana Turner and me backstage at Evita, *July 14, 1980.*

UPI/ANDY LOPEZ

roadway, opening night. After two weeks of previews, we opened *Evita* at the Broadway Theater on September 25, 1979. The day we opened, I had the flu. I threw up in the sink at intermission, then went out and sang "Don't Cry for Me, Argentina." A review from one of the critics called my performance "colorless." No shit.

One of the few positive moments of opening night for me was a telegram from Kevin. It was simply one word: "InEVITAble!" I was very touched, and treasure that telegram to this day.

Robert Stigwood, our producer, held the opening night party at Xenon, a popular discotheque. I entered the main room to hear "Disco *Evita*" blaring over the PA system. I stayed for about an hour and then left. The place was loud and packed with club-bers, as well as the throngs from opening night. My best friend and date for the evening, Jeffrey Richman, had to crawl on his hands and knees among the shoes, handbags, and fallen food to extract himself from our table. Hal didn't want to go to Xenon, so he and a select group took over what was then the back room of Joe Allen's. Jeffrey and I joined him there and we waited for the reviews.

In those days, the *New York Times* building on West Forty-third Street still printed the newspaper, and the first printing would come out an hour or two before midnight. Opening night parties were thrilling or excruciating, depending on the reception of the show you were opening. Somebody would run to the *Times* building, bring back the first edition, and read it out loud on top of a dining table to a hushed and anxious crowd. The *Times* review was and still is the only review that counts for a show's box office the next day. If the review is good, the party will continue into the wee hours. If it's bad, the party will break up, and everyone will exit rather quickly, taking bets on when they'll see the closing notice posted on the call-board.

No one runs to the *Times* building anymore, sadly a lost tradition. The critics attending opening night is another lost tradition. Opening night curtain is always at seven o'clock. In the past, when we took our curtain calls, we would see critics dashing up the aisles to make their deadlines. Now they see the shows during the final week of previews. So why is opening night curtain still at seven? I don't know, but I do miss seeing the backs of their heads as they made that mad dash up the aisle.

We opened *Evita* to indifferent reviews, cold reviews. At least a bad review elicits some sort of passion, but indifference . . . that's the worst. This stunning production that Hal had mounted, and the amount of work that Mandy and I had put into those characters, was dismissed. As Hal read Walter Kerr's review in the *New York Times*, I watched his face go a shade of red I'd never seen before. Hal's production was innovative, but his accomplishment received scant acknowledgment from the press.

Why? For one thing, I believe there was resentment in the theatrical community, and also in the New York area itself, that the Nazi sympathizer Evita Perón was being glorified. Not only was there an active community of Argentine expatriates, but many people still remembered who the Peronistas were and what they had done. They were fascists, and a lot of Nazis found safe haven in Argentina after World War II. To many it appeared that Tim Rice and Andrew Lloyd Webber—and all of us by extension—were glorifying fascists and the harborers of Nazi war criminals. Many in the theatre community were also upset because a British composer and lyricist were usurping what was an innately American art form.

In his review, Walter Kerr seemed to think that the creators were *telling* him what was happening rather than *showing* him. "It is rather like reading endless footnotes," he wrote, "from which the text has disappeared, and it puts us into the kind of emotional limbo we inhabit when we're just back from the dentist but the Novocain hasn't worn off yet. . . . We're not participants, we're recipients of postal cards (and photographs) from all over. Which is a chilly and left-handed way to write a character musical. . . . You go home wondering why the authors chose to write a musical about materials they were going to develop so remotely, so thinly."

It's kind of true. The musical is expositional. You really had to read the chronology of events in the program to know the life of Eva Perón. Who reads the programs, anyway, even if you do know the story?

A week or so later, Mandy asked after the show, "Do you want to go to Joe Allen's?" As we walked in silence down Eighth Avenue, the two of us simultaneously burst into tears—all that work ignored. It's easier to get a bad notice than to be ignored.

After the reviews were in, Mandy and I had to work even harder. We had to lasso the audience and bring them to the stage every night. It wasn't easy. The audience was pissed off the moment they walked into the theatre because they'd spent $35 a ticket on a flop. (Can you imagine how pissed off they'd be today, at $125 a pop?) They sat there scowling at the stage with their arms folded across their chests as if to say, *Prove it.* We ultimately did. The audience did get hooked; we turned it around. Word of mouth spread.

It took several months and seven Tony Awards, but *Evita,* a show that did not get good reviews in Los Angeles or San Francisco or New York, became a huge hit. If you didn't see *Evita* in L.A., you saw it in New York—if you were lucky enough to get a ticket. Scalpers were on the street outside the theatre every night. That Halloween, Evita in her white dress was the preferred costume, especially among gay men in Greenwich Village. People who had never been inside a Broadway theatre came to the show because of the TV commercial. It was directed by Bob Giraldi, who directed the videos for Pat Benatar's "Love Is a Battlefield" and Michael Jackson's "Beat It." The *Evita* commercial was on all the time, day and night, for years. When *Evita* toured the country, they kept using it.

Odd things started happening to me. I received death threats. I had an FBI guy follow me around for a while. He was very cute. We had bomb threats. In the seventies, there was always a bomb scare on opening night. You didn't have a proper opening night unless you saw the bomb squad and their dogs sweep the theatre before the seven o'clock curtain. It was kind of good luck for a show.

For this production we had several bomb scares because of Eva Perón, I'm convinced. One of my favorites was when I was onstage singing "Buenos Aires." As the song was ending, I saw the spotlights flicker and then go out. I exited stage right to see a scared house manager standing with several cops and firemen.

"What's going on?" I asked.

"Bomb scare," they said.

"What are you going to do?" I asked. The police and firemen were trying to figure out when to stop the show and get the audience out.

"We can't decide if we should stop the show now or after 'Art of the Possible,'" they replied. It was an artistic decision.

"What if the bomb goes off during 'Art of the Possible'?" I asked. Which, as far as I was concerned, was redundant.

Howard Haines, the general manager, was called on the phone. "Don't you dare stop the show," he said. "It'll kill our box office." So the cops and firemen went away. I guess they agreed it was better to kill a theatre full of people than future ticket sales.

One of my favorite things about Broadway is the juxtaposition—the incongruity—of guns and greasepaint, billy clubs and fishnets. Whenever you see a cop backstage, more likely than not he's a member of the "theatre squad." They protect you as you're leaving the stage door, and direct the traffic and crowds in the Theatre District. NYPD's finest from Midtown North and South are your best friends. I love to see them backstage. There's something about showgirls and cops hanging out together around a stage door—it's pure Damon Runyon, and it's one of the great allures of Broadway for me. I'm still very close to the cop assigned to West Forty-fifth Street during my run in *Master Class,* Patrick (Hollywood) Cassidy.

Regardless of *Evita*'s success, I was still struggling with the singing, I still had the subversive alternate, and I still had stage management who didn't lift a finger if they didn't have to. The walk from my dressing room to the stage felt like a war zone, but I showed up every night and prayed that I'd get through it.

There's no question that Hal Prince taught me invaluable lessons, but they came at a price. This was the beginning of the era of dual productions, which I abhor. Once you have dual productions, you have dueling performances, then comparisons—and some-one always loses. In January 1980, less than four months after we opened on Broadway, Hal rolled out the L.A. company, with Loni Ackerman as Eva. Nevertheless, we all soldiered on, even after Hal returned from L.A. and told our company that the L.A. company was better than we were. Working with Hal was both exhilarating and painful: I will always be grateful to him for giving me the op-portunity of a lifetime and for believing in me when others didn't. That's not to say there weren't bumps in the road on the way to that Tony Award. I didn't always understand his methods . . . or his madness. Looking back as I do on many of my trying theatrical experiences, I remember the words of a very wise person: What doesn't kill you makes you stronger. Or leaves you open to sec-ondary infections.

The discipline I needed to play the part was intense. It was still all about the singing, an unbelievable struggle I had to face by myself. There was no Kevin; I missed him and wished we hadn't broken up. There was also no life beyond the theatre. I was a monk—a very quiet monk. At home I turned the ringer off on my phone and turned down the volume on the answering machine. I was silent for at least fourteen hours a day. When it was time to vocalize, I turned on all the faucets in the apartment so I wouldn't have to hear the first sound coming out of my mouth. I muscled my voice every night onstage. I willed it to hit the notes.

Now, when I listen to the album, it doesn't sound to me like I was struggling, but I was, and I continued to struggle all through the New York run. It started in the first ten minutes of the musical. If I didn't hit the first D correctly, it affected the rest of the night, which affected the rest of the week. I was still working with David Vosburgh and he said great things to me: "Sing on your inter-est, not on your capital." "Remember where you're going tonight;

Costume and wig fitting for the "Charity Concert" scene in Evita.
PAUL HUNTLEY

remember where you're going for the rest of the week." It got easier as time passed, but I was never out of the woods.

I was now considered a "star." I didn't change personalities
or anything like that. I was trained enough and had been onstage
long enough to know that it's part of the territory. My reputation kept growing, however, as I fought more and more battles
backstage. Those battles became public, and fodder for the press.
There are moles in Broadway houses. No one knows who they are,
but things that only people working on the show would know get
printed in the most vicious ways.

Whatever. I would go to the theatre and leave the theatre
in my "poor actor" street clothes, because as I see it, what's the
point of getting dressed up to take my clothes off to get into costume to get out of the costume to get dressed to go home? Carlos

Gorbea, our dance captain, told me, "Patti, you're a star. You must dress up!"

In the past, if you were a star, you dressed to go to the theatre, you dressed to be seen leaving it, and you dressed with gloves and high heels just to walk around in life. I've been wearing costumes all my life. I don't know how to dress myself. I don't know how to shop. One of my favorite shopping sprees was buying a sweater, a pair of boots, and a car. During *Evita* I left the theatre in jeans, with my long brown hair and a clean face, having just taken off the stage makeup. As I came out the stage door, I'd look people in the eye, knowing that they were waiting for me—or Evita—and I'd walk right by them because they were looking for a tall blonde. I was completely invisible.

When the weather warmed up, I started walking regularly from the theatre to the Oyster Bar in the Plaza Hotel—a great bar that was also a discreet hangout for Central Park South hookers. I'd sit at the far end of the bar so I could watch the people coming in. The bartenders would say hello and talk to me. I remember in particular this wonderful Jamaican bartender. None of them ever knew I was Evita. All they knew was that this girl came in, sat in the corner, and drank two beers. When I was sufficiently buzzed, I'd grab a cab and go home. They must have thought, *That poor little hooker, she never manages to get a single customer.*

Sunday was my day off. Vocal silence all day, all night, all Monday until showtime.

At one point, one of my dearest friends in the world, David Ingraham, got through my telephone madness and invited me to go with him to a New York Rangers hockey game. David had four prime seats in Madison Square Garden, right on the ice behind the opposition net.

I had known David's family since I was a kid in Northport.

I grew up with the Ingraham kids, David's cousins. As grown-ups, David and I came together in the strangest way. He was a friend of Margot Harley, John Houseman's administrative assistant at Juilliard. She later became the executive director of The Acting Company. Northport and Juilliard collided. That gave me the creeps . . . too close.

When I was a kid, I went to hockey games when the Long Island Ducks—now the New York Islanders—played in the Commack Arena. I loved watching them play. On that Sunday in February 1980, the American hockey team beat the Russians at the Lake Placid Winter Olympics. I watched the game on TV. I was cheering and crying—silently, of course. Everything I did was silent when I wasn't onstage.

That same Sunday night I went to the Garden with David to watch the Rangers play the Islanders. The atmosphere in the Garden was electric because of what had happened just that afternoon at Lake Placid. Everybody in the place—eighteen thousand strong—was screaming, "U-S-A! U-S-A! U-S-A!" Except for me . . . on voice rest. After that, every Sunday I'd go to the Garden with David and whomever else he invited. I couldn't talk, but I'd bang on the boards whenever I felt I needed to express myself. I fell in love with ice hockey. It also gave me a social outlet from my self-imposed *Evita* isolation. Those Sunday games and the Oyster Bar were my only diversions from this musical, the musical that made me a star, and gave me a hostile reputation. Ah, the glory . . .

But back to the stage. Sometimes a hit requires a lot of proof that it's worth the audience's effort. In the case of *Evita*, with a book so sparse and convoluted and music so odd for a Broadway musical, we had to work at it every minute of the two hours we played. By now most of the audience knew who this woman named

*Mandy Patinkin and me in "Waltz for Eva and Che," the only time
these two characters interact onstage.*

Eva Perón was, and this created a moral dilemma for them as they
watched the show. How were they supposed to react to her?

I tried to make her human. I did my best to make her accessible to an audience, even though she is depicted quite accurately
in the musical. There are moments in the book when she is hateful.
However, I wrung a laugh out of the audience in "A New Argentina." And I was able to make them cry at her death in the second
act. I had to find ways to curry favor with the audience. How could
I tell the story if the audience didn't care about the character?

When the curtain came down is when the ambivalence toward
her really set in. When Mandy took his bows, he had it relatively
easy. He was the Greek chorus, and he had the audience on his
side immediately, but the applause level during my curtain call,
which followed his, used to dip. That was fun—I had the last bow;
they're supposed to go crazy for the actor who comes out last, but
Mandy consistently got the big cheers while mine were . . . polite.
As much as people may have wanted to applaud my performance,

they were ambivalent about the character I was playing. It's a testament to how much I love Mandy that I didn't want to murder him. I will say that by the end of my run, I was finally getting the reaction I wanted. I don't know whether I improved in the role or I just willed them to clap harder, but they did. Whew! (P.S. By then Mandy had left the show. . . .)

Nevertheless, the fever that made this show a hit remained constant. One night, a dentist from New Jersey brought his entire family. He had lived through the Peronista regime. He was anti-Peronista, but he still had every newspaper printed on the day Evita died. He came to my dressing room and gingerly turned every page of these old Argentinean newspapers, very carefully showing me his treasures. No one could touch the newspapers but him. He was obsessed. Evita had died in 1952, almost thirty years earlier. *If he was anti-Peronista,* I wondered, *why was he hoarding those papers?*

Sometime during our run, I gave myself permission to be social and went to see a cabaret act after the show. Pete Sanders was the press agent for the club, and suggested I do my own cabaret act.

At first I didn't want to do it. But then I remembered how my applause was dipping and thought, *What the hell, I want people to know who I really am, and it'll give me something to do during the day.*

I remember going to David Lewis's apartment once a week. He became my musical director and he put an act together for me. I learned it, but I don't remember actually rehearsing it.

I don't know where I got the nerve to sing more than just the musical *Evita.* I think I was desperate to get off this treadmill and have some fun. After the Saturday curtain I didn't have to sing again till Monday night. I should've been on vocal silence,

At Les Mouches, with Stephen Sondheim, 1980.

but on Saturday night I went down to Les Mouches, a club on Twenty-eighth Street and Eleventh Avenue, and performed at midnight. We opened at the beginning of March 1980, and we were going to do it for just four weeks, but it became a hot ticket. We kept extending the run—it was sold out every week for twenty-seven weeks. It was wild.

I performed there the night before the 1980 Tony Awards. My Tony dress was a disaster and I had to wear my sweaty Les Mouches tuxedo to the Tonys. Jeffrey was my date once again—between the show and the act, I didn't have time to scare up a boyfriend. Jeffrey told me that right before Faye Dunaway announced the winner for Best Actress in a Musical, I shoved my purse in his lap and said, "Here, hold this!"

"And the winner is Patti LuPone!" I was out of my seat and on that stage. I don't remember any of it.

In L.A. and in New York City, everybody came to see *Evita*—Jack Nicholson, Henry Fonda, Gregory Peck, Ginger Rogers, Helen Hayes, Lana Turner, Sammy Davis Jr., John McEnroe, Bjorn Borg, Andy Warhol, baseball players, hockey players, a couple of queens—actual royal ones—and Imelda Marcos.

Alongside my best friend, Jeffrey Richman, on our way to the Tony Awards.

Backstage with Maxene Andrews and Angela Lansbury.

They all came backstage. I was awestruck. When all is said and done, I'm still a fan and a tourist. Lana Turner came to see the show with her hairdresser, and they came backstage. I think she enjoyed the performance, but she sat with me for an hour, because the paparazzi had materialized out of nowhere and were hanging around the stage door. She was trapped. While the stage doorman was looking for another way to get her out of the building, she told me a story.

There used to be an Argentinean film festival during the Peronista regime, and all of the Hollywood movie stars would go. One time while Lana was in Buenos Aires, Evita kept sending her invitations to the Casa Rosada, but Lana kept declining them. As she was getting ready to leave the country, Lana found that her passport had been confiscated. Then the secret police showed up and took her by force to the Casa Rosada. She didn't know what was going on. She thought she was going to jail.

Lana sat and waited. When Evita was ready, they ushered Lana into her presence. "I just wanted to tell you," Evita said, "that I modeled my pompadour hairdo after yours." And with that, she gave Lana back her passport and wished her a safe trip back to Hollywood.

I don't know which I thought was more amazing—Lana's story about Evita Perón, or the fact that I was sitting in my dressing room, knee to knee, with Lana Turner. Every time someone famous came backstage, I was shocked.

And then my contract was over. I left *Evita* in January of 1981, even though they asked me to stay. They offered me a raise, though it wasn't anything substantial; I think I was only making three thousand dollars a week for that part. I left with nothing to go to, and everybody thought I was out of my mind. When they asked me why I was leaving, I said, "Because I've lost my sense of humor."

Closing nights in the theatre can be extraordinary events— and not just on Broadway, because I've had closing nights that were extraordinary in London and in Sydney as well. People who buy a ticket to celebrate that particular performance, that show, celebrate it in a way that lives in their memory forever. *Evita* was one of those nights. A lot of people who'd seen the show came back to see the closing night. I cried pretty much through the whole thing, but I was so relieved when it was over. The show was a success, I was finally a success in it. My contract was over. I was done. I'd played Evita for twenty-one months.

People think that if you have a success in a Broadway show, the doors open up, that it's a stepping-stone to Hollywood. Not in my case. However, I was invited by the renowned Romanian director Liviu Ciulei to come to the Guthrie Theater in Minneapolis to play Rosalind in *As You Like It* the following year. Because I had such enormous admiration for him as a director, and because I was dying to work with him, I said yes. I would go back to my roots, which was repertory theatre.

But this was not the end of *Evita*. I went home to my apartment with nothing to do. Three months after we closed, the phone rang. I picked it up on the first ring. It was Robert Stigwood, *Evita*'s producer. "Would you like to come to Australia to play Evita?"

Robert explained to me that Jennifer Murphy, who was playing the role in Australia, had severely damaged her voice, to the extent that she was now speaking the part, and would not be able to sing the role in Sydney, which was the final stop on their tour. I completely understood about the voice problem, and I bled for her. Every woman who has ever played the part onstage has been knocked off of it for a week, for a year, for the rest of her career. I said yes to him right away. *Nobody's ever going to ask me to work in Sydney again,* I told myself. *I'm going.*

It was a very long flight to Australia—New York to Los Angeles, Los Angeles to Hawaii, Hawaii to Sydney. I traveled with Richard Allen, my hairdresser, and one of the stage managers from the New York production.

When we got to Sydney, we were met by people from the press department and the general management for the Sydney *Evita*. They took me to my hotel, the Sebel Townhouse. I remember standing in front of the hotel and I heard, "Yo, Patti!" I looked up and there was Billy Joel's band—Liberty DeVitto, David Brown, Russell Javors, and Doug Stegmeyer—all Long Island boys.

I couldn't believe it. I'd flown twenty-four hours to Sydney, Australia, and landed on Long Island.

I partied with the band for a week and a half. Until I started rehearsal, I hung with these guys and they made me laugh. I hadn't laughed for so long. I was very glad for the comic relief the Long Island boys provided.

Before I left for Sydney, I somehow had the presence of mind to ask the producers, "Are you buying my performance for the Sydney production?"

"Yes, we are," they said, even if they weren't really sure what I meant. By "buying my performance," they were buying everything I did onstage in the New York production. I wouldn't have to relearn the part. I was speaking on instinct, but it was the smartest thing I could have said. When I started rehearsal in Sydney, I discovered that the company was doing everything on the opposite foot. For instance, on Broadway, when I did "Waltz for Eva and Che," I started with my left foot going backward. In Australia, the choreography began with the right foot going backward. If I had not asked that question about their buying my performance, I would be forced to relearn all the choreography in five days.

My New York stage manager argued, "For expediency's sake, Patti, just do it."

"Nope," I said, "management bought my performance."

It made relearning the show infinitely easier and the Australian company was happy to comply. After all, my being there meant the show wasn't closing.

Tony McNally, my wonderful company manager, found me an extraordinary apartment in Point Piper, where the "fourth wall" was the Sydney Harbor, the Harbor Bridge, and the Sydney Opera House. When the sun set over the Harbor Bridge, I knew it was time to get in the car and go to the theatre. On days off I explored every possible part of Sydney. I was so very happy in Australia. I had a Canadian hockey-player boyfriend who followed me to Sydney. I had someone to love and to share all this with.

The Australian people were great. I also got the reviews I'd always wanted. My favorite was, "She acts like an inspired witch." I said, "Yes, finally. Thank you." I just hope it wasn't a typographical error.

Perhaps my success was due to the fact that finally I was vocally secure in the role and I could have a blast playing the part.

I could sing it. I could sing it at last. I was doing something vocally that I hadn't done before, which helped me to relax, be comfortable, and have fun. I don't know what it was—maybe it was the three months off, maybe it was vocal cord memory—but whatever it was, I was able to sing the role with enough ease to get on a plane during rehearsals, fly to New York to sing "Buenos Aires" on the Tony Awards telecast, go to the after-party, fly back to Sydney in time for rehearsal, and sing the shit out of the part—all in twenty-four hours.

I was there through September of 1981. My closing night in Sydney was extraordinary. In Australia they have a candy called Jaffas, and it's come to mean good luck onstage. If the audience likes your performance, they'll roll Jaffas down the aisle to you. On my closing night, there were tons of Jaffas rolling down the aisles.

And then there were the streamers. The audience upstairs started throwing streamers from the balcony. These hit the mezzanine. The mezzanine streamers hit the orchestra, and then the orchestra threw streamers, which hit the stage. I'd never seen that in a theatre before. The orchestra pit and the company onstage were covered in streamers. It was a phenomenal closing night.

After I finished in Sydney, I went home to New York. I was back in the same apartment, waiting to go to the Guthrie Theater, which wouldn't happen for another year. I was waiting and alone. The hockey-player boyfriend only lasted through my Sydney run. I had just done the biggest show on Broadway, and at this point the rest of the world was thinking I was a huge Broadway star.

But the reality is that it's not what you think it is. It never is. Goddammit.

A Working Actor, Part 1

1982—1985

9

Oliver! *Ron Moody as Fagin, David Garlick as The Artful Dodger, Braden Danner as Oliver, and me as Nancy.*

ome. It felt familiar but not necessarily comforting to be home in Manhattan with time on my hands. Actually, it felt a lot like I was starting over: I was back in my apartment, I had no love life, and I had no work.

Worse than that, I had convinced myself that this was a permanent condition. Sitting there staring at the four walls, I was sure I'd never be hired again. Or loved again. But boyfriends could wait. I needed a job and no one was banging down my door. What if the banging had stopped forever? (Which could also apply to my love life, but I digress. . . .)

Crazy thinking? Not really. It's the actor's life. At the end of one play, most of us think we'll never work again—a feeling that lasts until the next play comes along.

Somehow it always does. The phone rings and someone asks, "Are you interested?" and you're on to your next role. No matter how many years I ride this roller coaster of emotional highs and lows—"I'll never work again," "I just got the best job!" "I'll never work again," "I landed the biggest musical since *Oklahoma!*"—it's impossible to be completely reassured. I've never entirely gotten over the panicky feeling that my career is over after I've packed up yet another dressing room and said, "Good-bye, I love you," to yet another backstage crew and allowed that nagging question to creep back into my brain: *Now what? I'm hopeless at everything else. How much could I get for that Tony on eBay?*

At least I knew not to hold my breath for another major role on Broadway immediately following *Evita*, much as my agent might have thought I should. Even the actors who are considered "Broadway working actors" don't just go from one Broadway play to another. Life in the theatre doesn't work that way. After *Evita* it would be years before I again set foot on a Broadway stage. If I'd turned down everything that came up in between, I would have starved. But more important, I would not have grown as an actor. I would've missed truly enriching personal and theatrical experiences.

I was fortunate that my midnight show at Les Mouches had opened up a whole new way for me to make a living on the stage. But I wanted another acting role, and was not about to wait for the next *Evita.* I went back to my roots. I was a trained actor—an actor who earns a living on the stage. I would pursue my craft and take the part that was offered, whatever and wherever that may be, knowing that not every show is a blockbuster musical, and not every play is a hit. Good or bad, hit or flop, each one teaches you something. I ended up doing some of my best work in these productions. The work was done mostly in plays. People say to me, "You've had the most wonderfully diverse career, moving from musicals to plays to TV to opera to cabaret." The simple fact is I go where the work is. It's not planned.

After *Evita,* I went back to repertory theatre. Early in 1982 I headed for Minneapolis in the dead of winter to Liviu Ciulei's production of *As You Like It* at the Tyrone Guthrie Theatre. Ciulei's staging of *As You Like It* was internationally famous, and I was so flattered he wanted me in his production. I had seen his work at Juilliard and was very eager to play Rosalind under his direction. My agent insisted that it wasn't a smart career move. I could see his point—his commission would be about twelve dollars.

Minneapolis was experiencing the coldest and snowiest winter in a hundred years. The icicles were three stories high, and potentially lethal if they broke off. From time to time they plunged to the ground, like huge daggers. We were constantly looking up.

On our first day of rehearsal, the stage manager handed out a *Good Housekeeping* article entitled "I Froze to Death—and Lived."

Rosalind in As You Like It, *1982.*

© GIANNETTI 1985

With Val Kilmer as Orlando in As You Like It, *1982.*
© GIANNETTI 1985

The story took place in Minnesota and described a woman whose car broke down at night on the side of the road. Not properly dressed for the cold, she left the car on foot and started to head for the light of a distant farmhouse. In the morning the farmer opened his door to find the woman, frozen stiff as a board, on his front step. He put her in the back of his pickup truck and brought her to the hospital. They defrosted her. She survived, but she couldn't remember anything about the incident—about slipping into unconsciousness or how she got to the farmhouse. . . . So how the hell did she write that article?

I lived in the refurbished attic of the home of two artists, a Swedish woman and her husband, a Chippewa Indian—Hazel Belvo and George Morrison. It was recommended that I put a heater on the engine block of my car before I left New York. I did just that and at night before I went to sleep I would plug my car into an electrical socket on the outside of the house. I thought it was peculiar, but apparently this was not unusual in Minneapolis.

Liviu had assembled a wonderful company of players, one of whom was David Warrilow. David was considered to be one of the foremost interpreters of Samuel Beckett's plays. Rehearsals were master classes. Liviu is a scholar as well as a great director. There were wonderful lectures all through the rehearsal period. I remember an actor asking Liviu what style was. "Style is what suits you," he said. It was so simple and clean.

His concept for *As You Like It* was a play within a play. We actors were cast as a troupe of eighteenth-century repertory players, costumes and performances frayed at the edges, playing the roles in *As You Like It*. Liviu's production was miraculous. My reviews, however, were a different story. If it's a hit and the critics say nice things, people will tell you. Unfortunately, if the critics don't like you, people will find a way to tell you that, too. I wouldn't have known about my reviews had David Warrilow not called me the day after we opened to tell me how sorry he was.

"Sorry about what, David?"

"Oh, your terrible reviews . . . just terrible, but no worries, Patti, you're lovely in the part."

"Oh, dear . . . Well, how were your reviews, David?"

"Well, Patti, they were . . . GLORIOUS!"

Great, David. Thanks for calling.

The *Village Voice* said my casting was "a brainstorm at night and a nightmare in the morning." Getting panned is never fun, but it was harder this time around because now the question from the critics was, What was a musical theatre star doing at the Guthrie in a Shakespearean play? It was like *Evita* gave me a career and then ruined it.

Great, Evita. Thanks for calling.

Over the three-month period I was there, I learned that the Guthrie had a curse on it, that the sister city, St. Paul, was the seat of the occult in America, and that Minneapolis was a Mafia strong-hold. I loved working with Liviu but couldn't wait to get out of there at the end of the run for a lot of reasons—three months in the cold, in a cursed theatre, working off lousy reviews being three of them. Oh yes, and I was thrown out of Prince's music/dance club for unruly behavior and unsavory language. Minneapolis bars taught me to drink a Bloody Mary with a beer chaser. It's the only way they're served. Mmm, delicious. Wait a minute, what am I talk-ing about? Minneapolis was fabulous!

It was barely spring when Peter Weller picked me up and drove me home. He and I were about to reprise our roles in *The Woods* at the Second Stage Theatre. We started out after the clos-ing night party, so it was rather late. Not ten minutes into our jour-ney, we were stopped by a state trooper. When Peter went for his wallet in his bag in the backseat, he pulled out a cat turd instead. My cat had taken a shit in his bag. You had to laugh. Or I did, anyway. Peter not so much. The cop took Peter's license and regis-tration, called it in, and when he came back to our car, told Peter there was a warrant out for his arrest in the state of New York. It's a long story and has something to do with a truck Peter was driv-ing and the Park Avenue underpass—the truck was too tall and got stuck in the underpass, which snarled Park Avenue traffic all day, and they had to cut part of the historic underpass out to move the truck—something like that.

Peter and I rehearsed and opened the revival of *The Woods*. My bad reviews continued. John Simon of *New York* magazine said that I was a poor reason to revive *The Woods*. (I forget now which "friend" told me that.) I remember one performance where audience members had obviously read our reviews. At a particularly poignant moment in the play, they laughed out loud at us.

I also remember a knock-down, drag-out fight Peter and I had during a rehearsal. It was early morning and it was a staging dispute on the verge of getting really violent. David Mamet defused it by taking Peter to a bar, and then me antiquing. Peter drank, I shopped. David is a great leveler.

In February 1983, I did *America Kicks Up Its Heels* at Playwrights Horizons in New York. As *The Baker's Wife* had proved to me earlier in my career, great music and a fine cast are not enough to make a musical work. Bill Finn, our composer, had written a wonderful score. The cast was extremely talented, and included Dick Latessa, Lenora Nemetz, and I. M. Hobson. Nevertheless, this was not a pleasant experience. Something prevented this show from gelling and becoming a really good musical.

The production was a mess from the beginning, perhaps because we had no director, for one thing. I can't remember who our first director was, but whoever it was didn't last long. I think the choreographer took over directing, until she got colitis and left. After the choreographer took off, Bill Finn attempted to direct, but that was a bad idea. He couldn't write, rewrite, direct, and handle us as a company all at the same time.

As rehearsals continued to disintegrate, we became known as "the snake pit" by the Playwrights Horizons management. We were sold out through their subscription series, but the word of mouth was not good. I couldn't understand why management wanted to officially open it. I remember threatening to walk if they brought in the critics, which they initially intended to do. We would've gotten butchered. It would have been sticking a dagger in the already bloody heart of this company. We didn't officially open, and we finished our run as best we could. So much talent was wasted on that stage.

In the fall of 1983, I appeared in *The Thornhill Project,* written by Meade Roberts. The cast was fabulous, and included Ben Gazzara, Murray Hamilton, Carol Kane, George DiCenzo, and Polly Draper. This was an odd but wonderful experience. The wonderful part: I was being directed by John Cassavetes and playing opposite Ben Gazzara. The odd part was that *Thornhill,* a play about Eugene and Carlotta O'Neill, was five and a half hours long and it was terrible. Why was it being done?

We workshopped it at Westbeth, the artists' community in the far West Village, with the intention of moving it to Broadway. Our producers were Fran and Barry Weissler. As I rehearsed the play (I played Carlotta to Ben's Eugene), I kept thinking that this would be my longest one-night stand on Broadway because that's all it would last—five and a half hours, one night.

Meade Roberts was a very temperamental man who treated John Cassavetes like shit. During rehearsal he would beckon John to his side by wagging his finger at him with a withering look of disapproval on his face. It didn't faze John. I can't remember if Meade rewrote while we rehearsed, but the play never improved. One night I got a telephone call from him. Meade was in a state of delirium, and I told him to come over to my apartment. He did and we talked—or rather, he talked and I plied him with scrambled eggs and Valium. That was my go-to dish in those days.

In the middle of the rehearsal period I was fired, along with Carol Kane, Murray Hamilton, and George DiCenzo. We were fired because Carol had wisely told us not to sign our workshop contracts; they contained no guarantee that we would be the actors to reprise our roles on Broadway.

So I didn't sign my contract, and as a result I was fired—except nobody bothered to tell me until I showed up at rehearsal one day. John looked at me strangely and said, "What are you doing here?"

"I came to rehearsal," I replied.

"You've been fired," he said. "The Weisslers fired the four of you."

I was shocked, first, because I was fired, and second, because of the way I found out I was fired—from John, who was surprised that the Weisslers hadn't told me, or my agent. Because of the Weisslers' underhanded method of producing this project, a major battle erupted between John and them. He broke off his association and ended up buying the play from them in order to continue rehearsal. Once that happened, he rehired all of us.

We continued rehearsing. I remember one afternoon when I had to deliver a long, convoluted, and emotional speech in front of Gena Rowlands, who had come to visit John. That was intimidating. She is a great actress, and she was boring holes in me, or so I thought. I never found out if she approved or disapproved.

Still, the play never got any better—or any shorter. We opened *Thornhill* at Westbeth, played a couple of performances, and that was the end of that.

In the spring of 1984, I was cast as Nancy in Cameron Mackintosh's Broadway revival of *Oliver!* I don't remember singing for the director. I believe it was Cameron who wanted me to play Nancy. I went to the Mark Hellinger Theatre and met some of the creative staff. The director showed up much later.

This should have run longer than the two weeks we did run. I mean, it's *Oliver!* It starred Ron Moody, the original Fagin. We were being directed by the original director, Peter Coe; we had the original sets by Sean Kenny; we had all the original costume designs, the original blocking. . . . Hmm . . . maybe *that* was the problem.

After Ron, Graeme Campbell (who played Bill Sikes), and I were set, the rest of the ensemble was cast by the assistant director, Geoffrey Ferris. We went into rehearsal with Geoffrey for I believe two weeks. When the director finally did show up at rehearsal, two things happened:

1. He pointed to a chorus woman and said, "I remember the woman who played your part twenty years ago." I thought, *Oh no, we'll never be good enough.*

2. He fired Oliver. I left the rehearsal room clutching my throat thinking, *I'm next.*

It was a blow to everyone, and a bad way to start rehearsal. In reality we never actually rehearsed. We were given the blocking from the original production. There was no exploration, no discovery, no nothing.

I asked the musical director if I could change the keys to Nancy's songs. "Absolutely not!" I had to sing in Georgia Brown's keys, which were much lower than mine. I had major battles with the musical director. One battle I remember concerned the definition of the musical term *vamp*. Typically a conductor will repeat a musical phrase until an actor is ready to sing. This is vamping. But he never waited for me to finish my dialogue. I believe I said, or perhaps yelled (yes, that's more like it), "Vamp means vamp till I'm ready." He was the only one in the building who yelled at the kids. I did not like this man at all.

One night in my dressing room, Cameron saw me in my Nancy costume and said I would be perfect for a character in *Les Misérables*, a new musical being done with the Royal Shakespeare Company.

I said, "Where and when?"

He said, "London, nine months from now."

I sighed and let it go.

Oliver! is such a wonderful musical. I wish we had run. Ron, Graeme, and I were happy onstage. We played so well and so fair together. The kids were great. Just recently I reconnected with my Artful Dodger, David Garlick. We were a happy company once we opened, but we didn't sell tickets, and so it goes. We closed. I packed up my dressing room, said my farewells, and headed to Lancaster, Pennsylvania, to begin filming *Witness*.

Witness, directed by Peter Weir and starring Harrison Ford, was shot in Amish country in 1984 and released on February 8, 1985. This was a great experience because of Peter and Harrison. I played Harrison's sister. It was a small role and I wasn't on the shoot for long, but I had a great time doing it. Harrison was completely generous to me and Peter is among the best film directors

I've worked with. I'm not on movies long enough to become involved with the politics or intrigues. This one was just a good experience. I remember laughing a lot.

With Harrison Ford, on the set of Witness.

After *Witness,* I returned to the stage in Dario Fo's *Accidental Death of an Anarchist.* This is a really interesting Italian play based on a true story. A man who was (or was not) an anarchist was arrested, and while he was being interrogated at the police station, he mysteriously fell (or was pushed) out of the window and died. It's a political farce that began as street theatre during his actual interrogation.

Jonathan Pryce was our star and was unbelievably brilliant as Antonio D'Antonio. He taught me an incredibly valuable lesson: "Get to the end of the line."

Make your point is what he was saying. I had no idea that I wasn't making my point. What I was doing was taking too much time within the line, and as a result I was losing all sense of it by the time I got to the end. I was being indulgent onstage. Thank you, Jonathan. I quote him all the time. Jonathan is such a smart actor, and he remains a great friend. I remember see-

Jonathan Pryce and me on opening night, 1984.

ing him in *Comedians* and being electrified by his performance. He is one of the greats, and howlingly funny.

This turned out to be another short-lived Broadway experience—fifteen previews, twenty-five performances, and we were done. My Midas touch again. Before we opened, Dario Fo was denied entrance into the United States as an "undesirable" because he held leftist political beliefs. (About twelve years later he was awarded the Nobel Prize for Literature. So much for undesirable.)

After a vigorous protest by American writers, he was allowed to enter. The dustup made headlines and gave us millions of dollars of free press. It didn't help nearly enough. Our reviews were not good. Mine especially. Frank Rich of the *New York Times* questioned my involvement in the play. Again, as at the Guthrie, I had to deal with "What is Evita doing in this play?" I don't know why the critics were so obsessed with me taking roles in straight plays or why my friends were so obsessed with telling me why the critics were so obsessed.

I left *Evita* as a musical theatre performer, but when I initially won the part, I was "refreshing" casting because they had cast an actress. Now it seemed that I couldn't go back to doing what I had done before *Evita*, namely plays. Show business has a short memory. I persevered, however, and continued doing what I had been trained to do. It took a long time to get over the hump of not being allowed to move from a musical to a play. I got over it by continuing to play the parts that were offered to me, and fortunately, many people knew me as an actor before *Evita*.

The year 1985 started out with a joint phone call from Peter Sellars and Timothy Mayer. Peter had just been named director and manager of the newly formed American National Theatre. He was just twenty-six years old. Peter and Timmy offered me roles in ANT's first two plays, *Henry IV, Part I*, directed by Timmy, and *The Count of Monte Cristo*, directed by Peter, both at ANT's new home, the Eisenhower Theater at the Kennedy Center in Washington, D.C.

I was to play Lady Percy in *Henry IV, Part I* and Mercedes in *The Count of Monte Cristo*. I couldn't believe my good luck. I accepted, of course, which meant that I would be in D.C. for five months. The first production was *Henry IV*. Timmy began directing, having just given up drugs, alcohol, and smoking. His opening remarks were stunning, but then it went downhill from there. I can't remember the details of what happened, but we lost our Falstaff, and John McMartin, who was playing Henry IV, was asked to take on Falstaff as well. He did so expertly.

We were saved—for the moment. Rehearsals seemed to be going well, but it turned out to be a lifeless and pretty boring production. We got terrible reviews and closed after just thirteen performances. This was getting ridiculous. I had done almost a dozen plays since *Evita* and none had been hits. Or even semi-hits. And all my reviews stank. And I still didn't have a boyfriend. I've gotta get out of this chapter quick. It's depressing me.

That particular company disbanded, except for those of us staying on for *Monte Cristo*. The premature closing of the very first production was unexpected and a little devastating for this new company.

On the other hand, *The Count of Monte Cristo* was a staggering experience and a benchmark in my career. It was as odd and as talented a company as I have ever worked with. The cast included Richard Thomas as Edmond Dantès, Zakes Mokae, and Roscoe Lee Browne. In a reversal of typecasting, Roscoe played the noble good guy and Zakes was the bad guy. David Warrilow and Tony Azito (from Juilliard's Group I) and I were reunited.

Peter's production was so expansive and so unexpected. It employed the physical space of a theatre like no other production I'd ever been in. The upstage firewall was raised for the exit of a spinning desk. The prison was the fly rail and the stairs leading up to it. The set was green and black patent leather, and every inch of the Eisenhower Theater's bare stage walls was used. There were no teasers or tabs that as a rule identify the difference between backstage and onstage.

Peter took the James O'Neill script and interpolated the Bible, the original novel, and Alexander Pope into O'Neill's very thin adaptation. We were schooled in melodramatic acting, which was to be the style of acting for the play. As Mercedes, I was constantly falling to the floor in a dead faint. This was problematic—I had to figure out how to do it so as not to provoke laughter from the audience. *Slowly* turned out to be the answer, as if I were doing a balletic move. I conquered it eventually, but it took several rounds of audience snickers and guffaws to get it right.

The show was long, three hours and forty-five minutes long. We would have symposiums after some performances, and members of the audience were, among many other things, angry. Angry at the length of the play, at the interpretation of the play, at the direction, whatever—it was definitely live theatre in the house during these heated discussions. Nonetheless, I was privileged to be acting in this play. I loved working with Peter as much as I'd loved working with Liviu Ciulei. What I would give to work with both of them again. How proud I was to be a part of this production.

Unfortunately, ANT itself didn't last long. Peter is too innovative, too avant-garde, for a town like D.C. What a pity. I really wanted to be a member of a permanent national company. This could've been it.

10

The Cradle Will Rock, Les Misérables, LBJ, A Sicilian in Sicily

1985–1987

"I Dreamed a Dream."

PHOTOGRAPH BY MICHAEL LE POER TRENCH © CAMERON MACKINTOSH LTD

*T*he summer of 1985 found me in London, reprising my roles as The Moll and Sister Mister in Marc Blitzstein's play *The Cradle Will Rock*. As The Moll, I sing what may be the best-known song from the show, "The Nickel Under Your Foot." This was the second time we'd presented it; the first time had been two years earlier at the American Place Theater in Manhattan.

The cast that first time was made up entirely of alumni from The Acting Company. I'd been surrounded by familiar faces—David Schramm, Mary Lou Rosato, and Henry Stram in particular. John Houseman directed us. For him, *The Cradle* was very much a sentimental journey, and not just because we'd all been part of his repertory company.

To give you a brief history of this musical, in the fall of 1936, John and Orson Welles formed WPA Project 891, also known as the Classical Unit of the Federal Theatre. Their third production was *The Cradle Will Rock* by Marc Blitzstein, described by its author as "a Labor Opera—composed in a style that falls somewhere between realism, romance, vaudeville, comic-strip, Gilbert and Sullivan, Bertolt Brecht, and agit-prop." Someone in Congress concluded that Marc Blitzstein had written a leftist, antiestablishment, even communist play using taxpayer money. It had to be stopped, and with the collusion of Actors' Equity, they proceeded to shut it down. Three days before opening night in New York City, a dozen WPA security guards took up residence at the Maxine Elliott Theater to ensure that the costumes, props, sets, musical score, and the leading man's toupee did not leave the theatre, since everything was considered government property.

Welles and Houseman barricaded themselves inside the ladies' powder room, the only room off-limits to the government, and scrambled to put the show on despite everything. Defying the authorities and with unbelievable cunning, they secured an empty theatre twenty-one blocks uptown from the Maxine Elliott, and rallied the opening night audience to follow them, gathering more people along the way. The house was filled to the rafters. Alone onstage, Marc Blitzstein sat at a piano and played the opening chords. Although the cast had been forbidden by Actors' Equity to perform onstage, they had not been forbidden to perform *in the house,* so they played the scenes in different and unexpected parts of the theatre, with the stage managers finding and illuminating them with handheld spotlights. It was a huge success. John and Orson were subsequently fired for insubordination.

It was this version that we presented at the American Place Theater almost half a century later. The only thing onstage was a piano and black chairs. Before the performance, John Houseman, now eighty-three, stood in front of the audience and told his very moving personal account of the turbulent opening night of *The Cradle Will Rock.* The play itself is the story of an industrial town in the grip of Mr. Mister, the villainous boss of the steel plant.

Highbrow himself, he uses lowbrow threats, coercion, and violence to keep his workers and the townspeople under his thumb. *The Cradle Will Rock* is an amazing piece of theatre, a legendary piece of theatre history, and a show that is still relevant today. We played to full houses. John said it was an audience he hadn't seen in a long time, made up of theatre students and the Old Left. One night at the end of the show, as we were descending the stairs to our dressing rooms, peeling off bits of costumes and wigs, we heard a commotion in the audience. We all turned around, raced back up the stairs and into the wings. A man was reprimanding the audience and all we heard was, "The Mr. Misters still exist today and the only way to stop them is to JOIN THE COMMUNIST PARTY!" Live theatre. That moment was truly exciting and paralyzing. But what is theatre if it doesn't incite, doesn't move, doesn't change us in some way?

After a successful run at the American Place Theater, we closed *Cradle* and I went on to do and prematurely close two Broadway shows. Then I left for D.C. and the American National Theatre. When my five months with ANT were over, the *Cradle* company left for London and the Old Vic Theatre, where we enjoyed minor celebrity in the English theatre world. Vanessa Redgrave became fascinated with our show and especially with John. We became "theatre darlings" with a host of English actors who had never seen the play or might have had leftist beliefs. We were in English theatre heaven. One of my most treasured memories is of John's birthday party in the lobby of the Old Vic after a performance. We were drinking and chatting away when a Bentley or a Rolls-Royce pulled up to the lobby doors. The chauffeur got out, went to the back door of the car and opened it. We froze on the spot, silent and breathless staring at the scene unfolding before our eyes. "Who's going to get out of the car? Norma Desmond? The queen?"

Mom and Dad (above, center) on their wedding day, July 1, 1931, in Jamestown, New York, and (left) during World War II.

Twin brothers Bobby (left), Billy, and me.

Members of The Acting Company (left to right): Kevin Kline, Jed Sakren, Sam Tsoutsouvas, Gerry Gutierrez, me, and Ben Hendrickson, in Saratoga Springs, New York, c. 1975.

Prince Edward III in Edward II: *my first pants role, 1974.*

Photographer Martha Swope's iconic photograph of Evita.

With Howard McGillin as Billy Crocker in Anything Goes, *1987.*

Royal Variety Performance for Queen Elizabeth, 1991.

Sunset Boulevard, *1993.*
Costume fitting with Anthony
Powell. PAUL HUNTLEY
Right: "As If We Never Said
Goodbye." © FRITZ CURZON/ARENAPAL.COM

Steve giving me insight into Nellie for the New York Philharmonic's
Sweeney Todd, *2000.* © STEPHANIE BERGER

John Doyle's Sweeney Todd, *Broadway, 2005. Clockwise from left: Michael Cerveris, me, Donna Lynne Champlin, and Mano Felciano.*

PHOTO BY © PAUL KOLNIK

Below, left: Passion, *"Live from Lincoln Center," 2005.*

PHOTO BY RICHARD TERMINE

Right: The Rise and Fall of the City of Mahagonny, *my Los Angeles Opera debut, 2007.*

ROBERT MILLARD © 2007

The Ravinia Festival's Gypsy, *one of the best companies I've ever worked with.* JIM STEERE/RAVINIA FESTIVAL

Broadway closing night of Gypsy, *2009, hugging Arthur Laurents.*

Bobby, Mom, and Billy in Australia, 1980.

My family at our beach house: Matt, Joshua (holding the late Lucky), Pearl (in front of Joshua), me, Scout, and Indiana.

SAMMY LEDBETTER

Joshua, me, and Matt celebrating my Tony win in 2009.

BRUCE GLIKAS/BROADWAY.COM

He reached into the car and retrieved a single red rose, came into the lobby and presented it to John. It was from Vanessa. She's in a class unto herself. We were awestruck. John took it in stride, as if this happened to him every day. He was amused but nonchalant. That was John—so nonchalant that he planted his Emmy Awards in his flower garden. When the garden was full, he used them as doorstops.

Vanessa visited him quite often and they had long talks. We ended up doing a benefit for the Workers Revolutionary Party, a far-left Trotskyist group, at the behest of Vanessa and her brother, Corin. I had to give up my dressing room to John, who had to give up his dressing room to Lady Rachel Kempson, Dame Wendy Hiller, and Dame Peggy Ashcroft. I so wanted to burst open their dressing room door and sing, "Dolls! There is nothing like a dame, nothing in the world!" John forbade me.

While we were performing *The Cradle Will Rock* in London, I started rehearsals for another musical: *Les Misérables*. I played the role of Fantine, a young wistful girl forced into prostitution to support her illegitimate child.

Cameron Mackintosh again offered me a part. I love this guy. He'd seen my picture in a London paper announcing the upcoming run of *The Cradle Will Rock,* and before I left for London, he came to my apartment and played me some of the music. I knew it was going to be a hit after hearing the first four bars.

"Yes. I'll do it."

I should have told him to call my agent, but I said yes right away because I was excited by the music, and perhaps even more excited by the significance of his offer. I was an American actor being asked to work in London with the Royal Shakespeare Company (RSC). I said, "Yes, yes, yes." Then I thought about the really bad position my "yes" put me in when it came time to negotiate.

When the *Cradle* company had arrived in London in August, I'd started coughing nonstop. I coughed for the entire seven months I was there, through *The Cradle Will Rock* and all through *Les Misérables*. A cold, wet North Atlantic wind chilled me to the bone. I had a beautiful complexion but I was freezing all the time. It didn't do much for The Moll in *Cradle*, but it worked for *Les Miz*, because Fantine was consumptive. However, it's very interesting how Dr. Broadway takes over when one hits the lights. I'd be backstage and I would see stars on the first cough and the coughing could last for forty-five seconds, but the minute I hit the stage, I never coughed once.

Les Miz was rehearsing at the Barbican, then the theatrical home of the RSC. I would leave rehearsal early each day because I was still performing *The Cradle* at night. One of the stage managers escorted me to the door every afternoon. "The Barbican is a maze," he told me. "You won't find your way out by yourself." The maze at the Barbican brought me back to my days at Juilliard, which had a similar tangled network of hallways and corridors. I began to realize that there was something so right about my decision to stay in London for this production. It felt as if I had come full circle.

Les Miz had two directors, Trevor Nunn and John Caird. Early on in the rehearsal period, they assembled the company and said that when the principal players finished their roles, they would then become part of the ensemble and partake in the varied events that made up the story of *Les Misérables*. . . . *I don't think so,* I said to myself. I sure as hell didn't come to London to be in the chorus of a four-hour musical. I had to think quick. During rehearsals, I had a bulletproof excuse. I was still performing *The Cradle Will Rock* at night.

After Fantine dies twenty minutes into the first act of this four-hour extravaganza, there's a big waltz that introduces my daughter,

Cosette, to the proceedings. After Fantine finished "dying" in rehearsal one afternoon, John said, "Patti, my dear, you should be part of this next section, the waltz."

"Oh, darling John, I simply can't," I purred. "I've got a show to do tonight and I must . . . go . . ."—think quick!—"lie down." I kind of did need to lie down. Thanks to *The Cradle,* I got out of that scene and a few others.

At the end of our rehearsal period and before the technical week began, the company was given five days off so that the set could be loaded onto the Barbican Theatre stage. By this point *The Cradle* had completed its run, so I was free to return to New York to see my fourteen-year-old cat and my boyfriend at the time. When I got back to London, I went to the Barbican, looking for the company. All I found was the cook in the green room snack bar. "They're not here," he told me. "They're rehearsing at another theatre because we're loading in the set." I had totally forgotten.

I went to the other theatre and entered from the lobby just as they were staging the barricade scene. I was standing at the back of the orchestra when a member of the cast and my friend (so I thought), Sally Mates, spotted me. I didn't duck fast enough.

"Patti's back!" she hollered.

You bitch! I thought.

John turned around and said, "Oh, smashing. Patti, come join us."

Fuck! Busted. I begrudgingly walked up onto the stage and was now a member of the ensemble in the dreaded barricade scene. However, I did everything I could to shorten the length of my stay. I entered as a grown man, a smelter in fact, not even knowing what a smelter was, but when the character Enjolras tells the women and *children* to leave the barricade, I beat a hasty retreat as a little boy clinging to the hem of Sally Mates's skirt. However much I hated being in that damn barricade scene, I was lost in reverie every night Colm Wilkinson sang "Bring Him Home." Now, *there's* a voice. The barricade scene is the only scene the actress playing Fantine is in, and only because Sally Mates called me out, the raving bitch, as I stared at the rehearsal onstage too jet-lagged to react with my usual lightning speed. I never forgave Sally. She laughed her head off at me every night in the scene.

We opened at the Barbican on October 8, 1985. Before we opened, Trevor Nunn and John Caird prepared us for what they thought would be the Barbican subscription audience response to our little play: "Nothing," they said. "Because they are used to and want Shakespeare." During the curtain calls on opening night, people were standing, crying, and screaming, "Braaavooo," waving their arms and wildly clapping over their heads. We were a hit. Despite snippy reviews, audiences loved it. As the *New York Times* put it, "Rarely has there been an occasion when so many nasty reviews counted for so little." Ticket scalping was a regular occurrence. I was so right. I smelled a hit. This guaranteed our move to the Palace Theatre in the West End in two months' time.

We played this musical to delirious audiences. However, we had major technical problems. Our barricade set kept breaking down. One night as it was revolving and lowering halves onto each other, the stage-left barricade didn't lock into place and slammed into the proscenium as it was revolving with actors astride. We all left the stage for forty-five minutes, time to go to the pub next door. It was one of only two times we got to go to the pub. *Les Miz* was so long that all the pubs were closed by the time it was over. *Everything* was closed by the time it was over. Anyway, on this particular night, the set was repaired and the show went on. One night at the Palace Theatre, we had to cancel the show at the beginning of the second act because the barricade repair couldn't

Fantine's death scene, with Colm Wilkinson as Jean Valjean.

PHOTOGRAPH BY MICHAEL LE POER TRENCH © CAMERON MACKINTOSH LTD

be made—the only time I've been sent home from the theatre because of a technical problem, and the second time we went to the pub on a show night. My cast mate Roger Allam, who played Javert, and I went next door and got drunk. Whoopee!

Royalty came to the show. Early in the Barbican run, Princess Diana was at the performance as the chair lady, or something like that, for the Mary Rose Trust. The money raised at the benefit performance went to the excavation and preservation of the ship-wreck *Mary Rose*. When Princess Di arrived, the orchestra played eight bars of "God Save the Queen," but they didn't play the whole thing because she wasn't the queen. It sounded so crazy. I guess there's no "God Save the Princess" song.

I was so starstruck that I gave my entire performance to her. I sang "I Dreamed a Dream" to her and even bowed to her. After the show, the cast was invited to the Barbican atrium to meet the princess. I was the first one up there, just waiting, waiting, for her to arrive. We were all lined up, except for the few Republicans who didn't show because they despised the monarchy. One of our cast members refused to take his curtain call in protest. As the princess came in, she was backlit, followed by a ton of press and photographers.

It was a Hollywood movie-star entrance, no question. But after all that anticipation and excitement, she moved down the line, speaking only to the men, skipping right over all the women. Being a little boy-crazy myself, I wanted to say, "I totally get it, girl." But I just stood there and stared at her, disappointed but mesmerized.

I was busy onstage but my personal life was a wreck. It was early autumn when one morning I got a phone call from the States. It was my boyfriend—breaking up with me. I started screaming and crying. "What am I doing here?" I wailed.

My friend and cast mate Michael Ball was living with me at

the time. My crying woke him up. He went to the liquor cabinet, got out a square bottle, and pushed it in my direction. It was still morning. In our pajamas we walked on Hampstead Heath as I threw back gulps from this square bottle in between the wails and torrent of tears. I have no idea how I performed that night. I was drunk on my ass by eleven in the morning. I still don't know what kind of alcohol comes in a square bottle, but if you're an emotional mess and somebody offers you a swig, take it.

It was as if melancholy was my permanent condition. From Kevin on, all of my relationships had ended without any resolution. I was in London, in a musical hit, acting with the Royal Shakespeare Company, but I went back to that spectacular house at 87 South End Road in Hampstead Heath by myself every night, lonely and miserable . . . *misérable* . . . ha-ha. The interesting thing about my breakup this time was how well it informed the role of Fantine. There's a lyric in "I Dreamed a Dream" where Fantine sings, "He slept a summer by my side, but he was gone when autumn came." Life imitates art—that and the coughing. Apart from the cowardice of the guy who broke my heart, my misery was magnified because I wasn't home. I "wasn't surrounded by my lovely things," as Sada Thompson put it when a Thanksgiving dinner she was giving while on the road was not going as planned. Jack O'Brien told me the story and I love that expression and use it from time to time. It says it all. Somehow things become intensified when we're on the road. To see a picture in a frame or use the familiar coffee cup or sleep in one's own bed can chill out the most dire of emotional upheavals. I travel with a pillow all the time. I once left it at an inn in England and almost had a nervous breakdown until I had it in my arms again. I paid a king's ransom to get it back. Like I said, things intensify when we actors are on the road.

While I was being totally miserable every day and performing every night, I learned two things about the theatre in London: (1) A fireman presides over each and every theatre once we all have left, and (2) A priest or minister presides over the souls of the inhabitants of these theatres. The firemen protect those glorious and historical theatres from fire and destruction. The priests and ministers introduce themselves to the company and are there for anyone about to self-destruct and in need of their guidance and prayer. When I arrived at the theatre despondent, I met with the Barbican's minister and he talked with me for weeks. I can't remember his name or even what he looks like, but he never failed me and was so diligent in his concern over my mental and emotional well-being that I almost converted to the Church of England, or worse, returned to any kind of organized religion.

Oh yes, in the midst of my upheaval I was nominated for an Olivier Award, London's equivalent of the Tony Award. When I was told in my dressing room one night before the show that I was nominated, I asked between sobs, "What's an Olivier?" I was actually nominated for both *The Cradle Will Rock* and *Les Misérables*. I was totally chuffed. I was astonished when I won. It was an out-of-body experience. There we all were at the Criterion Theatre. I think we did a piece from *Les Miz* and I sang a bit of "Dream." Then my name was called and I won Best Actress in a Musical. Claude-Michel Schönberg said to me, "Patti, I weel never know eef you won for *Les Miz* or for zee ozzer show." "No, Claude-Michel, you never weel know." I won for both, but which show tipped the ballot, we'll never know. I adore Claude-Michel and love to tease him . . . him and his cigar. He used to come to music rehearsals smoking a cigar, but I excused him because he's French and they can do no wrong as far as I'm concerned—even when they're insulting me.

I had another experience at the Barbican I will never forget. One day after the matinee, the stage doorman told me I had visitors. Vanessa Redgrave and Frankie de la Tour. I knew who Vanessa was but the other one . . . sounded like a stripper to me. "Show them in." Vanessa and a stripper? It was Frances de la Tour, the highly respected actress. They asked me out for tea between shows. "Me? Okay." We went to Chinatown and Vanessa started to talk. She would very much like for me to perform my cabaret act in mining camps all over England for the Workers Revolutionary Party, she told me. *But I'm an imperialist pig,* I thought. I was drinking in every moment of this wacky scene. We finished tea and I think I said yes. The bill came and we split it down to the last pence. *But you asked me out,* I thought, *and you have a Bentley!* I went back to the Barbican, my head spinning, actually excited that I might be hanging out with Vanessa Redgrave in mining camps. Would she be my producer, my company manager, my assistant? Oh, the possibilities were endless. It never came to pass. I didn't see Frankie again until she came to New York in *The History Boys* and won the Tony for her performance. I recounted the story to her. She vaguely remembered it, or she was humoring me. I stay somewhat connected to Vanessa, seeing her every time she sets foot on a stage. I sadly last communicated with her over the death of her daughter Natasha Richardson. I bled, as so many others did, for her and her family.

Our run at the Barbican ended, my broken heart was mending, thanks to a lot of laughs with cast mate Roger Allam, wacky teas, and an unexpected award in my hand. We reopened *Les Miz* at the Palace Theatre in the West End on December 4.

On opening night, Trevor Nunn came into my dressing room. "This is so right," he told me. "If anybody belongs here, Patti, it's you." I was so grateful he said that to me. Not because I felt I didn't belong, but because it validated the connection I was already experiencing.

One of the great figures in the history of the RSC was artistic director Michel Saint-Denis, who along with John Houseman cofounded the Drama Division at Juilliard. That was my connection, the key to my sense of belonging. For me, continuity is very important in my profession and in my loyalty. My choices over the years may seem haphazard, but they've been shaped by the way I was trained and by the people who have influenced my life. When continuity reveals itself to me, as it did when I was walking the halls of the Barbican, linking it back to Juilliard, then having that reaffirmed by the head of the RSC at the Palace Theatre, it deepens all those connections that are so important to me.

Again we were sold out with the same delirious audience reaction. It was pretty amazing to be having this experience. I had absorbed and deflected so many bad reviews and premature closings and now I was in a mega-blockbuster hit. You can't predict. . . .

Les Miz is a long show. And it was a long time between my cues. One night a couple of months into the Palace run, I got really tired of listening to the score. It happens. One just gets sick and tired of the play. It's actually when I start to do my best work. When I'm bored, I stop "acting." However, after the barricade scene this one particular night, I went back to my dressing room, took off my wig, my costume, my microphone, and my contacts. I turned off the Tannoy (the intercom), stuck some gum in my mouth, put my glasses on, lit a cigarette, and began reading the Madonna issue of *Interview* magazine. I was sitting there in my long johns because it was wintertime and the Palace Theatre was freezing. Just as I began thinking, *I wonder where they are . . .* , Roger Allam burst open my dressing room door with his foot.

"LuPone!"

"Whaaaat?"

"You're on!"

"Holy shit!"

My wig, my costume, and I flew down three flights of stairs. By the time I hit the bottom step, I was fully dressed. (No contacts, no mike, no time.) The ghost of Fantine is supposed to make an entrance in the closing minutes of the show as Jean Valjean is dying, but I had left Colm Wilkinson onstage alone, dead, sitting in a chair, head listing to the right, barely breathing—enough to keep him alive—for sixteen bars of music. Yeah, I royally fucked up. I've often wondered whether Colm opened his eyes at some point during those sixteen bars and looked around to see if he was really onstage or in some dream/nightmare?

Since I had missed my entrance, the dance captain told me to enter from the other side of the stage with the other ghost, Eponine. I said okay . . . *But what do I sing?* I seemed to think I only knew my lines in order. I finished the show totally freaked out, and during my curtain call with Roger, I was hissed by the RSC. I never did find out if they were serious or not. It's the only time I've ever missed a cue.

A lot of Americans who came to London that winter contacted me. I saw people I wouldn't necessarily have seen if I was on the stage back home. Vincent Gardenia found me. Vinnie was doing the movie *Little Shop of Horrors* with Rick Moranis and Ellen Greene, whom I knew very well because of our time together in Israel Horowitz's *Stage Directions* at the Public in 1977. I also connected with Michael Bennett and Bob Avian, who were mounting *Chess* in the West End, and Sigourney Weaver and Paul Reiser, who were filming *Aliens*.

One day Paul, Rick, and I were having tea at a hotel when Rick said, "I miss pancakes. And I can't find maple syrup."

"I know where the maple syrup is," I said. And so the Day of the Yank Breakfast was born. I invited Roger Allam and Michael Ball from the cast, as the English contingent. Michael Bennett, Bob Avian, Sigourney, Paul, Vinny, Ellen, and Rick comprised the American faction. We had a drunken revelry on a Sunday morning in this incredible house in Hampstead Heath.

I was now having a great time there. I was working on the London stage and I was living in Hampstead Heath, a section of London that remains so romantic to me. Roger Allam became my closest London friend, and I was reunited with Colin Stinton, my Edmond from a few years earlier, who had moved to London. And then some shit just had to hit the fan, now, didn't it? It just wouldn't be me if it was smooth sailing.

First, I found out that I was not being paid commensurate to the highest-paid RSC actor, which was a contractual point. And that it had been going on since the beginning of my contract. Where the hell was my agent? I found out because I talked with another actor. Why do producers think actors don't talk to one another? Their excuse was that they didn't want to upset the senior members of the RSC. Huh? Whatever happened to a contract is a contract? You agreed to it, you signed off on it. They never paid up. A fissure between the management and me started to form. Then, after we had recorded the album, and even though my contract stated that no single of mine could be released without prior negotiations, a single of "I Dreamed a Dream" was released without the said negotiation or a "Hey, Patti, guess what?" I walked off the show.

I walked off the stage and stayed away for three days. The company manager begged me to come back, but staying away was the only weapon I had to make them honor my contract. The day I walked, I called Colin Stinton and asked him to come to my house, but before he got there I bought a chicken and made a vat of chicken soup. I was a nervous wreck. Colin showed up and as I madly stirred the pot, I freaked out on him. "I've never walked off the stage in my life, but I'm sick and tired of being abused by producers. Until they honor my contract, I'm not returning to the stage. I don't care if I get on a plane tomorrow." I looked in vain for a square bottle. In the end I did return, a negotiation took place, but why, why, why was I forced to walk off the stage to have this issue resolved?

Over the years, nobody's fought my battles for me. This is my career, my livelihood, and my talent. I will protect it if nobody else does. Too much experience has come through trial and error. I now have a very strong agent and lawyer and a rider that, in the words of one general manager, "reads like every mistake in Patti's career." He's right, but with each new contract I try to make sure that every problem I've had in the past will never happen again. It's impossible. Theatre keeps changing.

I came home from London $25,000 in debt, but *Les Miz* is one of my strongest and most treasured experiences.

I was only going to do Fantine in London for six months. Before my visa expired and I had to come home, I started to get a little nervous about the next job. "Next" started with a phone call while I was still in London from producer Sandra Saxon Brice in L.A. She wanted me to come to Los Angeles for the television movie *LBJ: The Early Years*. She wanted me to play Lady Bird Johnson. Thank God for the next job. I got out of the *Les Miz* debt.

"We're going to have to dye your hair brown," she warned, "because Lady Bird is a brunette."

"I have brown hair," I said.

"No, you're a blonde," she insisted. Ever since *Evita*, I'd had trouble convincing people I was not a blonde and Evita was not me. Nevertheless, I got the part, and Sandy, who's from Texas, flew me there to meet Lady Bird. After listening to seven hours of taped interviews she had made with the producers, I paid her a visit.

"Do you have any questions?" she asked.

Seven hours of tape, I thought. *What could I possibly ask that she hasn't already talked about?* I was silent, racking my brains trying to figure a way into the conversation.

To break the ice she asked me, "What have you done?"

"I played Evita Perón," I said.

And while I jabbered some inanity, she said, "Well, it's a far cry from Evita to me. Evita was a bird of paradise, and I'm just a little mouse." The statement was revelatory.

That meeting, and the viewing in the Johnson Library of private home movies that she filmed on a Brownie camera, were my first clues that perhaps I'd underestimated Lady Bird. I have enormous respect for her. She's one of America's unsung and underestimated First Ladies.

We shot the movie in Los Angeles. Randy Quaid played LBJ. He was definitely in the boots. I was barely in the hair helmet. But shooting *LBJ* turned out to be the most remarkable experience—it was where I met my husband, Matt Johnston.

He was a camera assistant. I saw his beautiful blue eyes one day. I said no in my head and yes in my heart. One day between shots I sat on his lap wearing a wool suit (he's allergic to wool) and in third-stage makeup (Lady Bird in her sixties). I asked him out on a date. He was so shy. I think he said yes. All I know is I fell in love with this man, head over heels in love, and we've been together for twenty-three years. We have one son, Joshua. I don't know what would've happened to me if Matt hadn't come into my life. I don't know what I would do or how I would survive without either my husband or my son. Matt loves me, protects me,

With Randy Quaid on the set of LBJ, *1987.*

and balances me. He is funny, patient, charming, handsome, kind, sweet, and smart. Joshua has all the best qualities of Matt and a few of mine. We are so deeply proud of Josh and love him unconditionally. We couldn't have asked for a better son. I grabbed the brass—no, strike that—the gold ring.

I was still doing *LBJ* when my agent called. "How would you like to make a movie in Italy?" It was just like Robert Stigwood's invitation to work in Australia.

Nobody's ever going to ask me to work in Italy again, I thought. *I'm going.*

When shooting for *LBJ* ended in July, I was on a plane for Rome. The film was a movie for television called *A Sicilian in Sicily,* and it was a French-Italian coproduction with three Americans in the cast: Jimmy Russo, Vinnie Gardenia, and me. I played Vincenzina, the wandering gypsy. I said my lines in English and they were dubbed in Italian later. Even today I'm not quite sure what the film is about. I read the script three times and still didn't have a clue.

But so what—I was in Italy, the motherland! The producers were great, and I was able to talk them into sending me to the seaside before I started shooting. "I'm supposed to be a gypsy," I said, "but I'm so pale." They agreed and sent me to a resort on the sea, all expenses paid, to get a tan. I *loved* these producers! To get ready for the part, I was in makeup for three hours, and the last piece of makeup was the film equivalent of black underarm hair. "Don't pluck or shave anything," they told me. "Not eyebrows, not arms, not legs, nothing." They dyed my hair black and gave me a permanent. When I was done I looked as Italian as the local women. I've always known that my face was more European than American, but now I looked like a seriously hot Italian . . . at least until I started eating.

Matt and I were newly together as a couple at this point, and I gave him a ticket to Rome as a birthday gift. We were living in the Hotel de la Ville at the top of the Spanish Steps. It was so romantic. We shot for three weeks in Rome, then flew to Sicily for the last two weeks of the shoot. We flew into Catania, went south to Agrigento, and arrived at the Hotel Akrabello. Matt and I walked into the bar, which was packed, and from across the room I heard someone call out, "Patti!" It was Joss Ackland, who had been the original Juan Perón in the London *Evita*. What the . . . I'm in Sicily and I know someone?

Joss was part of a large cast and crew working on the film version of Mario Puzo's *The Sicilian*. That's who the rest of the people in the bar were. Now there were two film companies in this tiny, tiny motel. Every day around four P.M. they'd run out of liquor.

Joss was playing the *capo di tutti capi,* the Mafioso boss of bosses. Director Michael Cimino had sent him to Sicily to live with the real capo for six weeks prior to shooting. Can you imagine living with THE BOSS? He'd shoot me before too long because I'd ask too many questions.

"What are the Mafiosi like?" I asked.

"See for yourself," Joss said, and gestured toward the end of the bar. There sat four preppy young men, very handsome and very well dressed. These were the sons of the capo, and might easily have passed for Yale or Harvard grads. Where were the bad suits and the greasy hair I remembered from all the movies I'd grown up with?

Italians have a different mind-set about making movies, and I guess about life in general. We shot on location pretty much the whole time, and wherever we shot, there was amazing hospitality. In Sicily the women would greet the set in the morning with all kinds of food and pastries. Wherever we had our lunch breaks, they laid a feast on us.

And of course long lunches were routine. The art director would find a local restaurant; we'd eat the local meats and vegetables and drink the local wine—lots of local wine. Lunch would last two and a half hours. I'd be smashed on my ass and be expected to shoot when we got back to the set. I gained thirteen pounds in two weeks. I know I screwed up continuity. I was thirteen pounds less in this shot, then thirteen pounds fatter in the next shot. I've never seen the movie but I'll bet dollars to doughnuts (mmm . . . doughnuts) I was cut out of it. Matt gave me a lecture in Sicily on the roundness of me. That didn't stop me eating. It was Italy, for God's sake!

In true moviemaking fashion, there was a lot of time off. Matt and I traveled all over Sicily. The art director's father and stepmother, Leo and Pucci, hooked up with a local man who showed us rarities of the island that we never would have seen by ourselves.

Leo's description of Sicily was so perfect: a cross between the moon, the desert, and paradise.

We returned to Rome and shooting was winding down. Matt surprised me one day—he told me he loved me as we crossed a bridge in a little town outside of Rome. I was already in love with him. I'll never forget the moment.

I was sad when the shoot ended. I learned enough Italian to thank the crew. They were very happy I made the effort to say it in their language.

We came home. Matt moved into my apartment in Manhattan, and I was happier than I'd been in a very long time.

Then came one of the roughest choices I've ever had to make in my career. Cameron Mackintosh offered me Fantine in the Broadway production of *Les Misérables*.

It was a choice I'd already made. Two weeks into the London run of *Les Misérables*, I came offstage after the barricade scene and walked to the stage door. Cameron was standing there.

"I can't play this in New York," I told him.

"I know," he said. "The part's too small."

"No, that's not it," I replied. "It has nothing to do with the size of the part. I'm in the perfect theatrical experience. I'm in a perfect musical with a perfect company in a perfect environment. I can't play this in New York. It would never be the same." This is my company and my experience.

All a stage actor has is his or her performance and the memory of it. I didn't want anything to touch that memory.

Everybody expected me to reprise my role on Broadway. I'm sure people thought I was nuts not to. I forced myself to remember what I'd said in London about not wanting to spoil the memory, and told Cameron I couldn't do Fantine on Broadway.

Even though I'd said no, I still didn't want to be anywhere

near New York City when *Les Miz* opened. When the ship *Queen Elizabeth II* offered me the chance to lecture on a cruise through the Indian Ocean, I took it. It was a great way to escape. Matt and I had an amazing time and now we were on a plane home and about to land at Kennedy Airport when someone in the seat behind me tapped me on the shoulder. I turned around to see Colm Wilkinson's agent.

"We're really going to miss you tonight, Patti," he said.

It was March 12, 1987, and it was opening night of *Les Misérables* on Broadway.

Noooooooooo! Holy shit! How did this happen? How did I end up being in New York on the night I most wanted to be someplace else, *anyplace* else?

I cried my eyes out that night, second-guessing myself mercilessly about not being in the cast. Had I made the wrong decision? Had I done something really foolish? It took awhile before I had my answer. One night, several months later, John Caird called me. "Come on, Patti," he said. "I'm in New York. Let's go pick up Frankie."

In the year or so since I'd been in London, John and his wife had split up. He was now dating Frances "Frankie" Ruffelle, who played Eponine. She and Colm Wilkinson had been the only two original London cast members to cross the Atlantic with the production. As John and I stood in the back of the house to wait for her, I was immediately glad that I was not up there onstage. What I saw was a pale imitation of the show as I knew it. I must have had some sort of premonition that I would have been miserable. Knowing my temperament, if I had been involved in this imitation of the original production, I would have had a fit. Worse yet, I would not have been able to hold my tongue.

This is how producers mass-produce hits. They "freeze" the

show the way the first cast created it. When it's a hit, they want to impose the characterization that the original actor discovered onto every actor who follows in the part.

That's why they had wanted me to mimic Elaine Paige's every gesture as Eva. Now they wanted Randy Graff to duplicate mine as Fantine. They won't let the second, third, or fourth cast discover the play for themselves. It's not that the New York company didn't have competent actors and strong voices—they did—but to impose somebody else's interpretation on them was unfair. Like any carbon copy, it could never be as sharp as the original. At least that's what I thought I saw, and I knew I had made the right decision.

Anything Goes, Driving Miss Daisy, Life Goes On, A New Life

11

1987–1992

Reno Sweeney in Anything Goes.

© BRIGITTE LACOMBE

att and I were officially a couple living in
New York when I got a call to audition for a new production of
Cole Porter's *Anything Goes*. I mentioned the audition to the wonderful photographer Jack Mitchell during a photo session. Jack had
been photographing me since the early days of The Acting Company. His studio walls were covered with portraits of the leaders
and creative forces in the performing arts. It was an inspiring gal-
lery of dancers, opera singers, writers, and actors. When I told him
I was up for the part of Reno Sweeney, he gave me the last photo
he took of Ethel Merman, who had originated the role in 1934.

It was my good-luck charm. At the beginning of my audition,
I turned upstage, then turned back to the room with the photo
of Ethel in front of my face as I spoke my line. I don't know what
possessed me, but it got a laugh.

I got the part and started rehearsing this fantastic piece of
American theatre history. We were extremely lucky to have Timothy Crouse, the son of Russel Crouse, who was one of the 1934

revisionists for the original *Anything Goes* book, and John Weidman as our new book writers. Timmy had his dad's original script to refer to with the original gags and all . . . the history.

We rehearsed in the bowels of the Vivian Beaumont Theater. As I wandered the hallways, peering into every room and exposed crevice that made up the rehearsal spaces, scenic shop, wardrobe room, and offices, I felt as though my moment had finally arrived. It validated all the time and money my mother had invested in me for those Long Island lessons. It validated the Juilliard experience—all of it—good, great, and painful. I was working at Lincoln Center, something I had aspired to so long ago. I remember a day at Juilliard when I was looking out of a window over to the plaza, just daydreaming. The dream was to one day walk that plaza on my way to work at Lincoln Center Theater. It took me twenty years to achieve that dream. Another twenty years have passed and I'm back where I started, wishing I could work at Lincoln Center Theater. If they wait much longer, look for me in a revival of *The Gin Game*.

I was reunited with Bernard Gersten for the *Anything Goes* production. I had met Bernie at the Public Theater when my brother Bobby was doing *A Chorus Line* in 1975. Joe Papp and Bernie were running the Public then. I ended up there a year later in the play *Stage Directions* with John Glover and Ellen Greene, who became my fast and lifelong friends. Now that Bernie was executive producer of Lincoln Center Theater, I was coming full circle. Everything made sense. More dots were connected. I felt safe, happy, and productive knowing that Bernie was upstairs in the Beaumont offices. To me, Bernie has always been a benevolent producer and protector.

Our director was Jerry Zaks and the choreographer was Michael Smuin. Howard McGillin and Bill McCutcheon were my leading men and great fun to work with. Howard remains one of my favorite leading men. He was so beautiful to gaze at every night, always had a smile in his eyes when we played our scenes together, and stopped me dead in my tracks whenever he sang "All Through the Night" and "You'd Be So Easy to Love." He wasn't singing to me. I was offstage doing yet another twelve-second quick change.

"Friendship."

© BRIGITTE LACOMBE

Tony Walton, responsible for the genius sets and costumes, dressed me like I've never been dressed before. Pat White, my very own Thelma Ritter, worked those quick changes like an entire pit crew in a NASCAR race.

Our rehearsal period was inventive, crazy fun, and long. It was the longest preview period I'd ever had, which was a very good thing and I wished happened more often. The longer you play the part, the more familiar the character becomes to you, obviously. It sounds simplistic, but the longer you play the play, you know that environment and the audience that much better. The audience is half of a stage actor's performance. They supply information an actor can't possibly know until there's that interaction. When that extraordinary rapport occurs between actor and audience, the fun begins. Our long preview period for this production garnered great reviews, the icing on the cake. This time I didn't have to be afraid of opening the *New York Times* the morning after.

Our opening night was October 18, 1987, forever known as

Black Thursday because the stock market took a huge dive that day. David Ingraham, my old friend and an arbitrage stockbroker, had tickets for opening night but never showed up. His company took a massive hit. In the opening moments of the show, Eli Whitney (Rex Everhart) talks about a stock he wants Billy Crocker (Howard McGillin) to sell. Those audience members who did show up opening night—we played to about half a house—laughed uproariously at the reference. It was a sudden bit of unexpected magic.

Matt and me at the Anything Goes *album release.*

Frank Rich gave *Anything Goes* a rave review in the *Times* and wrote me a love letter. I wrote him one back. The show was a hit, and I was a hit in it. I didn't escape bad reviews entirely, however. Several complained about my diction. It was the second time in my career my diction was brought to my attention. I didn't know what they were talking about. I understood me—what was *their* problem? I think it was the sound mixer, I really do. He sucked. And that other time they complained? That was someone else's fault, too, I'm sure.

Anything Goes went a long way toward finally freeing me from the tap-dancing blond fascist that *Evita* had made me. After years of what I used to call "crying and dying" onstage, not just in *Evita,* but in *Oliver!* and *Les Misérables* as well, suddenly everyone discovered that I could be funny. What happened to the Tony nomination for *The Robber Bridegroom* in 1976? That was slapstick and I was rollickingly funny in it. Broadway has a short memory.

A few months into the run, Bernie came into my dressing room and said, "Do you want to go to London with this production?"

"Yes, yes, yes!" I said out loud once again, only *this* time I also said, "Get in touch with my agent." No, I didn't, of course I said yes. I thought it would be the perfect contrast to my last West End appearance in *Les Misérables*—an American musical comedy classic and one of the great female parts in all of musical comedy history. From Bernie's question, I assumed that Lincoln Center Theater would be bringing its first production to London starring me as Reno Sweeney.

A short time later Tim Rice came to my dressing room one night after the show. "Just wonderful, Patti, great fun, what larks," he said. I soon found out that after my visit with Tim, he optioned our production for London to star Elaine Paige, and Lincoln Center Theater (LCT) gave it to him! Our show was a huge success, but LCT decided not to produce it in London. Howard McGillin was the only member of our company who made the trip. I was pissed off, but I also thought it was divine justice. I took Elaine's part, Eva Perón, here. She took my part, Reno Sweeney, there. It didn't soothe the wound, however. I still can't understand why Lincoln Center Theater didn't bring our company en masse to London and produce it themselves—like the RSC has done on Broadway. I wish there was greater reciprocity between London and New York, especially when it comes to entire companies.

By this time Matt and I were no longer just living together, we were engaged, but I was having trouble figuring out where to have the wedding. I couldn't decide between Northport, where I grew up, and Manhattan, where I was working. I told Bernie about my problem and he offered a wonderful solution: "My wife, Cora, and

Sealed with a kiss.
We're married.

I got married on the Ansbacher stage at the Public Theater twenty-
five years ago, and we're still married. Why not get married on the
stage of the Vivian Beaumont?"

Which is exactly what Matt and I did on December 12, 1988.
The finale in *Anything Goes* is a wedding scene, so Tony Walton
added extra doves and streamers to the existing set. My father
came back east from San Diego and walked me down the aisle.
Our processional music was *Wedding Day at Troldhaugen* by Edvard Grieg. The minister who officiated the service was Fred Ingraham, my dear friend David's twin brother. When the ceremony
was over and we were pronounced man and wife, the music blared
"Stars and Stripes Forever," Matt's choice. It was a wonderful, joyful event and it was the first time my mother and father had been
in the same room in more than twenty years. We were given Fred
and his then-wife Sally's villa in St. Barth for our honeymoon.
After a raucous reception in a place downtown called the Loft,

Jerry Zaks and Mandy Patinkin at our wedding, 1988.

serenaded by Kit McClure's all-girl Big Band, with tons of family, friends, and *Anything Goes* cast mates, Matt and I headed off to St. Barth for two weeks.

After the honeymoon I went happily back to *Anything Goes* because if there's one thing I love in the theatre, it's the sound of an audience weeping with laughter. This was a stunning and uproariously funny musical. We played to giddy audiences for months. One night I was feeling depressed while I was standing backstage at places. The show began, as it always did, with the taped voice of Cole Porter singing the first-act finale number, "Anything Goes," then our kick-ass Broadway band picked up where the tape ended, playing the glorious, romantic, and rambunctious overture. My face went from a frown to a huge smile. That show was just so infectious. You couldn't help but feel good.

I received my third Tony nomination, my second nod for Best Actress in a Musical. In fact, the production received ten nominations for the 1988 season. In all of the newspapers across the country, from New York to L.A., I was predicted to win—predicted to win hands down. I thought I was good in the part but this was a huge validation of my performance. I tried to keep it all in perspective, but as I said, we were a hit, and now with ten Tony nominations we became a gigantic hit. We were also the underdog. That season saw the original productions of *Phantom of the Opera* and *Into the Woods*. All three musicals received multiple nominations. The Tony Awards night arrived and I was dressed to the nines on my way to my big night. It had been eight years between nominations—eight years since my win for *Evita*. The company and I had to perform the musical number "Anything Goes" live. My microphone was still on as I turned upstage at one point during the song. The audience heard me wail, "Oh my God!" The nerves were so intense.

It was now time for my category to be announced. I waited patiently as the nominees were read. "And the 1988 Tony Award goes to . . . Joanna Gleason for *Into the Woods!*" I sat there and watched Joanna pick up her award. During her acceptance speech, I felt like I was having a flashback on an acid trip. She looked like the Tin Man from *The Wizard of Oz*. What happened? I was supposed to win! It was a bad night for me. Another lesson learned. Don't believe your own press. Somewhere, give it time, there's a banana peel with your name on it. I returned to the show, thrilled as we all were, for Bill McCutcheon's win for Best Featured Actor in a Musical, Michael Smuin for Choreography, and our Tony win for Best Revival.

Unfortunately, the longer our show ran, the more eager I was to leave. In a long run, things backstage can go rancid faster than you can sneeze, and it did with *Anything Goes* because of just a few discontents. Despite having a great director, Jerry Zaks, a great choreographer, Michael Smuin, and a wonderful cast of veteran actors, ultimately *Anything Goes* ended up not being a happy show. The problem in this one originated with the dancers, and to a lesser extent with the chorus, both of which were filled with first-timers. LCT is a nonprofit theatre, and salaries tend not to be the size of Broadway paychecks. As a result, we didn't get a full roster of A-team dancers and singers. We ended up with a group of mostly C-team players, and they conducted themselves that way. We did have some disciplined, experienced singers and dancers who knew backstage etiquette and their responsibility to the production, just not enough of them to make a difference. I take my hat off to Dale Hensley, Richard Korthaze, Jane Lanier, Gerry McIntyre, and Rob Ashford among those pros.

This inexperienced minority had no knowledge of proper backstage behavior. They had no awareness or a point of reference of how rarefied the air at Lincoln Center Theater really was. For instance, and this is a big for instance, everyone had a dressing room with a bathroom in it on stage level. For all they knew, it was like this in every theatre and always had been. They approached their roles in the show with a tremendous sense of entitlement and little sense of responsibility. The veteran actors in our company shared my frustration at the bad attitude of these few individuals. I would have traded my private bathroom for a company of professionals who understood how to conduct themselves onstage and off. (Okay, I wouldn't have traded *my* bathroom, but I would have been really, really tempted.)

Entitlement and arrogance is a virus in musicals because I think directors do not rehearse the book of the musical with the entire ensemble to include the dancers' and chorus's participation. It breaks down into quadrants from the first day of rehearsal. "Chorus, go here and learn music. Dancers, learn this choreography over there. Principals, scenes with the director in the next room." The unity isn't created from the start. Plays are much different. Each actor learns his responsibility in the play through the table reads, the importance of which musicals seem to ignore. Unbelievable care must be demonstrated from the beginning of a rehearsal period and a director needs to help each member own his part and his responsibility to it. It's the only explanation I have for the laziness and the amount of missed performances some Broadway companies have to contend with. Thanks to Arthur Laurents, I had a uniquely different experience with the *Gypsy* company concerning this phenomenon. We had table reads, lots of them, with the entire ensemble present. As a result, the performers owned their roles, loved this play, and wanted to be onstage every night. They never missed a show.

During my *Anything Goes* run, I became increasingly more unhappy. An opportunity presented itself that would perhaps shake things up. I was asked to read for a TV pilot. The producers were in New York and wanted to meet with me before my performance. I was now living in Connecticut and commuting to the show. My agent made the appointment. On the day of my meeting I didn't feel like going to the city earlier than I had to, so I canceled the appointment. They returned to L.A., but apparently they really wanted to see me, because they called my agent again and asked me to audition on tape.

I had no expectation that anything would come of it. New York actors frequently tape their movie and TV auditions if they're not flown to L.A. by their potential employers, but in general we won't get the parts because the people doing the casting are not in the room. The lack of personal interaction puts us at a disadvantage. We're also not "local hires" for an L.A.-based show, so it costs money to put us up, rent cars for us, and so forth. And it's not as if there is a shortage of actors in Los Angeles, right?

When I started taping the audition, the first thing I did was speak directly into the camera and apologize for not showing up the first time. Then I read the scene. When they got back to me, they told me that my talking to the camera was actually more interesting than the audition I gave. Talk about a left-handed compliment. They then flew the director, Rick Rosenthal, to New York and had me tape about three scenes with a guy named Bill Smitrovich—for five hours on a performance day. I think I finally said, "Gotta go . . . lie down"—always a good excuse in a pinch.

It was oil and water with Smitrovich and me from the very beginning. At one point during those five hours he pressed both hands down into my shoulders and said, "We just need to relax."

What the fuck? I wondered. *I don't know who you are, but get your hands off me, and exactly* who *needs to relax?*

But I let it go. What were the odds of either of us getting cast in this thing, let alone together? Better than you'd think, it turned out.

I took a hiatus from *Anything Goes* and flew out to Los Angeles in April to shoot the pilot. During the filming I had three huge blowouts with Mr. Smitrovich, in a span of just three weeks. *This is a fucking disaster,* I thought. I actually called my agent and told him that this wasn't going to work, so find a way to get me out.

I phoned one of my dearest friends in the world, an actor I had worked with in Studs Terkel's *Working* and another Mamet actor. "I want to make sure I'm not the asshole here," I said. "What's the rap on this guy Smitrovich? I want to know what I'm up against." My friend checked with his friend who had done another series with him. Let's put it this way, if there was an asshole in the cast, it wasn't me this time. I faced a seven-year sentence with a thoroughly distasteful man. *Noooooooo!* Howard McGillin, save me!

We finished shooting the pilot and I chose not to return to *Anything Goes.* In April 1989, I left the production after fifteen months onstage and waited for the fate of the pilot.

While I was in L.A., however, I also met with Richard Zanuck and Lili Fini, the producers of *Driving Miss Daisy.* At first I had no idea why I was there. There was no audition, but right after I met Dick and Lili, I was told I would be playing Florine Werthen, Boolie's wife, a part written specifically for the screen. Dan Aykroyd would play Boolie. You mean that's it? I got the part?

I couldn't believe the role was handed to me like that, so I

The cast of Driving Miss Daisy *(from left to right):*
Jessica Tandy, Dan Aykroyd, Morgan Freeman, Lili Fini,
me, and Richard D. Zanuck.

called my friend Alfred Uhry, who had written both the play and the screenplay for *Miss Daisy*. "Did you think of me for this role?" I asked him.

"Yes," he responded, "because nobody wears costumes like you do."

My character Florine was based on a relative of Alfred's. She was a clotheshorse, so in this context Alfred was paying me a compliment. What a great way to get a part. You look good in clothes.

There I was, down in Georgia in a movie with Jessica Tandy, the original Blanche DuBois in *A Streetcar Named Desire* on Broadway. Our director was Bruce Beresford, a gentleman, an artist, and a man incredibly respectful of his actors. We felt welcomed on the set, which was always quiet and prepared. Everyone was especially respectful of Jessica, because she was carrying half of the movie at eighty years old. Despite being frail, she was radiant, both on-screen and off. At the time, I was reading *Blessings in*

Disguise, Alec Guinness's autobiography, and there she was in the book. Wow. And there I was in the makeup room ogling her and intimidated beyond belief. She was elegant and generous. I was happy to be working with Dan Aykroyd again. He was so terrific in that movie. Shooting for me was brief. I was sad to leave this experience.

I returned to Connecticut and the home that Matt and I had just built to learn that the pilot had been picked up and I would now be living in L.A. But I'd just moved into this brand-new house in the woods! I had to leave my new home, and in my first TV series, I would be working very closely with someone I couldn't stand. God does not give with both hands, I'll tell you that.

So began my time as Libby Thacher, the mom on *Life Goes On*. The show premiered on September 12, 1989, and ran for four seasons. Matt and I relocated to Los Angeles for the duration.

Life Goes On was an important show because it spoke specifically to the disabled community in America. It was the first time a Down syndrome actor was actually hired to play a Down syndrome character. Audiences loved it. I loved so many people involved in the show, including Kellie Martin, who played Becca; the original Paige, Monique Lanier; Chris Burke, who played Corky; as well as crew, directors, and writers. My biggest problem was that I had absolutely no chemistry with Bill Smitrovich. I found him to be a self-absorbed bully. If only he had been a talented or generous actor, his behavior might have been justified.

The star of our show was Chris Burke, the Down syndrome actor. Even though Chris was high-functioning, he was still a young man with a disability. Rick Rosenthal, he of the five-hour network test, directed many of the episodes. Once we went into production, he shot endlessly. It was as if he didn't want to go home and he was taking us with him on his descent into TV hell. He did take after take, shot after shot, piling up footage that never got used—over the shoulder, under the leg, the "I went to film school" crane shot. We were on the set for sixteen hours a day the first two years. The schedule was grueling on everyone and the long hours put a lot of pressure on Chris. He'd never done episodic television before, and sometimes the stress was too much for him to handle. Every so often he would have meltdowns, and when he melted down, we were sunk because our producers never prepared a "cover set"—another scene we could shoot without Chris in order to stay on schedule. The problem was no one knew exactly when Chris was going to melt down, but no one bothered to take his needs into consideration.

Rick never dealt with Chris very well. In one episode, Chris had to say the word *customer,* but he just couldn't get the plosive out, the *k* sound in *customer.* Rick made him do forty-two takes because he couldn't say "customer" without stammering—forty-two takes in front of all of us, a ton of extras and the crew. That would have been a nightmare for any actor, let alone one with Chris's challenges. Chris covered his distress well and just tried to please Rick. He did it, he finally did it, and we were all there to hug him and love him up a lot.

Frank Burke, Chris's father, is an ex-cop from the South Bronx. Frank has said that he could never leave the set when Rick Rosenthal was directing Chris. He and his wife, Marian, were always cool when we were at work, even though I know they were not happy with Rick's treatment of their son. What made them put up with it, I guess, was that *Life Goes On* was a tremendous opportunity for Chris. His being on the show was also symbolic, in that he was representing a part of society that TV had pretty much ignored until then. Chris Burke is a champion, the sweetest heart, and an angel.

Life Goes On was revolutionary because it pioneered the idea of showing a disabled child as a normal part of an American family. That said, the American family they created around Corky was anything but normal. It was a direct descendant of *Ozzie and Harriet*, or maybe *Father Knows Best*. For four years I played a docile mom in a patriarchal family. Libby Thacher was reduced to saying, "Yes dear, no dear, whatever you want, dear." I begged the creator to let me go. He wouldn't. Libby Thacher was unrealistic to me and the writers never could figure her out.

Nevertheless, every year we kept getting picked up, to our bewilderment. Every year another writer became a producer. It's common knowledge that *Life Goes On* was a problematic set at Warner Bros. Studios. We were the first ones back after hiatus and the last to leave before hiatus. Our executive producers would fire our best and most efficient directors, and the writers would then write, produce, and direct. If only they did one thing well and stuck to it. We did have two great producers—Phillips Wylly was one and Bob Goodwin was the other. There was hope when Bob joined our beleaguered set.

There were bright spots as well. Every time I worked with Chris or Kellie or Monique, I couldn't have been happier.

Monique Lanier played my stepdaughter, Paige, but she was only with the show for a year. She left the cast when she got pregnant. To give her a proper send-off, the girls took her out to Gladstone's in Malibu. She abstained from drinking. Not me—I was throwing back tequilas like crazy. But I should have stuck to water as well, since it wasn't long before I realized that Matt and I were expecting a baby of our own. You have to wonder whether there wasn't something in the water on the set of *Life Goes On*. There were forty pregnancies in the cast and crew during the four years we were on the air. Life went on and on and on over there.

We did an episode in Hawaii when I was about five months

along, but we may as well have stayed in Los Angeles. The producers gave us the gift of sending us to Hawaii, then took it back by making us shoot sixteen hours a day with Rick Rosenthal. I had popped at five months and told them I was showing, but the men didn't hear me. I was in misery with the heat and the long hours. It was a signal of things to come. The writers and producers took no notice of my condition until two weeks before I was due to deliver. Oh, they wrote it in the story line but paid no attention to the shooting schedule. Executive producer Michael Braverman came into my trailer one day and said, "Well, Patti, you leave in two weeks and we have a lot of work to do between now and then. You'll be working every day all day from here on out." I did work every day all day until just before I delivered. Thank God I'm strong like an Italian bull. Our son, Joshua Luke Johnston, was born November 21, 1990, at Cedars Sinai Medical Center in Los Angeles. On *Life Goes On,* Libby didn't give birth till the season finale in May 1991,

Our beloved son Joshua.

which means that I was pregnant or playing pregnant for something like twenty months. Elephants don't gestate that long.

I went back to work after a six-week maternity leave. I'll never forget being in my trailer with my infant son when I was visited by the current episode's director, Michael Lange, and makeup, hair, and wardrobe friends. It was good to be back. As they were goo-goo-ing over Josh in my arms, Michael said, "What do you think he's going to be when he grows up?"

Without missing a beat I said, "He's going to stage his mother's comeback!"

I know exactly when I got pregnant. It was when Matt and I went to Washington, D.C., in February 1990 so that I could sing in a PBS Presidents' Day special called *In Performance at the White House*. In April 1991, I was invited to sing at the White House once again, this time as part of *Points of Light, A National Celebration of Community Service*. After the performance, Matt, my mother, and I worked our way down the receiving line to shake hands with George and Barbara Bush. When President Bush told me that it was good to see me again, I blurted out, "The last time we were here, we got pregnant."

"Well," he said with a big grin, "come back anytime." And with that, Barbara Bush invited us to come upstairs and tour the living quarters. My mother and I raced for the elevator and were the first ones out of it, running down the second-floor hallway to see it all before they threw the theatricals out.

Meanwhile, back in L.A., on the set of *Life Goes On,* my relationship with Bill Smitrovich continued to deteriorate. By the end of the fourth season we were no longer on speaking terms. Can you imagine? We played love scenes, we played parenting scenes, we kissed, we hugged, and when the director yelled "Cut" we never even looked at each other. That's acting. (On my part. He just stunk.) Kellie and Bill were not on speaking terms, either. He tried to direct her in a scene they were both playing. At fifteen years old this child/woman shut him down simply by telling him not to direct her. Bill didn't speak to Kellie for six weeks.

In 1992, during shooting, I was offered a way to escape L.A. and the TV show. Andrew Lloyd Webber wanted me to perform in a workshop production of his new musical called *Sunset Boulevard*. Oy vey. *Anything Goes* and *Life Goes On* were the opening acts. The Main Event was about to begin.

Sunset Boulevard, Part 1

SEPTEMBER 1992–JULY 1993

12

Trevor Nunn and me after the Sydmonton performance.

a lot of the jobs I've had throughout my career have started with a phone call—the phone rings, I pick it up, and someone says, "Are you interested?" I almost never get the part when I audition. Equally, I almost never turn down an offer. And the offers have come out of left field, believe me.

When my phone rang in August 1992, I thought the offer of this role and experience would be one of the highlights of my career. Instead, it is still the worst experience I've ever had in the theatre.

In the summer of 1992, I got the "Are you interested?" phone call from David Caddick, Andrew Lloyd Webber's musical supervisor. Did I want to come to London to sing through a new musical that Andrew was writing with Christopher Hampton, a work in progress called *Sunset Boulevard*? The music would be performed in workshop at the Sydmonton Festival on Andrew's estate in early September.

"Hmm, let me think about it . . ." *Are you kidding?* I was in my fourth season as Libby Thacher on *Life Goes On*, and I was suffocating from boredom. I missed singing. I missed being onstage.

I knew the Billy Wilder film, which starred Gloria Swanson as faded movie star Norma Desmond and William Holden as Joe Gillis. How could I resist? If nothing else, I could get out of L.A. for a couple of weeks. Kevin Anderson would be playing Joe. He and I worked with David Caddick and pianist Steven Cahill
for three weeks in L.A. before we
left for England. I was so lucky to
have Kevin as my leading man.
We'd met in London when I was
doing *Les Miz* and he was doing
Orphans with Albert Finney. He
is a wonderful actor, a wonderful
singer, and a great guy. I adore
him. I asked my producer Michael
Braverman for permission and got
excused from *Life Goes On* to perform at Sydmonton.

*With Kevin Anderson
at Sydmonton.*

There were a few rehearsals
in London before we all trooped
out to the country estate of Andrew Lloyd Webber. They told me I could hold the book onstage—that I didn't have to memorize the role. I wasn't about to hold the book. I wanted to act the part, and you can't do that when you're reading from the script. Although it was billed as a workshop, I knew I was being given the chance to prove I could play Norma Desmond in a full-fledged production.

We rehearsed for about five days before giving just a single performance in Andrew's "theatre," a desanctified chapel on the grounds of the estate. Even though I knew that this, in effect, was an audition, I didn't know what a three-ring circus it would turn out to be. What's the matter with me? Hadn't I gone through *Evita*? It wasn't a workshop. It was a full-on event. We were costumed and propped and wigged and the performance was videotaped.

On the night of our workshop performance, the chapel filled with Andrew's invited guests, and there wasn't a civilian in the house. Broadway producers and theatre insiders had flown in from America just to see it. Trevor Nunn was there. Bernie Jacobs and Gerry Schoenfeld of the Shubert Organization were there. Meryl Streep arrived.

The pressure that night was intense. I stood behind the make-shift curtain and watched the audience take their seats. I actually do that in every show I'm in. I like to see the audience before I perform for them. I saw Meryl and we waved to each other. I waved to everybody I knew. I tried to dispel the nerves by getting smiles from the colleagues I knew and respected.

*Me, Andrew Lloyd Webber, Meryl Streep, Don Gummer,
and Robert Stigwood at Sydmonton.*

Several people in the audience that night said Meryl was crying at the end of the play. I didn't see Meryl or anyone else for that matter, because when the lights came up onstage, they were blinding. I couldn't see a thing beyond the set, although at the end I did hear sniffles from the audience. *Okay,* I thought. *They've stuck with it to the end of the play. I didn't bore them at least.* Meryl found me after the performance and was gracious and complimentary. I appreciated it so much. These things, these "one-offs," are more difficult than anyone can possibly imagine.

Apparently my delivery of the role was good enough to get the offer that night at the lavish dinner laid on for all of the guests and the *Sunset* company. Andrew drew me aside and said, "Name your price." We hugged.

"Kevin Anderson," I told him.

What I didn't say again was, "Call my agent." Why do I keep forgetting those three simple words? Call . . . my . . . agent.

The company and I stayed at the dinner for a while, then retreated to the local pub. Ah, the trip was finally worth it! Meryl showed up with Christopher Hampton, I think, or was it Andrew? Who can remember? We were drunk and having a blast releasing all the pent-up energy from this tornado of a "workshop" we'd just completed.

I was on a flight back to Los Angeles to resume my life on TV as Libby Thacher, but with the expectation of returning to the London stage in *Sunset Boulevard.* I had another meeting with my producer, Michael Braverman, and asked him to release me from my *Life Goes On* contract. He had refused in the past, but this time it was easier for him to say yes. The story line had shifted to such a degree that it was mostly about Kellie Martin's and Chad Lowe's characters. It's the reason I could rehearse for three weeks before I went to London and why I could rehearse and perform a two-act concert at the Westwood Playhouse in L.A. I was working maybe four hours a week. Michael told me that he didn't want to prevent me from playing "Nora" Desmond. I didn't have the heart to tell him I wouldn't be on *The Carol Burnett Show*. I thanked my lucky stars and waited for the negotiations to begin.

Despite Andrew Lloyd Webber's assurances that the role was mine, as soon as I got back to L.A., the rumors started to fly. Who would play Norma Desmond—Meryl Streep or me? I was befuddled because nobody was claiming responsibility for releasing this information and Andrew's company, Really Useful Group, was not denying it.

There was a piece in the *Daily News* just ten days after the Sydmonton performance about the "battle royal" to play Norma, and how Meryl had told her agents at CAA to "get me *Sunset*." In early November, Marilyn Beck's column actually announced that Meryl would play Norma.

My agent was just beginning my contract negotiations when all this appeared in the papers. It was a long and disturbing negotiation. I should have taken it as a sign. The same day that the Beck column appeared, I received a note from Trevor Nunn, who would be directing *Sunset Boulevard*, saying how thrilled he was that he would be working with me again. It was all very confusing, to say the least.

Then the media got ugly: MERYL MAKES A SONG AND DANCE OF LOSING, the headlines said. STREEP THROAT WASHES OUT. According to the papers, Meryl was furious because Andrew had told her that her singing was not good enough for her to play Norma, and as a result she'd been held up to "public ridicule."

Meryl and I have never been close friends, but I believe there has always been a mutual generosity and respect between us. She, Mandy Patinkin, Kevin Kline, and I were all on Broadway together, in 1975, across the street from one another—Meryl and Mandy in *Trelawny of the Wells,* and Kevin and me in *The Robber Bridegroom.* Through all of this, Meryl herself said nothing publicly, and I don't for a moment believe that she or her people had anything to do with this mean-spirited speculation in the media. But if it wasn't coming from me, and it wasn't coming from Meryl, where was it coming from?

My guess is that Andrew's company, Really Useful Group, was planting rumors and innuendos in order to generate interest in the show. Nobody was controlling the gossip because nobody wanted to. Who else would have benefited from the hype? Still, through all of the speculation in the press followed by all the reassurances from Andrew, the contractual negotiations were turning ugly and threatening. I remember saying to my agent, "Is this worth it?" I was made to feel that even though the part was handed to me by Andrew himself, I was lucky to get what I was getting monetarily and I was replaceable if I wasn't satisfied, and generally I should go fuck myself. Ooh, I couldn't wait to get on that plane and work my ass off for a company called Really Useful Group. Useful to whom?

Finally, at the beginning of December 1992, Andrew and I faced reporters in London and it was announced that I'd be playing the role of Norma Desmond. Andrew was gracious: "Patti LuPone played the role when we performed the show at my Sydmonton Festival earlier this year. To say that she was a tremendous success and left the audience exhilarated and moved by her performance is an understatement." That night, Matt, Roger Allam, my cast mate from *Les Miz,* and I went to see Sam Mendes's Donmar production of Steve Sondheim's *Assassins.* I wondered two things:

1. Would Andrew be pissed off that I chose to see a Sondheim musical?

2. Why couldn't I be in a Sondheim musical?

In the wake of the announcement, the buzz in the press was amazing and positive. Liz Smith said that *Sunset Boulevard* was already being talked about as "the theatrical happening of 1993." I returned to Los Angeles to finish *Life Goes On*. Through my best friend Jeff Richman, I met lyricist Scott Wittman and composer Marc Shaiman at their housewarming party in Laurel Canyon. As I left the party, I just happened to say to Jeff, "Do you know anybody who could put together an act for me?"

"Scott," Jeff said. I approached this new person in my life and asked him if he would create a show for me. We started working at his house with musical director John McDaniel. During the rehearsal period, John came to me with an offer—ten nights at the Westwood Playhouse, now the Geffen. I accepted the engagement and we billed it as my farewell to Los Angeles. I again had to get permission from my producer from the TV show. No problem. I was barely on the show anymore. Now I was starting to have fun in L.A.! Isn't it always the way? You meet lifelong friends ten minutes before you leave the city?

One night my new friend Scott Wittman, Matt, and I went to the Queen Mary, a drag club on Ventura Boulevard in Studio City. We got very drunk. At one point I went to the ladies' room and came face-to-face with two six-feet-tall drag queens, both prettier than me. I said, "Girls! Guess what? I'm playing Norma Desmond in Andrew Lloyd Webber's new musical, *Sunset Boulevard*!" They squealed in delight. Afterward I felt so tawdry. That's where I chose to make my personal announcement. Drunk in the ladies' room of a drag club. Hmmm . . . another omen missed, one could say . . .

Life returned pretty much to normal in L.A. I worked on the set and rehearsed my concert with Scott and John. My agent was still in negotiations with Really Useful, even though my getting the

Sunset Boulevard role had already been announced in the press. One day I received a very funny gift from Stephen Sondheim. He sent me what he called the *"real* score" from *Sunset Boulevard.* In the late 1950s, Gloria Swanson made the first effort to get a musical version of *Sunset Boulevard* produced, but nothing had ever come of it. The composer was a man named Richard Hughes, who was said to have been her lover at the time. As an added bonus, Steve also included a track of Swanson herself performing the climactic song on *The Steve Allen Show.* It is something only he could have found. It is a treasured gift and quite a listen. Steve has a wicked sense of humor. Gloria's musical adaptation? Not so good.

In February I taped my last episode as Libby Thacher. It was a wrap for the season as well. I said my good-byes to my favorite people, packed up four years of Los Angeles right before the earthquake, the riots, the fires, and the mudslides, and headed back home to Connecticut. Rehearsals in London weren't going to start until April, but there continued to be a lot of media coverage anyway, relentlessly fueled by the PR machine at Really Useful Group. It is an article of faith that the opening of any Andrew Lloyd Webber musical must be a highly anticipated extravaganza, a newsworthy event. Everything leading up to *Sunset Boulevard* was news, even buying a ticket.

Even though by 1993 we were well into the age of telephone ticket sales, it was impossible to buy a seat for *Sunset Boulevard* except in person (unless you were overseas). This meant that when the Adelphi Theater box office opened, the queue on that first day supposedly stretched for more than a mile. Some will say it was a photo op manufactured for the TV cameras. Andrew Lloyd Webber himself sold the first tickets. That first day's advance sales amounted to £500,000. Before the curtain finally rose in July, advance bookings had risen to £4 million. That's roughly $6 million, and *Sunset Boulevard* was pretty much sold out for the first six months of the run. It was a new record for the West End.

On Palm Sunday in early April I was in the midst of packing for London, when my friend Philip Caggiano called and asked me whether I was mad at Barbra Streisand. "Why would I be mad at Barbra Streisand?" I replied.

Why? Because the *New York Times* was reporting that she had recorded both "With One Look" and "As If We Never Said Goodbye"—Norma's two most powerful ballads—for an album that would hit the stores before we even opened. That's why.

What? Again? This is exactly what happened when Andrew let Barbra sing "Don't Cry for Me, Argentina" before we opened *Evita* on our pre-Broadway tour. When I was cast as Evita, one of my first tasks was recording "Don't Cry for Me, Argentina." It was never released. I never knew why, except I found it odd that Barbra had recorded it as well and her recording was out there for all to hear. Was I mad at Barbra? No, I was mad at Andrew. When I'd done my concert at the Westwood Playhouse, I had been specifically forbidden to sing anything from *Sunset Boulevard*. The story from Really Useful at the time was that Andrew wanted to hold these songs in reserve so we could premiere them with great fanfare on the cast album. Now Barbra had been given the chance to cherry-pick the best of the score, and put her imprint on the songs that I should have been originating *before* I was even in rehearsal. And according to the *Times,* she'd recorded them in February. What a bunch of crap. Yet another portent I chose to ignore.

I felt as if something had been stolen from me—again. It's insulting for an actor who is originating a role to be barred from originating the musical material associated with it. Certainly under these circumstances I felt insulted, devalued . . . but I'm not sure that mattered to Andrew in the slightest. Having Barbra record these two songs was part of the global hype to promote the greater glory of *Sunset Boulevard.*

This was yet more proof of the total disregard Andrew seems to have for the directors, designers, and actors who present his work to the public. From his point of view, there was nothing collaborative in the success of any of these shows; they sprang purely from his own musical genius. The rest of us who took what we were given—shaped it and made it work—had nothing to do with it. And we did make it work—not to take anything away from the writing, but you can't put a score on a bare stage and have an audience feel and care and stay interested for two and a half hours. It's a collaboration.

During negotiations, Really Useful informed my agent that there would be a production of *Sunset Boulevard* in Los Angeles before the show opened on Broadway, but they refused to let me be in it. This angered me beyond belief. I was supposed to be the original Norma, in England and in America. I was caught between a rock and a hard place. They insisted that I do London, skip Los Angeles, and then go to Broadway. Their argument was that because Los Angeles would open about four months after we did, my doing it wouldn't give me enough of a run in London. L.A. would keep running after we opened on Broadway.

It was going to be *Evita* all over again. There would be two U.S. productions running simultaneously, inviting comparisons and setting up competitions. I told my agent to tell them I'd skip London and just do it in L.A. and New York. That didn't fly with Really Useful. I seriously don't know why I agreed to take on the part in the first place. Everything was a battle and I was on the losing side. I was not getting what I wanted in the deal, so why did I stick with it? What was so important to me about doing this role? It's a question I still ask myself.

My agent finally came to an agreement with Really Useful, but not without a lot of screaming and tears—screaming from me, tears from him. (Kidding.) Because the negotiations had been so bloody, I told him that I was not leaving my home until I had a signed contract for both the London and New York productions in my hand. When that finally happened, I sent my family's luggage—five trunks—to London.

On the day Matt, Josh, and I were to fly to London, we closed up the house and waited for the car to take us to JFK. The phone rang. It was my agent. "Are you sitting down, Patti?"

"Oh no, now what?"

"Andrew Lloyd Webber just announced that Glenn Close will play Norma Desmond in Los Angeles."

I was stunned.

Before I started rehearsal in London, Andrew Lloyd Webber had called a worldwide press conference to announce Glenn Close as the L.A. Norma ten months in the future. My agent had been right to ask if I was sitting down. I was blind with rage.

Just then the car arrived. I handed the driver our three tickets and said, "This is what you came for. Take them back to Really Useful in Manhattan." Matt, Josh, and I went back into the house. There would be no flight to London that day, or the day after that. Why didn't I stay home altogether? It's another question I still ask myself.

It took three more days of negotiating to actually get me on the plane. I had several conditions Andrew Lloyd Webber had to satisfy, starting with Glenn Close not attending the London premiere, or being anywhere in the vicinity while I was rehearsing the part. Having ambushed me with the announcement the way they did, there was no way I would now let them parade someone about who would be playing the part almost a year later. I so wanted the drama to end right there in Connecticut, nurse my wounds and look for another job. Worse yet, the fact that the timing of the announcement coincided with my leaving for London was enough to rekindle the gossip fires in the press. For the second time now, Really Useful had orchestrated what would look to the media like a catfight between two actresses.

Having been through the Patti/Meryl rumor mill in the fall, I was now confronted with endless Patti/Glenn speculation. And the biggest irony of all is as I was setting foot on a British Airways flight to finally start rehearsal for *Sunset Boulevard,* I got a call from the Director of Musical Theater for Lincoln Center Theater, Ira Weitzman, asking me if I was interested in the role of Fosca in Steve Sondheim's new musical, *Passion.* Finally a Sondheim musical. But I was grudgingly on my way to London. My five trunks were sitting in the house they'd rented for me. They'd never send them back if I just bagged the whole thing. I cursed my luck. Why did I send those damn trunks? Another question that has a stupid answer at best.

Andrew Lloyd Webber had created dueling Normas. Immediately after the announcement, Baz Bamigboye, who was and still is the Liz Smith of London, reported that there was "unconfirmed talk" that Glenn Close would take *Sunset Boulevard* to New York. His column drew a staunch letter of denial from Andrew: "Patti LuPone will give the world premiere of *Sunset Boulevard* in London," he wrote to the *Daily Mail,* "and will repeat that role on Broadway." He was never quite that unequivocal again.

Matt, Josh, and I arrived in London in mid-April, just before my birthday. Our home for the next year was a stunning six-story house located at 17 Stanley Crescent, in Notting Hill. The back door opened out into a very mature two-and-a-half-acre garden, more like a private park, really. It was great for our three-year-old son, who learned how to talk in London and came away with a proper British accent. The house became known as "The House of Good Vibes," and it was my refuge the entire eleven months I lived in London.

I had missed three days of rehearsal, but before I began, I wanted a meeting with Andrew, Trevor, and Patrick McKenna, Andrew's something or other. My agent calmly explained to them the emotional damage they had caused me already, and I tried to explain how they had set up a competition between two actors and someone was bound to lose. They assured me it was not true, I was the most important Norma, blah, blah, blah. It was useless. The three of them didn't hear a word I said. I felt no satisfaction after the meeting. It deflated me even more. But I forged ahead. I don't to this day know why I didn't walk away. I was given all the signs and I recognized them, but it didn't stop me from this crushing force that kept me heading into the *Sunset Boulevard* disaster. Legally I couldn't walk away. I had a signed contract in my hands. I had to uphold my part of the deal.

Sometime after the meeting, Andrew said quite casually, "Let's go to the studio." What for? I had just gotten off the plane. My body and my voice were still somewhere over the Atlantic. Nevertheless, he was herding me off to sing in the studio. At the time I had no idea why, but I was pretty sure I wasn't getting paid to be there. I recorded Norma's two big numbers—the Barbra Streisand songs.

That night, Andrew threw me a welcoming cocktail party. What did he play at the party? The songs I'd just recorded, over and over and over. They were running a musical backdrop for

Ah . . . happier times.

the party, and it made me feel like an organ grinder's monkey, performing for the pleasure of his guests. Monkey had to leave early. I had a previous invitation. Cameron Mackintosh was giving me a birthday party upstairs at the Ivy restaurant. I don't think Andrew was happy I left his cocktail party, especially for another producer's celebration, but like everything else that swirls around Andrew, the recording was a surprise and his cocktail party was a surprise. I truly felt as though my freedom had been usurped now that I was employed by Andrew and his company.

It was finally time to rehearse. We started working at Riverside Studios in Hammersmith. The rehearsal period was fun. I love English companies. In this one, there were no psychodramas, no personality conflicts, no backstabbing. If there was an issue, it was discussed sensibly and resolved in the best way possible. I also love the dialogue British actors have with their directors. There *is* a dialogue. Plus, my dear friend Bob Avian was the choreographer, so I had a pal on the creative side. I was so happy to have Bob there and to be working with him. He remains one of my very closest friends. We all would walk along the river to the local pub every day for lunch. Kevin Anderson and I were back playing Joe and Norma. Everything was fine until technical rehearsals began at the theatre. In preparation for *Sunset Boulevard,* Andrew had acquired, gutted, and completely refurbished the Adelphi Theater, at a cost of some £1.5 million. Everything was new. Moreover, John Napier's set was very ambitious. Everything was done on a grand scale, and everything moved. The problem was that you couldn't always be certain *when* it was going to move. John Napier had done the sets for *Les Misérables.* I love John and his brilliant mind.

Getting taken for an unexpected ride by the scenery was another matter entirely. The *Sunset Boulevard* set had tremendous problems, and the technical rehearsals were brutal. The biggest scene changes involved what was then state-of-the-art electronics, but they couldn't get the bugs out . . . for my entire run of nine months. At entirely random moments, the sets, including Norma's living room and grand staircase, would jump downstage at will— as much as four feet at a time—with Kevin and me on them.

There were times when the house wouldn't fly in and times when it wouldn't fly out. It turned out that whatever radio frequencies they were using to trigger the hydraulic lifts on the sets were the same frequencies every cell phone . . . and every taxicab . . . and every courier service in the city were using. Anyone in the West End passing by the Adelphi could give me a thrill ride just by picking up the phone. When they finally figured out what was wrong, they started making modifications to the lifts and the set, which meant we couldn't rehearse onstage. It got so wacky that one day when I was sitting in the mezzanine, I witnessed a huge fit Andrew was throwing at the entire creative staff, ending with him pulling the score from the show. I thought to myself, *It's the theatre of the ridiculous now. You pulled the score from yourself. You're the producer, you dimwit.*

The public eagerly followed every bump on the road to our premiere. Because this was an Andrew Lloyd Webber musical, the buzz in the media continued to intensify. In the lead-up to opening night, the British press corps often asked me about my interpretation of Norma Desmond, and my response was consistent. Above all I wanted to avoid camp—Norma had already been satirized by generations of drag queens, and I had no intention of becoming one of them.

I wanted to create a character, not a caricature. Norma had to be real—extravagant but real. To me, the Norma written for this musical was what was left of the star that the Hollywood machine had created, then mercilessly spat out when the movies learned to talk. She never got over what happened to her; the wounds to her psyche never healed. Her ostracism made her unstable, and her rejection by Joe Gillis finally pushed her over the edge. To be sure, Norma Desmond was a woman who was larger than life, both as a great actress and as a movie goddess, but at the same time she still had to be recognizable as a flesh-and-blood human being.

This was in keeping with what Christopher Hampton, who wrote the book and cowrote the lyrics, had in mind. "We are making her more human, making the relationship more understandable," he said at the time. "You feel for her, and that's the point."

We began previews on June 28, 1993. Opening night would be two weeks late. The technical problems were severe enough that the premiere, originally scheduled for June 29, had been delayed to July 12. This made for a lot of tension—some onstage because we knew we were short on rehearsal time, but even more at the box office. Really Useful had to coax, cajole, persuade, or strong-arm the existing July 12 ticket holders to give back or ex-change their seats to accommodate opening night dignitaries and celebrities, including Nancy Olson, the movie's original Betty, Billy Wilder, who had written and directed the film, and members of the press.

Those members of the press included theatre critics, both British and American. After initially saying he wasn't going to do it, Andrew eventually chose to invite U.S. theatre critics to the London opening. This was an unusual change of heart—much had been made in the press of the allegation by Andrew that U.S. critics had it in for him, above all Frank Rich, who was then lead theatre critic of the *New York Times*. Even when it was announced in December that I'd be playing Norma, the papers reported that *Sunset Boulevard* was "skipping" Broadway and opening in London to make the show "critic proof," because Andrew believed "he can't win" with Rich.

Nevertheless, we continued barreling toward opening night, and the media circus was really ramping up. If I didn't have Matt and Josh with me, and if I hadn't been through it all before with *Evita*, I don't think I would have handled it as well as I did. I had friends and family flying in for opening night, so when I got the "we have a problem" call from Madeleine Lloyd Webber, Andrew's wife, I was not prepared for what she had to say. She was insisting that I had to disinvite some of my guests. She needed the tickets back.

Opening night parties have become mob scenes, which doesn't necessarily make them fun, but that's what they've become. I hate them. The invitation list goes way beyond the cast and crew, and includes celebs, journalists, and twenty-five thousand friends of the twenty-five thousand "producers."

Madeleine actually said to me, "You know, Patti, the opening night party can make or break the success of the show." Now, I've been on Broadway for more than thirty years, and not once did an opening night party affect a show's success. The reviews and word of mouth did. *You dilettante, you poseur,* I thought. *My tickets are a contractual point—nothing you can do about it, lady.* But what I said out loud was, "Oh, dearest Madeleine, you can have twenty back." In truth, I gave back nothing. I'd cushioned my guest list for the opening night party so all my nearest and dearest would get in without a problem. On opening night I was surrounded by the people I love and by the London actors I knew and loved from *Les Miz.* I don't know who was sitting at Madeleine's table.

I barely remember the first night's performance. I must have been very nervous. It went on, I know that much. Murray Lane and Caroline Clements, my beloved dresser and hairdresser, respectively, kept me in costumes, laughing, and on the stage. We didn't have any technical difficulties that I can recall and we got through it. There was a standing ovation, bravos, and general raucousness in the audience. I remember my dressing room after the performance much more vividly than the show itself. It looked like a wake. There were so many bouquets that we had to put half of them in the tub in the bathroom. The dressing room was soon filled to overflowing with friends, family, the creative staff, and well-wishers. Champagne was uncorked and everyone was jubilant. I was exhausted and relieved.

The opening night party was a zoo, but that's how it goes. I don't remember where it was or how long I stayed. It was loud and busy. I did talk to Billy Wilder, though I can't remember what was said, but he seemed pleased. I kissed and hugged everybody, stood on a chair and waved, and then I went home. There's not much to do at an opening night party. It's work and hype. My dressing room before the party was so much more fun.

Now there was nothing to do but wait. When the reviews came in, the British press was somewhat mixed, but on the whole positive; the Americans were almost uniformly negative, sometimes brutally so. Perhaps predictably, Frank Rich was hard on us, and on me, calling me "miscast and unmoving."

Robert Osborne in the *Hollywood Reporter* was particularly cruel: "LuPone should take the 'Sunset' off-ramp. . . . She is a distinctly negative hurdle if the show is to go further. LuPone never seems to have a clue as to how a great star would behave. As Norma Desmond, she has no mystique, no elegance. She often runs up and down stairs like Irene Ryan in *The Beverly Hillbillies*. . . . Glenn Close is a cinch to be an infinitely better Desmond; for one thing, she already possesses an imperious air that suits the role extremely well."

She wasn't opening for nearly a year and she was already getting better reviews than I was.

Sunset Boulevard, Part 2

13

"With One Look."

PHOTOGRAPH BY DONALD COOPER © 1993 RUG LTD

By the way, the reason I ran up those stairs "like Irene Ryan in *The Beverly Hillbillies*" was because Andrew refused to write any more music for Norma to exit with, and the stage-left exit was a long way up that staircase. Why he didn't want to address the design of the staircase and the number of stairs it took to exit is beyond me. I remember the conversation with Trevor and I remember the "no."

Once the excitement surrounding opening night died down, we settled into the run. We played to sold-out houses. I was getting standing ovations every night. In the London press there was no bad word of mouth, nothing about how I stank in the part. America was a different story. "Patti LuPone doesn't seem crazy enough," griped the *Philadelphia Inquirer*. "The part demands a sense of danger, of holding on by a thread, that the actress doesn't manage. . . . The core of the character, the white hot purity and dignity that underlie the ragingly destructive fire, gets lost." Yup, I got me some bad notices.

Despite the sniping coming from the United States, things were fine in London. Not only were Kevin Anderson and I great acting partners, but we all became a close-knit, happy company. During our technical rehearsals we were given membership to a private club down on its luck called the Green Room, across the road in Adam Street. It had been around since Victorian times, and when we started rehearsals at the Adelphi, it was full of nothing but old English actors playing snooker and falling off their bar stools. You could join for something like ten pounds a year, which we did. Peter Ustinov was once a luncheon speaker at the Green Room. He said it was like "addressing sailors in a submarine." The place was painted a puke color green, the plaster walls were peeling, and you had to descend to the basement before the bar and game room revealed itself. It was a sad picture of a bar, but we made it one of our homes after the performance. The other place was the Spot, a club located diagonally across the

Opening night gift to Trevor:
his head on a platter.
I wonder if he still has it . . .

road from the stage door in Maiden Lane. Andrew would come to the Green Room, as did John Napier and Trevor. It gained in popularity throughout our run, and when I brought Goldie Hawn in one night, the membership skyrocketed the next day. Eventually we couldn't get in ourselves.

The goodwill was too good to last. Sometime in September

I was having lunch at Orso in the West End when Richard Polo, who owns the restaurant in partnership with Joe Allen, came over to the table. "Just heard the ads, Patti," he said. "They're fantastic."

I looked at him blankly. "Excuse me? What are you talking about? I don't remember recording anything."

Shortly thereafter I heard myself singing on the radio. Really Useful was running radio and television ads promoting *Sunset Boulevard.* The reason I didn't remember recording anything was because they were using the same birthday recordings I made in April on the day I arrived, right before Andrew's party in my honor.

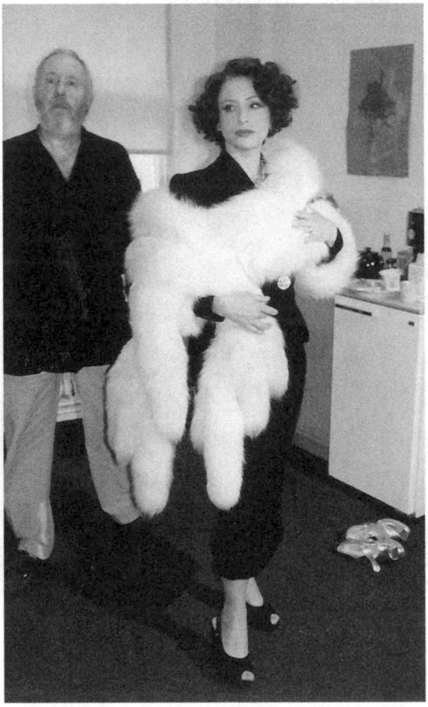

Norma Desmond costume fitting with Anthony Powell, one of my all-time favorite designers.

PAUL HUNTLEY

I felt violated—*shit*—again. They were using my voice without permission, without compensation. It was the worst kind of exploitation, not to mention a breach of contract. The attitude at Really Useful seemed to be that I was their property.

This was not very different from what had happened years before during *Les Miz,* and I had the same emotional reaction. I walked off the stage. I went home and called my agent, then waited for somebody from Really Useful to call me. I refused to perform until the matter was resolved. Really Useful invented a fig leaf for themselves, saying I'd come down with tonsillitis, but there was nothing wrong with my throat. As it turned out, their timing was not to their advantage. They had rolled out the radio and TV ad campaign while Carol Duffy, my understudy, was on vacation. Alisa Endsley, who was a member of the chorus and second understudy, went on as Norma. At the curtain of her first performance, Andrew made the in-your-face-Patti grand gesture, appearing onstage to present her with an armload of red roses. Then they blew up her notices and posted them prominently in the lobby. What Alisa said to the press, I'll never forget and will be always be grateful for: "If it weren't for Patti LuPone, I wouldn't have been able to do it." I wonder what Andrew was thinking when those words came out of Alisa's mouth?

I think it was about this time that I started to be undermined by Really Useful. It was a kind of psychological warfare. I got the feeling that they were sabotaging me, trying to make it as unpleasant for me as possible. One of the most upsetting ploys was a financial one. They sent me a £35,000 invoice; that's almost $53,000. Unbelievably enough, it was for the Sydmonton Festival workshop. Really Useful billed me for my airfare, my hotel, my meals—and they sent the invoice to the theatre. I opened up the bill as I was preparing to go onstage. I was still reeling from it when they called places. I remember feeling faint and confused. That's a lot of money. I told Kevin about it and he shrugged it off, calling them Really Useless. I never asked him if he got a bill as well.

They also cranked up the rumor mill again. PATTI'S TRIP TO BROADWAY FADES INTO THE SUNSET, trumpeted the headline to Baz Bamigboye's column in the September 17 edition of the *Daily Mail*. "It seems Andrew Lloyd Webber wants a new Norma for Broadway, and I hear he has approached another actress," he wrote. A few days later, the rumor jumped the pond. *New York* magazine was reporting that Really Useful had offered me $1 million to give up the role before the show came to Broadway.

Nobody suggested this to my face, but there wasn't much doubt where this insider information was coming from. It had to be coming from someone in the Really Useful organization. Who else would have anything to gain from planting this tidbit? Who else would a journalist have accepted as a credible source?

Warfare or no warfare, I had a contract that guaranteed I would open as Norma in New York. I believed I was contractually safe, so I wasn't too worried. In hindsight, of course, I should have been. It's no secret that Andrew Lloyd Webber has a thin skin when it comes to bad reviews. He takes them very personally. And now he was obsessing over Frank Rich's review.

Andrew sought me out in the Green Room one night in the early fall. He was leaving for Los Angeles to start rehearsals with the second company, and all he could do was cluck and wring his hands about how disastrous Frank Rich's review had been for the show. I was so over his greed, his insecurity and megalomania, that I was fresh out of sympathy, especially since it was his own fault. Andrew himself had invited Mr. Rich to London to see the production, after he'd initially said he wasn't going to do it.

It had already been announced that portions of the show would be substantially revamped for L.A. because of the review. To be sure, the London production had its problems, but *I* was not the problem (and if I was, I'd like to think I would admit it—and if I admitted it, I'd like to think I'd put it in this book). Nevertheless, everything written about *Sunset Boulevard* from New York or Los Angeles still seemed to zero in on me. American critics didn't like the show, so it was shoot the messenger, pretty much. "I feel like I don't have a soul on my side over there," I said at the time. "They like me so much better here than they do in the States."

*Norma's mad
scene in the finale
of the musical.*

PHOTOGRAPH BY
DONALD COOPER
© 1993 RUG LTD

LuPone bashing was the order of the day. "*Sunset Boulevard*
has one liability that can't be rewritten: Patti LuPone," said the New
York *Daily News*. *Variety* reported that Andrew Lloyd Webber had
wanted to get rid of me as soon as the Frank Rich review came out.

Director Trevor Nunn went with Andrew to Los Angeles to
launch the second production. He sent me occasional bulletins
from L.A. as the work progressed:

Andrew has made a number of changes in the score . . .
but I doubt whether somebody who had seen the London
production once would be able to tell you what the changes
were. I mean, Norma still blows him away and then goes
nuts—we don't suddenly have a happy ending here. . . .

The pioneering work we all did in London made it
easier, but it's still a very tough show. Everybody in the L.A.
cast is in a state of true and genuine admiration for the orig-
inal company in London who had to ride the bronco first
and prove it was possible to stay on.

While Andrew was in Los Angeles preparing to open the show, he got more and more noncommittal about my playing Norma on Broadway. "Ms. LuPone is reportedly under contract to repeat her role on Broadway, though Mr. Lloyd Webber was faintly elusive on that subject," wrote Bernard Weinraub in the *New York Times* in early December. "It all really depends on how things go here," Andrew replied, meaning in Los Angeles. If I had a contract, why would that affect me? Andrew also told Weinraub that Glenn Close's Norma was "darker." "Patti's a great singer," he continued. "She's primarily a musical-comedy star." All of this hurt me tremendously and yet I was supposed to have a thick skin and go on night after night after night.

After *Sunset Boulevard* opened in L.A., the gossip really intensified. Glenn Close received rave reviews, but then again, she didn't have to sing the same high notes that I did. Andrew lowered the keys for Glenn. The score was extremely high, and again, only a few agile singers could sustain these songs eight shows a week. Lowering the keys also took the excitement out of the songs. Nevertheless, critics adored her. Her performance "catapults her into the sphere of megastars," gushed Vincent Canby in the *New*

York Times. "Ms. Close's triumph seems certain to complicate the question of who will be playing Norma if the $10 million show comes to Broadway next fall. . . . There's bound to be pressure now to bring in the star of the L.A. company."

The rumors were still swirling in January when Kevin Anderson decided to leave the production. "Why are you leaving, Kevin?" I wailed, clinging to his pant legs.

"Because I can" was his answer. Kevin had his reasons and it's not for me to discuss them here but it broke my heart. I loved being onstage with him. He left and I was lucky his understudy, Gerard Casey, was as good as he was, but Kevin's absence left a hole in the show. He was a great Joe Gillis. He took an extended vacation and when he returned to London we went out to dinner together. I asked him if he was going to do the New York production, hoping he'd say, "Not without you, Patti darling." He said he hadn't decided. Kevin was not asked to reprise his role as Joe Gillis. Kevin was also not told he wouldn't be reprising his role. A bunch of cowards, is all I can say. When I saw Trevor a couple of years later, he said he hadn't heard from Kevin. I looked him in the eye and asked him why he was surprised. Apparently he didn't know Kevin wasn't told he would not be playing Joe in New York. "You're the director, for God's sake." It was hard to believe, as much as I love Trevor.

At one point early in the new year, I received a call and had to make an emergency trip to New York for a funeral service. A childhood friend from Northport had died. It was a shock. She was only forty-two when she died of ovarian cancer. I called Richard Oriel, the company manager, and told him I had to go home. I knew I couldn't miss very many performances, so I had my travel agent book a round-trip on the Concorde. The plan was to go to the funeral, stay overnight, and head back to London the next day.

I was only going to miss one performance; I'd be back in plenty of time for the evening show.

Or so I thought. This was January of 1994, and the East Coast was in the midst of another snowy winter. It was blizzard after blizzard. I boarded the Concorde the day after the funeral. We were supposed to take off at nine A.M., but an hour later we were still on the ground because they were de-icing the plane. Even though it was only a three-hour flight, I knew that between getting through customs and getting through London traffic, I was in trouble for making the eight o'clock curtain. I asked the flight attendant if there was a phone on board and explained to her I was performing onstage in the West End. I needed to call the theatre and let them know I was going to be late. "We have no phone," she said. "This is the Concorde." I still don't know what that meant—the plane goes fast, so they couldn't possibly have phones in it?

I fell asleep and slept through takeoff. When I woke up, we were airborne and there was a note by my tray table that said, "The captain would like to see you." *What did I do wrong?* was my first thought. I pushed the call button and the flight attendant took me up to the cockpit. I felt like I was going to the principal's office. They opened the door and there I was in the cockpit of the Concorde with a true force of nature, Captain Terence Henderson.

"Take a seat right there, young lady." He pointed to the engineer's seat. I sat down, my eyes saucers as I stared at the cockpit controls. It was *Star Wars,* I swear to God. "I understand you want to make a phone call. Whom do you want to call?" he asked, picking up a phone.

"I have to call the stage door of the Adelphi Theater to let them know I might not be there tonight," I said.

He finally got a dial tone somewhere over Nova Scotia, made

the call, and Graham, our stage doorman, answered. "Hello, Adelphi Theater, Graham speaking."

"This is Captain Terence Henderson from the Concorde calling. We'd like to speak to Miss Tina Marshall," he said, then handed me the phone. Graham had a very distinguished voice, but it leapt up two octaves when this statement sunk in.

"Tina, Tina, pick up the phone!" I heard him squeal.

"Hello, Tina speaking."

"TINA! IT'S PATTI. I'M ON THE PLANE BUT I'M GONNA BE LATE!" I screamed. "CALL REALLY USEFUL AND FIND OUT IF THEY'LL HOLD THE CURTAIN, OR SHOULD I JUST GO HOME?"

"Can I call you back?" she asked.

"NO! YOU CAN'T CALL ME BACK!" I almost said, "This is the Concorde, we don't have phones!" but then I remembered I was on one.

"Oh, yes, she can," my captain said. "Call 1-800-Concorde."

"WHAT? NO WAY! TINA, CALL 1-800-CONCORDE!"

We hung up, and at that point Captain Henderson swung around in his captain's chair and bellowed, "You'll go on tonight and you'll give the performance of your *life*! The audience did not pay to see an understudy. They paid to see you! Now, get some rest. We'll get you there. No worries!"

What the fuck just happened? I went back to my seat, fell asleep again, and woke up to another little note on my tray table; this one said, "They'll hold the curtain." Now, come on. If I stunk in the part, would they bother to hold the curtain? That's my question. Anyway, we were close to landing. I found the flight attendant and said, "I have to vocalize—I have to get ready for the show."

"Well, you can use the galley," she said. The Concorde was already loud—tiny but loud. I could see passengers turning around and looking in my direction, wondering what was going on. I was hidden behind a little curtain, but they could still hear me doing my vocal warm-up. I don't think I sold any tickets based on that performance.

When we landed, I was rushed off the plane first. A British Airways special agent met me and whisked me through customs and immigration. We hit the floor running and I ran and ran through the very long terminal. I jumped in the waiting car, hoping the traffic would be light. It was now 7:15 . . . 7:20 . . . 7:30 . . . I was still vocalizing in the poor driver's ear. By the time we turned left into Maiden Lane, I could see Richard Oriel holding the stage door open, looking down the lane. We screeched to a halt. It was twenty minutes to eight.

I raced up to my dressing room. Stage management continued making the calls over the Tannoy: "Twenty . . . ten . . . beginners, please." It was now eight P.M. All the while I was chattering up a storm at my dressing table while Caroline Clements was pinning my hair, I was putting on my makeup, and Murray Lane was dressing me as best he could.

The stage manager called to check in. "How much longer will you be, Patti?" she asked.

I was standing and pacing the floor. "I'll be ready in . . . I'm ready!" I said. I was costumed, wigged, and the makeup was on my face.

We all stood there in a daze. I have no idea how but I'd done it all in eighteen minutes. Murray and Caroline had calmly worked around me while I talked their ears off. On a regular show day the process would have taken two hours. We went up on time and stage management told me that I cut two minutes off the show that night. The adrenaline was screaming!

Murray and Caroline kept me onstage in all kinds of weather.

We did laugh in that dressing room. It wasn't all bad. In fact, so much of it was good that it made the bad moments appalling. They remain dear friends and I can't imagine being on the London stage without either of them.

Eventually Captain Henderson of the Concorde and his wife came to see the show. When we talked afterward, he told me that he'd used every bit of aviation lingo short of Mayday to get priority clearance for landing that day. That experience was such a welcome diversion. It provided laughs in my otherwise tense existence.

I was still combating rumors, depressed as hell. My run as Norma in London would end in mid-March. I had only about two months left, and as much as I loved London and the house on Stanley Crescent, I was looking forward to getting home to Connecticut. I was unsure about New York. I had not a drop of support from anyone after they left for L.A.

On February 16, I was in my dressing room preparing for the show when I got a call from New York. It was my agent with the news. Liz Smith's column bore the headline IT'S GLENN AS NORMA. "It isn't even a bet; it's a fact," she wrote. "Although the Andrew Lloyd Webber company won't confirm or deny, Glenn Close will begin rehearsals as Norma Desmond in New York on August 1." I got fired in Liz Smith's column. I didn't take it well.

The same day, my oldest friend in the world, Philip Caggiano, sent me this fax. It reads:

Dear Patti,

I'm sorry about this nightmare they've put you through, although I admire the dignity that you've maintained in dealing with such a horrible situation. As Tennessee Williams said in concluding his

"Memoirs"—"After all, high station in life is earned by the gallantry with which appalling experiences are survived with grace."

You know I love you.

Best to the boys,

P.

Dear, dear Philip, so much for grace . . .

From the outside, I'm sure it sounded like all hell had broken loose in my dressing room, which in fact it had. I was hysterical. From the beginning of my involvement with *Sunset Boulevard,* I'd been in a snake pit of innuendo. Meryl, Barbra, Glenn . . . Every day I had to read that someone else was singing my songs, or that someone else was taking my place, or that someone else *should* have taken my place. After months and months of escalating speculation and rumormongering, followed by denials from Really Useful that were at first ironclad but grew less and less convincing by the day, to be handed this kind of public humiliation—in the worst possible way—overwhelmed me.

I took batting practice in my dressing room with a floor lamp. I swung at everything in sight—mirrors, wig stands, makeup, wardrobe, furniture, everything. Then I heaved the lamp out the second-floor window.

Not surprisingly, Richard Oriel came running in to see what was going on. "I've been fired from the New York production," I said. "I'm not going on tonight. I don't know when I'll return. Bye." I was sobbing. I do remember cast members hearing the screams and sobs and coming in and trying to console me, hugging me and feeling helpless. I can still see their faces. Remember, this was a tight company. When one of us hurt, we all hurt, and they'd been watching me, silently helpless to do anything.

I fled the theatre and returned to Stanley Crescent just as two of my friends, Bryan and Lindy Watson, arrived from Washington, D.C. They'd just gotten off the plane, having flown all the way to London to see me perform.

"I'm fired," I told them. They started laughing. "No, really," I said. "I've been fired. Pick up your bags. We're leaving town."

The Watsons, Matt, and I got in the car and drove to the Yew Tree Inn in Newbury, a charming seventeenth-century inn that Cameron Mackintosh had first told me about. We proceeded to get shitfaced. I stayed away for two or three days, just trying to pull myself together and figure out what to do next. The first question was whether to finish the run. Everybody in my camp told me that as painful as it would surely be, I had to stay on the stage. Why? Because I had a contract. "You have to perform," they told me. "If you don't go on, it gives them a way to weasel out of the money they will owe you."

I must point out that none of this was Liz Smith's fault. Both before the incident and after, she has always been supportive and generous to me in her column. When she ran the piece, she had no idea she was breaking the news not just to her readers, but to me as well. After the initial bombshell, she was incredibly sympathetic. "This has been a cruel experience for Patti LuPone," she wrote. "I hope she wrings every dollar, and then some, out of her contract."

In the wake of the announcement, I could see that working with Really Useful had adversely affected all of us. One night the cast was at the Spot, and suddenly our fireman (just as there had been during *Les Misérables,* there was still a fireman who slept in every theatre in the West End) burst out of the stage door and ran across the road yelling, "Eighteen pence! Eighteen pence!"

"What's the matter?" we asked.

"I got a raise from Andrew Lloyd Webber—eighteen bloody

Mom and Andrew Lloyd Webber at the House of Good Vibes: the irony.

pence!" he spat. In other words, about a quarter, twenty-five cents. As disrespectful as that was, it turned out to be not that unusual. Within the cast and crew, it seemed that everyone involved with *Sunset Boulevard* had been subjected to this kind of treatment, the lack of care, the disregard. We'd all become so much chattel to him.

Meanwhile, back at 17 Stanley Crescent when my friends, Matt, and I returned, there was a circus outside of my front door. It was the one and only time I've been stalked by paparazzi. It was very interesting and cruel at the same time. Bryan would walk out of the front door every morning for the paper or coffee and they hounded him, thinking he was Matt. Bryan's a very funny ex–hockey defenseman. He had serious laughs with the British paparazzi. I was quite lucky to be able to sneak out of the back door and through the two-acre garden to another street. The photographers couldn't figure out how I escaped each night.

Andrew Lloyd Webber continued to be an unmitigated coward. He didn't have the balls to tell me in person; when the news broke, he sent flowers but no apology. Then he sent two of the most delusional letters I've ever read and which I actually tossed in the garbage, then pulled out and saved. I wanted to reprint them here, but though the letters were sent to me, incredibly, I don't have the legal right to reproduce them without approval from Andrew Lloyd Webber. So without reprinting them, I can still give you the gist.

On February 17, 1994, he wrote to say how sorry he was that he couldn't give me the news personally, because he was on his estate in Sydmonton. (For the record, Sydmonton is just sixty miles west of London.) He assured me that he was as upset about the situation as I was. He claimed to have put everything he had into his efforts to get me to Broadway as Norma, and that the bad U.S. reviews of the London production had almost killed any chance of mounting the show in New York.

According to Andrew, he was not the one making the decisions. Paramount Pictures (who owned the underlying rights, because of the original movie) and his financial investors were the ones really responsible for getting me fired. He expressed his sympathy that I was "unhappy," and suggested that I do my best to end my London run in triumph. He hoped that the two of us would work together on another major project sometime in the near future, and that "a joint commitment to each other would make a far better end to this sorry affair." He then repeated his sorrow that he couldn't present this letter to me personally, ending with "Much love, Andrew."

His February 28 letter, in which he wrote to say he'd had a "brainwave" on my behalf, was even more delusional. After fretting that "our sorry situation" was making the Really Useful creative team look bad, he put forward his modest proposal. Wouldn't it be fabulous, he suggested, if I took over for Glenn Close in the Los Angeles production when she went to open as Norma on

Broadway? He dismissed the "snide" piece about my performance in the *Hollywood Reporter* because it was, after all, just a trade paper, and declared that it would be a "real career move" and a "coup" for me. He suggested that we meet over lunch in a quiet location to discuss the proposal after I had digested the idea. In a few days, he would call me or I should call him and this time he ended the letter with "All my love, Andrew."

After letting me get fired in a gossip column, he was asking me to replace the actor to whom he had given my role. If there could have been a bigger slap in the face, I'm not sure what it would have been. Nevertheless, Andrew was apparently mystified that I didn't think his "brainwave" was a fabulous idea. I believe my response to these two letters was, "Go shit in your hat. I wasn't born yesterday." It's what I thought but only said out loud to a couple of friends.

He tried to get away with the same bullshit in the press. "This is more a personal humiliation for me than it is for her," he told Baz Bamigboye in the *Daily Mail.*

"The whole decision was taken out of my hands," he declared to the *Evening Standard* in March. Really Useful "has only ever owned half of the show. The rest belongs largely to Paramount Pictures, who made the original movie. . . . Paramount flatly refused to put up their half [of the $12 million Broadway budget] if Patti plays the lead. They want Glenn Close. It's as simple as that."

"We were all handpicked by Mr. Lloyd Webber," I said at the time, "and all of a sudden you're telling me somebody is telling Mr. Lloyd Webber what to do? No one in the American and British theatrical communities believes that one."

Paramount itself was quick to call bullshit on his trying to dodge culpability for his actions. "All creative decisions were made by Andrew Lloyd Webber," stated Paramount spokesperson Cheryl

Boone Isaacs to the *Los Angeles Times.* "Paramount had no conversations with him about casting. It was all in his court."

After the story broke, Andrew's press man told the *New York Times* that Glenn Close was concerned that she "not be seen as some kind of Eve Harrington, the backstabbing opportunist from *All About Eve.*" Well, if you don't want to be seen that way, pick up a phone and tell me how terrible you feel about all this. Which she never did. Never.

Do I think Glenn Close was complicit in what happened to me? Hard to say. But what I do know is that from the time she was announced in April, I never heard from her. No "Good luck from one Norma to another," no "Congratulations on your opening," no "I'm sorry for what happened to you, but I had nothing to do with it." Nothing. You might think it would have been common courtesy, if nothing else. When it was announced that Betty Buckley was going to take over for me in London, I called her to wish her well. After I'd been dropped from the New York cast, Betty went public right away with her opinion that I'd been badly treated. "What happened to Patti is an inanity," she told the *Sunday Mail* in late February. "She must feel a tremendous hurt. It is the big business machine that rolled over her."

I heard from other friends as well. "I want you to know that I am horrified by the way you are being treated, and sickened by the situation altogether," wrote Trevor immediately after the news broke. "Never in my professional experience have I known such an appalling breakdown of communication and disregard of humanity. . . . I am angry on your behalf."

I was incredibly angry at several members of the creative staff involved in the production, including Don Black, John Napier, and Christopher Hampton, because their silence had been so overwhelming when the firing first happened. Finally John Napier showed up in my dressing room. "Where the hell have you been?" I asked him. "Why do you show up now?" He claimed ignorance. John, John, John. The only person who was any comfort besides Bob Avian was costume designer Anthony Powell. He is a gentleman and such a compassionate human being.

I felt they abandoned me. Were they embarrassed for me? Did they just not care? A couple of weeks later, Trevor wrote back about this very subject:

> *This stinking situation envelops us all, and I understand entirely why you should think that nobody has been your ally. But let me say honestly to you that at no time during the period in Los Angeles and before seeing you on my return did I discuss the New York situation, nor was I consulted for my opinion. . . .*
>
> *I wrote a letter to the management group acknowledging that it was not my place to be the decision maker when matters of large scale finance were involved, but that it was my role to remind those concerned of their responsibilities and the humanity that was required in the situation in which they found themselves. I insisted that the first priority on their deliberations must be considerations for your position and the protection of your achievement and status while they were deciding what to do. I repeated in my letter several times that you were our star, and the talent on whom the London show was altogether based.*
>
> *I was assured verbally that nothing would be done without your interests being their priority. I left messages for Patrick McKenna saying that I thought it was unforgivable that rumours were circulating in the profession and in the press.*

*I am now about to start rehearsing in London with half
a new cast, knowing that the pallor of unhappiness and the
whiff of moral inadequacy hang over the enterprise. . . .*

*Your talent is giant, your heart even bigger, and what
you bring to audiences is never less than the real thing, every
element taken to the limit. It won't help you at the moment
to know that I believe in you, that your colleagues in the
show all believe in you, that your audiences believe in you—
because we haven't been hurt the way you have. But we do
all believe in you, and you must, must, MUST continue to
believe in yourself. Nothing else matters.*

Paradoxically, I think I was a better Norma after I got fired.
The *Philadelphia Inquirer* had said I wasn't crazy enough. They
should have seen me during that last month.

My performance got quite deep and bitter. Not crazy enough?
No "sense of holding on by a thread"? No "white hot purity under
that ragingly destructive fire"? Not anymore. Everything that had
happened to Norma Desmond now became more personal. There's
a scene in the show where Norma is looking at her old movies, and
she has a line about being discarded. I owned that line now.

Daniel Benzali, my Max onstage, gave me a blow-up doll of
Edvard Munch's *The Scream* that lived outside of my dressing
room door for the rest of the run. It was a fait accompli. I had to
keep moving forward, defuse the pain, eke out some laughs, and
play the play eight times a week.

It took a long time, but eventually I let it all go. I've never
been one to hold a grudge. I mean, you have to move on with your
life, right? (Oh, did I mention Glenn Close *never, ever called me?*)

As my involvement with *Sunset Boulevard* was ending, it
often felt as though the gods were playing jokes on me. Just days

before my last performance, I was nominated for another Olivier Award—for the role from which I'd been fired. And I don't believe the category was Best Actress Who Stinks in a Leading Role. I lost to Julia McKenzie, who was brilliant in *Sweeney Todd,* but to be nominated was vindication enough.

Matt and me in London at the Olivier Awards for Sunset Boulevard, *1994.*

Finally it was down to the last day. I'd been very specific with the producers. I didn't want anyone from Really Useful Group or Patrick McKenna or Andrew anywhere in the theatre on my closing night. They honored that.

I am very possessive of my theatre memories, and closing *Sunset Boulevard* in London is still a special memory for me. It was incredible agony, because there was both a matinee and an evening performance. Both were sold out, and then some. The house was chock full to the rafters. Scalpers outside the Adelphi were asking a fortune for seats—and they were getting it. The Theatre Gods continued their merry pranks. During the matinee, the set came to a screeching halt. The Paramount Studio slides would not open for the next scene. The show was stopped. We waited for a bit and then I instinctually stepped in front of the slides in my beautiful Anthony Powell Paramount suit and sang a Depression-era Victor Young/Ned Washington song called "A Hundred Years from Today."

Life is such a great adventure
Learn to live it as you go
No one in this world can censure
What we do here below

Don't save your kisses, just pass them around
You'll find my reason is logically sound
Who's going to know that you passed them around
A hundred years from today

Why crave a penthouse that's fit for a queen
You're nearer heaven on Mother Earth's green
If you had millions what would they all mean
A hundred years from today
So laugh and sing
Make love the thing
Be happy while you may
There's always one
Beneath the sun bound to make you feel that way

The moon is shining and that's a good sign
Cling to me closer and say you'll be mine
Remember darling, we won't see it shine
A hundred years from today

The song ended and the slides tracked offstage. The play resumed. At the evening performance the gods played their biggest practical joke on me. The fire alarms curiously went off backstage before the show. And there were more technical difficulties with the set. This time the house wouldn't descend on my entrance. I was in place, having said the line "You there. Why are you so late?" The music started to play and the house remained still; it just wouldn't move. I couldn't believe this was happening. I looked up to heaven and asked, *Why?* I was laughing at this point. It was a good four or five minutes before anyone acknowledged that there might be an issue. The assistant director came onto the stage and told the audience, "We're having problems. Everybody have a drink on the house." At the bar, the rumor quickly spread that technical difficulties had nothing to do with it. The buzz was that I wasn't coming out until I got another million from Andrew Lloyd Webber. If only.

The crew sorted out the house. It and I descended to a raucous ovation that went on for several minutes. There was no way to continue—I had to turn around and acknowledge the ovation before they would allow me to begin. The audience stopped the show again for five minutes when I sang "As If We Never Said Good-bye."

The whole night went that way. It was very moving, but also very difficult for me. In a situation like that you have to be like a lion tamer, a very gentle lion tamer. You must control the audience, but do it graciously, as if to say, *Thank you, but we have to do the show now.*

You have to play the play so the audience goes out remembering the performance. You can't give in to the maudlin sentimentality of it. Nevertheless, there were times when it was all I could do to keep it together. At the end of the show, people were throwing roses at the stage. It seemed like there were thousands of them. The standing ovation at the final curtain was twenty minutes long. In the midst of all this overpowering pain, there was this incredible outpouring of love that I will never forget. I have said that perhaps I went through the *Sunset Boulevard* saga to have the memory of that closing night.

A Working Actor, Part 2

1994–2000

As Maria Callas in Master Class.

© JOAN MARCUS

y final *Sunset Boulevard* performance in London was on March 12, 1994. I was relieved it was over but I was also depressed, demoralized, and exhausted. I couldn't wait to go home, but in a bizarre twist of cosmic merriment, I couldn't get out of London. Everything was packed and ready to go, including those five huge trunks, but just before we got into the cars to take us to the airport, the news reported that the IRA had lobbed a bomb onto the roof of Terminal 4, our terminal. NO!!!

We went to Heathrow anyway, only to find out that all flights had been canceled, so we stayed at a hotel near Windsor Castle. It turned out to be a lovely but totally frustrating day. We finally got out the next morning. My family and I arrived home in Connecticut and I began to mentally process the *Sunset Boulevard* experience.

The show wouldn't let me go. The song I disliked the most from *Sunset Boulevard* was "The Lady's Paying," when Norma takes Joe shopping and buys him a wardrobe. When we got home I was very fragile, but "The Lady's Paying" was the one tune from the show that my son, Josh, age four and a half, kept singing with an appetite for endless repetition that only a child that age can summon. It was absurd. The other amusing thing he did with the same regularity was point at me and shout, "Fire!," as in "fired." I wanted to shout, "Hey, little man! I was nominated for an Olivier Award!" But it made me realize, *Oh boy, this is gonna be a long healing process.*

I had never been in a psychiatrist's chair until *Sunset Boulevard.* Excuse me, there was one other time—Juilliard drove me to the chair, but only briefly. I thought the psychiatrist was crazier than I was, so I went back to class. Now I was in a psychiatrist's chair, on Prozac, my kid was singing the dreaded song over and over, and I started taking everything out on my husband. The experience almost broke up our marriage. Matt finally asked, "Why are you doing this to me?" I had so much pent-up anger, anger that I'd held in for such a long time. I couldn't unleash my feelings while I was performing, so I unleashed them when I came home, and I took it out on the person closest to me, my loving husband, Matt. People have asked me what I would do if I saw Andrew again. My response is, "It's not what I would do. It's what my husband would do."

It took a very long time to heal from *Sunset.* Shortly after we got home, the family went to Anguilla in the Caribbean for six weeks, but even that didn't start the recovery process. It was not until eight or nine months later that the clouds began to part. I went to Canyon Ranch in Tucson, Arizona, and hiked for twenty-one days. I don't know what made the difference. Perhaps being alone with my thoughts helped me to heal—that and the Prozac.

The open wounds closed, but even so, those scars never go away. I know I'm the same person I was before I went into the *Sunset Boulevard* debacle, and I'm the same person who came out of it, just wounded, bruised, beat up, and bloodied. So actually maybe I'm not the same person. Maybe I'm a little bit stronger for having survived it.

Sunset Boulevard was a devastating experience, and it had nothing to do with theatre, nothing to do with the reason I perform onstage. It was something else altogether—one man's megalomania and insecurity crushing an actor behind deceit and greed. Yes, Patti, it turns out show business can get rough. If only there'd been some clues, right?

My lawyer, John Breglio, began the difficult task of negotiating with Really Useful for my financial settlement. John had to fly to London, and apparently it took a straight fifteen hours to come to a conclusion. I was prepared to take it through the New York court system and I think that's what forced their hand to settle. They didn't want any negative publicity when the Broadway production was preparing to open. In May of 1994, Andrew Lloyd Webber agreed to pay for breach of contract. Newspaper reports at the time were surprisingly accurate. Yes, I got a very large check, but it felt like blood money. I spent it on our house in Connecticut, and among other improvements we built what came to be humorously known as the Andrew Lloyd Webber Memorial Swimming Pool.

Even with the settlement, the healing process was long because the damage was deep. When *Sunset Boulevard* opened on Broadway in November of 1994, I was still very lost emotionally. As anyone who has ever been fired from a job can tell you, it is a wrenching experience—all kinds of self-doubt and esteem issues bubble to the surface—and my termination was compounded by the fact that it was so public. I watched the *Sunset Boulevard* saga unfold very carefully. I took special delight when Glenn got furious with Andrew and Really Useful when they claimed that the

*The Andrew Lloyd Webber Memorial Swimming Pool
under construction. The only thing missing was the
crime scene outline at the bottom of it.*

box office didn't fall off when she took her vacation. He does what he does to everyone, it seems. When it closed, I was ecstatic.

I spent most of that year at home tending to my wounded psyche, but the damage seemed to turn physical. Three of us got really ill after we returned to the States from *Sunset Boulevard:* Bob Avian, our choreographer, came down with shingles while he was rehearsing *Sunset Boulevard* in Germany; Kevin Anderson— Joe Gillis—got into a life-threatening motorcycle accident; and I found out that both my retinas were severely torn and practically detached. I also lost my voice for a month after a strenuous hike. A vein in my left vocal cord had burst and the cord filled with blood.

As long as I can remember, I would blow out my voice. Every time it happened, I thought I must have been singing too hard. In a way, I was. I ran into Jessye Norman, the fabled opera singer, after my vocal cord operation. I asked her questions about my condition, and she told me that when women are in the middle of their menstrual cycle, their blood vessels become engorged. In centuries past, an opera singer could cancel a performance or postpone rehearsal if she was mid-cycle. She simply would not sing. But that's the opera world, not the Broadway world. I doubt many Broadway singers are aware of this condition, or the damage that may occur from singing with an engorged vein. Most likely, I had been singing with an engorged blood vessel and it would burst with exertion—as it turned out, any kind of exertion.

I found out about the blood vessel five years earlier, when I was doing *Anything Goes*. I lost my voice and went to my throat doctor. He stuck a camera down my throat and gasped—not a reaction you want from a medical professional. He told me that my cord was filled with blood, and that I couldn't sing or talk until the trapped blood had subsided. It totally freaked me out, but at the time I didn't think that this would be a recurring problem. I just laid low and returned to the show when the cord was clear again. It happened again in 1993, when I was in L.A. doing *Life Goes On* during the day and singing the Westwood Playhouse concert at night. Halfway through my run, my voice was gone. Dr. Hans von Leden got me through the remaining shows but warned me that before I did another musical, I had better get the vein taken care of. He recommended Dr. Robert Sataloff, an otolaryngologist and microsurgeon at Jefferson Hospital in Philadelphia, but I put off going to see him.

I lost my voice again in London during *Sunset Boulevard*, and then when I got home from London, it happened yet again when I wasn't even singing. I went on the hike. I took Advil before I started the hike to prevent a headache. I didn't know it then, but Advil is a blood thinner, not good for singers. I got home, had dinner, and when I tried to speak I had no voice. When I could squeak out a sound, I called Dr. Sataloff. I went to Philadelphia to see him. Dr. Sataloff is a singer himself, and one of his specialties is care of the professional voice. He looked at my cord, but it was so filled with blood that he sent me home and told me to come back in a month. Now I was scared.

When I returned to him a month later, he assessed the problem and explained to me what my vocal cord operation would entail. He also told me that it was a relatively simple operation, and that after it I would sing better and sing twenty-five years longer. We scheduled the surgery very close to Christmas of 1994. I remember this because I woke up after the operation to the sound of a baritone voice in the atrium outside my hospital window. It was Dr. Sataloff singing a liturgy. You'd think a hymn-singing surgeon would give one pause, but the operation saved my voice. Apparently I had more than one broken blood vessel in my left cord, and Dr. Sataloff cauterized all of them. Post-op recuperation eventually led me to Joan Lader, who rehabilitated my speaking voice, and finally, after all of my years of singing, taught me *how* to sing. She gave me technique. I'm still studying with her, and still trying to understand the craft of singing. I can't imagine what would've happened to my voice or my career without her.

Each time I take a lesson with Joan, I learn something new about vocal technique and how to apply it. Singing is the most natural thing I do, and the hardest thing for me to do naturally. As a kid, I developed bad habits singing along with the radio—habits that were hard to break because they were the only thing I knew and could trust. I muscled my voice to hit the high notes. It's how I got through *Evita*. Now I can't conceive of learning a score without Joan. She is a godsend and savior for a lot of singers.

I was supposed to return to Broadway in *Sunset Boulevard,* but that didn't happen. What did happen was a self-imposed isolation and healing process, both emotional and physical. To be honest, it was wonderful. I loved being home with my husband and young son, but as I was recuperating from my vocal cord operation, I got a phone call from two old friends, Lonny Price and Walter Bobbie. They wanted me to play Vera Simpson in the Encores! production of *Pal Joey*. I said no for two reasons:

1. It was still too early in my rehabilitation to sing.
2. I wasn't ready to get back onstage.

But I loved these two guys. Walter said, "Patti, you'll be hanging out with your friends." I said I'd think about it. They sent the musical director, Rob Fisher, up to my house to convince me. I gave him lunch and sent him on his way without committing.

I don't remember when I said yes, but I finally agreed to do it with Joan Lader's cautious blessing. I wasn't totally healed. My voice was fragile but I started rehearsal, and I remember laughing my way through it, thanks to Lonny. There were lots of *Sunset Boulevard* jokes at my expense. It was a great cast in a great environment—the City Center theatre crew and the Encores! management.

We had a very limited run in May of 1995. When I made my entrance on opening night, I received an ovation that practically knocked me off my feet. It was a New York audience saying, *Welcome home, Patti. This is where you belong.*

I was deeply moved by it. It made me very nervous, but it also closed up some of the holes in my heart and spirit even more. I was so grateful. I thanked the ever-capricious gods that preside over the theatre and my life. I played the play. We did three performances and recorded it. And that was that.

A few months later, with my voice fully recovered, I returned to Broadway with a concert at the Walter Kerr Theatre: *Patti LuPone on Broadway*. This was the same show I had done at the Westwood Playhouse as my farewell to L.A. before I was to leave for London and *Sunset Boulevard*. It became my Broadway return. I was happily working again with Scott Wittman as director, Dick Gallagher as my new musical director, and Jeff Richman, who was supplying the dialogue and jokes for the show. Jeff has kept me laughing for the thirty-three years we've known each other. The show was sold out and the audience incredibly supportive. Scott made me sing "As If We Never Said Good-bye" from *Sunset* as an encore. It wasn't easy.

One night during the run, I was two bars into the opening number, "I Get a Kick Out of You," when over the house intercom the stage manager stopped the show and asked if there was a doctor in the house. A man who was sitting in the orchestra was now lying flat in the aisle surrounded by his family. Doctors came out of the woodwork. The houselights remained down and all of us remained onstage, truly lost, and wondering what to do. I went to the stage-right wing. Scott and Vinnie the Nose, the house electrician, told me to stay onstage. I did. Portia Nelson, a friend and colleague, came to the foot of the stage and told me that the man's name was John and that he was in cardiac arrest. I told the audience. As calmly as I could, I just kept everyone aware of what was going on, for about twenty minutes. There is a firehouse on the corner of Forty-eighth and Eighth, but it took them what felt like forever to show up.

The family was saying to John, "Come on! Pull through! Come on, John!" The paramedics finally showed up and put John on a stretcher. They left up the house-left aisle with the family behind the gurney.

I said to the audience, "We'll take a ten-minute break and start again."

From the back of the house a man shouted, "Don't do it, Patti. Don't do it. Tony Bennett wouldn't do it."

People turned around and shouted at him, "We didn't come here to see Tony Bennett." Then they turned back to me.

I was dumbstruck. I said, "I'm as confused as everyone else." The man on the gurney and his family left the theatre. In true New York fashion, four people from the balcony raced down the stairs for the four vacated and still-warm orchestra seats. We took the break. I started the show again and felt a strange breathlessness over the audience. It was totally surreal. We got through the show and I thought that was the end of that.

About a year later, I had just finished shooting *24 Hour Woman* and was on a shuttle flight to Boston to start rehearsal for *The Old Neighborhood*. I took an aisle seat, and in the window seat sat a woman reading the *Wall Street Journal*, all curled up in a knot, legs crossed, arms close to her chest, newspaper hiding her face. I thought, *Well, there'll be no talking on this flight*. And so it went, until we were about to land, at which point she reached across the empty seat between us, grabbed my arm, and said, "I can't thank you enough for what you did for John."

I gasped. I knew exactly what she was talking about. "Were you there?" I asked.

"No," she replied, "but John was a very dear friend. He had just eaten dinner and was late, so he ran to the theatre." I asked if he died, and yes, she said, he had died. I said I was very sorry, and we parted ways thinking about John and sending his family and friends our thoughts. Oh, and by the way, the man who yelled at me from the back of the house turned out to be a homeless drunk who had just aimlessly followed the empty gurney into the theatre.

While I was still in London with *Sunset Boulevard,* a friend told me about a new play by Terrence McNally being produced by Robert Whitehead, starring Zoe Caldwell as Maria Callas. He said, "It's a part you should play." This discussion took place close to the

The playwright (top left) and cast of The Old Neighborhood.
© JOAN MARCUS

end of my run. In fact, I had already been fired and was just playing out the end of my contract.

As fate would have it, I was performing my concert, *Patti
LuPone on Broadway*, at the Walter Kerr Theatre while Zoe was
portraying Maria Callas down the street at the Golden Theatre. I
had afternoons free, so I went to see her in a matinee of *Master
Class*. I was bowled over by her performance, and by Terrence
McNally's play. I left the Golden and took the alleys through the
Theatre District back to the Walter Kerr. I wrote Zoe a note that
said I was a student in the theatre that afternoon and that her
performance was a master class all its own. I felt truly inadequate.
Zoe is a great actress. She was mesmerizing in that role and I was
schooled that day. Her performance stays with me still.

At the end of my run, I went home to Connecticut. One day

out of the blue, Robert Whitehead called and asked me to replace Zoe when her contract expired. I said no, immediately. I told him I was sure that I had all the information I needed to play the part but that I'd have to be a complete fool to follow Zoe in that role. She was definitive. That was the end of that, or so I thought. Around that same time, I was offered a working cruise that would take me to the Indian Ocean. I love sailing and I loved where this cruise was going, so I said yes. Off we went—me, Matt, Josh, and his nanny, Liz Webb. I was in a Bangkok hotel when I got a phone call from the director of *Master Class,* Leonard Foglia. He tried to persuade me himself to at least read the play before I finally said no. "Okay, I'll read it," I said.

Robert's office sent a thirty-two-page fax to the hotel. I couldn't believe it. It was another truly theatrical moment, like the time Dino De Laurentiis found me in the Australian outback and offered me a role in his next movie. The next day I took the family and the thirty-two-page fax with me to Phuket. I read the script on the beach. I finished it and said to myself, *I'd be a fool to follow Zoe in this role. But I'd be a fool not to play this part.* I talked it over with Matt, and we both agreed it should be the next step in my career. I said yes to Lenny and Robert, and asked Zoe for her blessing. In mid-1996 I went into rehearsal with most of the original cast, but sadly without Audra McDonald. I played *Master Class* at the Golden Theatre on West Forty-fifth Street for seven months and was well received except by the *New York Times,* whose critic just had to bring up *Sunset Boulevard.*

In the spring of 1997, we took *Master Class* to London. During rehearsal one day, a note was sent to me from *Sunset Boulevard*'s stage management asking me to come to *Sunset*'s closing night.

Whaaaaat? I was quite sure Andrew Lloyd Webber knew nothing about this. Stage management and front of house wanted me there. Nobody from the original company was still with the show, but people I'd worked with at the theatre wanted me to come.

When I got home from rehearsal that day, I said to Matt, "Wait until you hear this one. They want me to come to the closing night of *Sunset Boulevard.*"

"Let's go," he said. He was actually excited by the prospect. I couldn't figure him out.

On closing night, I entered through the lobby of the Adelphi Theatre, which was a new experience for me. As soon as I walked in, the first three people I saw were Trevor Nunn, Christopher Hampton, and Anthony Powell. I walked right up to them—I think I actually punched Anthony Powell in the arm, not the person I should have punched hello. I was very nervous, as you can imagine. They turned around and looked at me as though they had seen a ghost. Trevor turned white.

I took my seat with Matt in the orchestra and started watching *Sunset Boulevard*. It was boring and slow. The black, white, and gray set didn't help the production, in my opinion. At the intermission I saw David Caddick, and I actually said to him, "David, were we this boring?" He said no. Clearly the show had gone downhill in the two or three years it had been running, as shows can do. That's not unusual.

I went to the closing night party for a while. When I talked with Trevor, he said the show didn't deserve to close. I just looked at him and said, "But, Trevor, it was so *boring.*" He gave me a stupefied look. *Well, it was, Trevor.* I walked away knowing that whatever was wrong with the show wasn't entirely my problem. I may not have been the ideal Norma for a lot of people, but *Sunset Boulevard* was a deeply flawed musical—with me or without me.

Master Class opened and closed rather quickly in London. In fact, London is the only city worldwide where *Master Class* failed.

Left to right: Dick Gallagher, Marc Shaiman, and Scott Wittman—all three deep and dear friends—the creative team for my Carnegie Hall solo debut.

Somehow they just didn't get it. Strange, a hit in one place, a flop in another. Pack up the trunks—we're out of here.

In the summer of 1999, Scott Wittman was approached by New York's Gay Men's Health Crisis to put together a benefit concert, which would become my solo Carnegie Hall debut. The two of us started brainstorming a new show with my musical director, the late and dearly missed Dick Gallagher. Jeff Richman would once again write the dialogue and the jokes. (He hates me calling them jokes. But there's no one better at writing them.)

That fall I was rehearsing the Carnegie Hall show, which was called *Coulda, Woulda, Shoulda,* in New York, and living a sweet life at home in Connecticut with my family. I cooked dinner, I did laundry, I attended my son's hockey games, and I had doctors' appointments. One was a routine mammogram.

I had the mammogram and waited in the office for the official dismissal—that everything looked good. I didn't wait long, and I didn't get the all-clear. A radiologist told me that there was a suspicious cluster of cells in my left breast and that I needed a more detailed mammogram to determine whether I had breast cancer or not. Apparently this cluster had been visible the year before, but now the radiologist felt it was time to do something. I asked why I hadn't been told the previous year about this abnormality. No answer or a lame one at best came out of his mouth.

Matt and I now started the rounds of interviews with breast surgeons and radiologists. We settled on a New York radiologist who believed there was nothing wrong with me, and we settled on a breast surgeon at Mass General in Boston in case there was. I went to New York and had the more detailed and excruciatingly painful mammogram. I continued rehearsing, with the concert looming just a mere week away.

Finally the concert was upon me. I was in the Parker Meridien hotel the day of the concert when I got a phone call from the radiologist with the bad news: I had breast cancer. She was sorry she had misled me, but she told me that I had the kind of cancer that, if I was to get breast cancer, was the kind to get. What a statement.

I heard every word she said, while in the back of my mind I was saying to myself, *I'm singing at Carnegie Hall tonight. Get to the point.* When I hung up the phone I was a total blank. Matt was with me and he figured out what was happening. We just looked at each other. What can you say at a time like that?

The phone rang again. It was Scott. I blurted out, "I have breast cancer."

He said, "You have a sound check."

It was perhaps the wisest thing to say. I went on with my life. I sang at Carnegie Hall that night without thinking of the cancer cells my body was now producing. There was no time. I went back to Connecticut, revisited Dr. Barbara Smith at Mass General, scheduled the operation, and had a lumpectomy, followed by six weeks of radiation treatments at the New Milford Hospital.

I was grateful that the cancer was caught early and that I had a great surgeon and radiologist. I am deeply grateful that I'm now ten years out, but it is never far from my mind that I could produce cancer cells again. I had a trainer at home who was well versed in what a woman should and should not eat during radiation. I lived on fish and soy. I viewed it as yet another test. There was no other way for me to process breast cancer.

The day I finished my last radiation treatment, I drove to New York City and started rehearsals for the New York Philharmonic production of *Sweeney Todd*. Finally I would sing my first Sondheim role, in an inspiring production that would be the third benchmark in my career.

Several *Sweeney Todds,* and Sondheim

2000, 2001, 2005

"The Worst Pies in London."
© STEPHANIE BERGER

*"A Little Priest," with
Michael Cerveris.*
PHOTO BY © PAUL KOLNIK

t began with another one of those "Are you interested?" phone calls. Was I interested in playing Nellie Lovett in a concert production of Stephen Sondheim's *Sweeney Todd* with the New York Philharmonic that was still several months away?

"Are you kidding?" It was a dream production—operatic and Broadway singers performing with the New York Philharmonic, in their home, Avery Fisher Hall at Lincoln Center. "Does Steve know I've been asked to play Nellie?" My agent said he would find out. Of course I wanted to do it, but I wanted to be sure Steve knew and approved. He did, and I was elated.

This would be my first Sondheim role, a role I never imagined I would play. I had seen the original production on Broadway, and was gobsmacked by Hal Prince's concept, by Len Cariou's and Angela Lansbury's performances, and by Steve's very complicated and heartbreakingly beautiful score. But it just wasn't a part my name would normally be associated with. This casting choice came out of left field.

I asked my agent who exactly thought of me for the part, and we found out that it was the brainstorm of Welz Kauffman, who at that time was the artistic administrator of the New York Philharmonic. Welz was embarking on a five-year birthday celebration in honor of Stephen Sondheim—from his seventieth to his seventy-fifth—a retrospective of Sondheim's work, and *Sweeney Todd* was to be the first production.

With Welz Kauffman, my theatrical muse.

Welz had already cast the opera singers for the concert. Welsh baritone Bryn Terfel was cast as Sweeney, soprano Heidi Grant Murphy was Johanna. He also cast Neil Patrick Harris as Tobias. His greatest gift to me, however, was the chance to work with Audra McDonald, who played Lucy. The two of us became friends and have performed together many times, but it was Welz who initially brought us together for *Sweeney.*

Welz approached Walter Bobbie to direct the show. When Walter fell out, I was asked for suggestions and Lonny Price immediately came to mind. We had worked together on two concert productions, *Pal Joey* and *Annie Get Your Gun.* He knew how to get it done.

Mrs. Lovett was a massive role to learn. I knew that I had to come in knowing my part, because the rehearsal time for concert productions is brief, often as little as a week. One of my favorite memories from our brief rehearsal period was seeing Steve read the *New York Times* in the theatre while orchestrator Jonathan Tunick corrected mistakes in the score as the Philharmonic rehearsed. It made me proud to be a New Yorker. I was envious of all of the actors who had these two men in their rehearsal room every day.

For this *Sweeney,* the orchestra was massive, approximately seventy-five musicians filling the entire stage of Avery Fisher Hall. Lonny solved the blocking limitations by installing ramps everywhere. This meant that during the performance, actors were moving in front of, through the middle, behind, and onstage left and right of the orchestra. The musicians' space is usually sacrosanct; they were definitely not used to seeing actors within their orchestral cocoon. Now, all of a sudden, they were in the thick of it, with people's legs, feet, arms, props, costumes, and wigs all around them. I remember watching the musicians watch the actors and thinking, *They're involved with the play.* They were as engaged as the actors—not that they wouldn't be focused when they were playing the score, but in this production they were far more than that. It was pretty amazing to experience, and a gorgeous production to play in.

About two weeks before we were to perform, Bryn Terfel suddenly had to cancel due to a recurring back problem. The question now was who could replace him on such short notice. Welz tapped George Hearn, which turned out to be nothing short of a stroke of genius.

George was no stranger to the role. He had replaced Len Cariou as Sweeney in the original 1980 Broadway cast and had sung the part with both Angela Lansbury and Dorothy Loudon. Because he lived in rural New York and I lived in rural Connecticut, George came to my house for some early rehearsals. George had gone to college in Memphis, Tennessee, where he learned to love hard cider. Coincidence: My neighbor down the road made hard cider—scrumpy, it's called—and I gave some to George before we started rehearsal. We had some tipsy, scrumpy-fueled blocking and script-analysis sessions in my house. Now, *that's* how to develop a character! When push comes to shove, drink the "miracle elixir" from a square bottle. . . .

George Hearn was a blessing for this production. He led a company of *Sweeney Todd* virgins through the tricky channels of a Sondheim score and style. Nobody in the company had done it before except for him. George knew the Grand Guignol—its macabre, over-the-top violence—and led the rest of us merrily into the gore. He also led us, by his interpretation of Sweeney, to find our own interpretations in the style of the piece. Without him we would have been more frightened to take the theatrical leap. I'm always grateful when an actor has generosity of spirit, and George is both generous and a gentleman—on top of being a great actor. He's another of my favorite leading men.

George Hearn and me as Sweeney Todd and Nellie Lovett.

© STEPHANIE BERGER

It was a fun new experience to watch the opera singers at work, especially Heidi Grant Murphy and John Aler, who played Beadle Bamford. I was thrilled that George, Neil Patrick, and I connected onstage. Audra was there with her undeniable goddess presence. It was an exhilarating time. *Sweeney* is the most difficult score I've ever sung. To this day, I've never sung a section of "God, That's Good!" correctly, and I've played Nellie three times. In the midst of all this exhilaration, I was actually able to forget that I had just completed radiation treatment on my left breast. I had too much to do and too much was at stake. I couldn't fail in this part in front of the heady crowd attending these performances in Avery Fisher Hall—fans of the Philharmonic and fans of Steve Sondheim.

We played for one weekend only, May 4 to 6, 2000, and were enthusiastically received.

Not only was I finally singing a Sondheim role in one of the greatest musicals ever written, but there I was, on the stage of Avery Fisher Hall, singing with one of the world's greatest orchestras, the New York Philharmonic. It's just not a frequent occurrence for Broadway actors to be in that environment. I was stunned by my good fortune. I was also working across the street from Juilliard, thus pulling together so many various threads of artistic life. It was the classical musician's world, the opera world, and Broadway all wrapped into one, and it all culminated in this moment on the stage of Avery Fisher Hall. What a great feeling it was when I walked through the stage door.

The following summer, I played Mrs. Lovett once again. The Louise M. Davies Symphony Hall in San Francisco was host to the identical concert production of *Sweeney Todd* that we had done in New York. Most of the cast (including George, but not including Audra) appeared with the San Francisco Symphony, with Rob Fisher conducting. Although the New York Philharmonic version had not been recorded, this one was. Our three-concert engagement of July 19 to 21, 2001, was videotaped for broadcast on PBS. They also issued a DVD, and of course, cuts from the show have been immortalized on YouTube.

In August of 2001, just a month after doing *Sweeney* in San Francisco, George and I performed it again, this time at the Ravinia Festival just outside of Chicago. The fact that we were reprising the New York Philharmonic production once again was no coincidence. Welz Kauffman had moved on from New York and was now the president and CEO of Ravinia. When Welz left the Phil, he took his long-planned Sondheim retrospective with him. This production, with George, once again kicked off his five-year celebration of the works of Stephen Sondheim.

Ravinia has been a part of my theatrical life for more than thirty years. The first time was in 1976, with The Acting Company's production of *The Robber Bridegroom*. We played the Martin Theatre. I returned in 1984 with *The Cradle Will Rock,* again at the Martin Theatre. Since 2000, it's become my annual August event and something I so look forward to because Welz Kauffman is my theatrical muse. Only he would have thought of me for Nellie Lovett, only he would have brought Jake Heggie's original opera *To Hell and Back* with soprano Isabel Bayrakdarian and me to the Martin Theatre, and only he would have suggested a Kurt Weill evening that included *The Seven Deadly Sins* at the Pavilion Theatre. Each year I wait for another creative idea from Welz. He makes me work very hard, and I only get deeper and better through the work and creative stretch. There is no one else who has so wholly embraced who I am, and who has had the vision to create productions around my talent. It's because of Welz that I've been able to play the Sondheim roles: Desiree in *A Little Night Music,* Fosca in *Passion,* Nellie in *Sweeney Todd,* Cora Hoover Hooper in *Anyone Can Whistle,* and Rose in *Gypsy.* None of those roles would have happened without Welz Kauffman.

In April of 2005 I was home briefly before leaving for Portland, Oregon, to perform my concert *Matters of the Heart* when I got a telephone call from my current agent, Gary Gersh. This time the question was not "Are you interested?" This time the question was "Do you play an instrument?"

"I've played the piano, the cello, and the tuba in my lifetime," I said. I began studying music in the Northport, Long Island, public school system, whose educators believed that a music education was as crucial to the development of a child as math or sports. Their music department is equally as strong today and those students are unbelievably lucky.

"Why are you asking? Because I haven't played any of those instruments for a very long time."

"Because they're mounting a Broadway production of *Sweeney Todd,* and they need singers who also play instruments," he answered. I had an edge on snagging this Nellie. The London Nellie played the trumpet. *Tuba, trumpet—close enough,* I thought.

Since I was leaving the next day, the producers arranged for the director, John Doyle, to fly from London to Portland to meet me. I finished the show and went to my hotel lobby to find my visitor. There was a gentleman sitting in a chair, looking very jet-lagged.

"You must be John Doyle," I said. "I'm Patti LuPone."

He nodded.

"I'm sorry you had to travel such a long way. It must be about five A.M. London time."

At this he stood up and asked, "Where can we get a drink?" *My kind of director,* I thought.

I took him to a great little wine bar that was right around the corner from my hotel. I drank lots of wine, he had several gin and tonics, and we talked about life, our families, and our backgrounds. It was the best meeting I'd ever had with a director. As we were walking back to the hotel, we stopped in front of a shirt store. We looked in the window, and I saw a shirt that I thought would look nice on Matt. I said so. "You've got the part, Patti," he later told me he'd thought at that moment. Being a normal person clinched the role for me in John's eyes.

John Doyle's concept for *Sweeney* was spare, and based on the very successful production that he had previously directed in England at the Watermill Theatre in Berkshire, and in the West End transfer. It was also very different from what I'd been doing. For the concert productions I'd participated in, Lonny Price had built ramps for the actors that ran through the midst of the orchestra. For John Doyle's production, we *were* the orchestra. And there were just ten of us in the company. We, the actors, would be making every sound that came from that stage. During that production, I became a proud card-carrying member of Local 802, the musicians' union.

As we came into September 2005, both Michael Cerveris, who had been cast as Sweeney, and I were performing in Sondheim's *Anyone Can Whistle* at Ravinia. As a result, we missed the first week of *Sweeney* rehearsal in New York. Previews were to begin in early October, so both of us had to catch up quickly. I played several instruments in the show, not the least of which was the tuba. I became very fond of my tuba—so fond I actually named her "Irene." I had a teacher in Connecticut whose friend lent me her tuba while I studied. Her name was Irene. Irene, the ¾ tuba, was placed in my dressing room closet every night, and as I closed the door I always said, "Good night, Irene." (Okay, it's not the best story in the book, but it's a happy memory, and you can never have too many of those.)

John Doyle's patience, and the clarity with which he presented his vision of the show to the cast, made this a great rehearsal period. I think that there is a scarcity of good directors in my world. When you are blessed to be working with a director who knows what he is doing in the *rehearsal* process, then you have an exceptional experience.

John was phenomenally prepared when he came into the rehearsal room. He was both inspired and inspiring. Not only did he motivate us with his opening remarks, but at the end of the day he left us with wonderful ideas to think about and to bring into the next rehearsal. Because we were both the cast and the orchestra, the process was complicated. Although none of us had ever worked onstage in quite this manner before, it never felt difficult, because he knew how to rehearse us and how to inspire confidence. It came down to the simple task of drill.

John said that he could not cast musicians because they would never memorize the music. For actors, the music would become an extension of the character. A musician sits in an orchestra and his music is in front of him on a music stand. We couldn't have music stands—we were moving around the stage with our instruments most of the time. John expected every note to be memorized. As I learned the music, my prop track and blocking cues became easier. Eventually, memorizing the music became an integral part of everything I did in the production. I would get up from playing the tuba to pick up a bucket of blood, move to stage left, and on a note from Judge Turpin's trumpet, pour blood from one bucket to another. Every piece of music became part of my character: I walked onstage. I hit the orchestra bells. I hit the triangle. I picked up my knitting. I poured blood. All integrated. All of us relied on one another for physical safety as well. Props, instruments, and blood were flying on that stage.

The rehearsal process was so complete that when we left the Ripley-Grier rehearsal rooms and moved to the Eugene O'Neill Theatre on West Forty-ninth Street, the transition was seamless. We all realized as an ensemble that nothing had changed from the rehearsal room to the theatre. We had been prepared with such discipline and such nurturing under John and under Sarah Travis, our musical director, that we were comfortable onstage immediately.

The Eugene O'Neill is a great theatre, and it was well suited for *Sweeney Todd*. It's one of Broadway's smaller houses, and seats an audience of about 1,100. It's also one of Broadway's haunted houses. I had a ghost in my dressing room. The ghost let me know he was there one day when I thought I'd stepped on one of my dresser's feet as I backed away from the closet. I apologized and Lolly said, "For what?" She was ten feet away. The ghost was right behind me, or so we both thought. Our ghost would turn the shower light on and close the dressing-room door to let us know he was there. I liked him. He was friendly and a male. I asked our head property man about ghosts in the Eugene O'Neill and he said, "You should be here on a painting call. They're running all over the stage-left side of the theatre." My dressing room was stage left.

Our *Sweeney* company was an incredible group of actors. In addition to being a great director in rehearsal, John also has a keen eye for casting actors in the right roles. Then he brings out the best in the actors he's chosen, and he trusts his decisions. That's one thing that can bother me about creative staff. They cast us—then they second-guess their own casting decisions and get mad at the actor for whatever reason. (See *Sunset Boulevard* chapters.) John is a different story altogether. He is decisive: *These are the people I want. This is what I know I can bring out of them.* And he does. All of us in the cast were the best we could possibly be in that production because of our director, John Doyle.

Everything about that show worked—the rehearsals, the staging, the company, the director, and great stage management.

One of the best parts was Michael Cerveris. The actor playing Sweeney Todd carries the show. Nellie Lovett is the comic relief. Like George Hearn before him, Michael always gave me plenty of room for the laughs to register. That does not always happen if you're the comic relief and a female. We had a shared history, having worked together at Ravinia, and our relationship onstage had developed a shorthand. We played well together. You pretty much have to in those two complicated roles. We went out there every night without a safety net. There was danger, but it was never scary, because I knew he was there for me, as I was for him. In fact, you could say that about every member of the cast: There was a mutual support onstage all the time, from one actor to another. Our production stage manager, Adam Hunter, likened us to a band, not a company of actors. High praise indeed.

We had a long period of previews, about a month; official opening night was November 3, 2005. When the reviews came in, we were a hit, not just with the public but with the critics as well. And we were a hit for the right reasons—they actually got what we were trying to do.

"Though it uses only ten musicians, this *Sweeney* never stints on the music's drama, intricacy, or sheer beauty. . . . Every note and sound, whether from a plucked violin or a tinkling triangle, seems to count fully," wrote Ben Brantley in the *New York Times,* in a highly positive review. "Because the performers are the musicians, they possess total control of those watching them in a way seldom afforded actors in musicals. They own the story they tell, and their instruments become narrative tools."

Exactly. For example, the two lovers in the show, Anthony and Johanna, played dual cellos, so they played their love scenes, sang their love scenes, and acted their love scenes. The fact that John

Michael Cerveris and me as Sweeney and Nellie in John Doyle's production.

PHOTO BY © PAUL KOLNIK

had been able to find two actors who each played the cello is phenomenal in itself.

You could see that with every cast member—the instrument became a part of them. Many members of the company played more than one instrument. These actor/musicians blew me away. To watch Alex Gemignani or Donna Lynne Champlin on three or four instruments was intimidating. They were the backbone of the production and another reason music in schools should never be cut from the curriculum. These actors were triple threats in a whole other way—actor, singer, musician. Alex and Donna Lynne made up two members of a piano tag-team quartet. When one of them who had been playing the piano had to act in the next scene, another actor, either Ben Magnuson (Anthony) or my beloved Mano Felciano (Tobias), would just slip into the seat and start playing without missing a note. It was all closely choreographed, and very impressive to watch.

Early in the run, Angela Lansbury, the original Mrs. Lovett, came to the perfor-mance. Our portrayals of Nellie were so very different,

Mano Felciano as Tobias Ragg.

PHOTO BY © PAUL KOLNIK

yet she was on her feet at the end of the show and came backstage to congratulate us. This *Sweeney Todd* was just so wild that even if you'd seen the show ten times before, you had never seen it quite this way. Before we opened we knew we had something special on our hands. We just didn't know how special. The piece was so dark, so modern, so scary, and the small space of the Eugene O'Neill enhanced that feeling—audiences were frightened and fascinated. Whenever someone was killed, we poured buckets of blood and the stage lights glowed red. But no blood came out of the human cut. It was deceptive and deeply theatrical—bloody and extremely intimate.

The intimacy was one of the things that made *Sweeney* very powerful to the audience. Too often audiences can't achieve an emotional connection with the characters because Broadway pro-ductions have become so electronically overproduced. In several musicals that I've attended, the singer's voice doesn't sound like it's coming from the stage where my eyes are looking. There's a subtle disconnect, which ultimately prevents the audience from having a theatrical experience—a listening experience and an emotional connection to the characters onstage.

With *Sweeney Todd,* there was no way to avoid the emotional connection. We all wore microphones, but the Eugene O'Neill is one of those Broadway houses with perfect acoustics, and our sound designer was such a master that he didn't disturb the acoustics but rather sparingly enhanced the human voice. Our voices sounded real and came from the stage, allowing the audience to connect their eyes with their ears. It was great. There's nothing more exciting than hearing a deafening silence from the house because an audience isn't dealing with distractions and can focus and listen.

Because of the gruesome subject matter of *Sweeney Todd,* we had a peculiar relationship with the audience. The premise of the show was that we were inmates in an asylum, performing our little skit for our families, the nurses and doctors. Each night we deliberately made eye contact with the audience and it was great to watch them look back at us in horror.

It was particularly interesting because of who was in the seats. With student rush tickets, *Sweeney* attracted a much younger audience, adolescents and young adults in their late teens and early twenties. One night after a performance I called Steve on my way home to Connecticut. "The theatre is alive," I told him. "There are kids in the house." The show became known as the "slasher musical," and they came back, again and again, with their friends in tow.

One of the many rituals that came about with this show happened before I even took the stage. My dressing room was on the second floor of the theatre, facing West Forty-ninth Street. Each night I was transformed into an East End grunge barkeep—or Goth cupcake, as I liked to call myself—with a tight little black skirt, corset, and a severe black hairdo. The traffic on Forty-ninth Street is westbound, and every night the Waterways bus slowed down because of traffic as I was getting dressed. I guess I could have drawn my blinds, but I kind of enjoyed being the nightly entertainment for a busload of suburban commuters en route to catch their ferry to Jersey.

Even without the busloads, it was one of my favorite dressing rooms. All kinds of Broadway types passed through there—cops, playwrights, composers, ghosts, and even private investigators. It was a Damon Runyon–esque dressing room. Steve Sondheim would often join me. Sometimes he left for dinner after the show went up; sometimes he saw all or part of the show with friends. To me, this was New York theatre—Steve backstage in my dressing room, with a glass of wine, some raw almonds, reading the *New York Times*. I had two rooms, an outer room and a private room, but the door was always open between them. Sometimes we'd shout back and forth to each other. He once asked my dresser, Pat White, if I sang through "The Worst Pies in London" every night before the show. Pat told him yes, I did. That's what I had to do to "speak with distinction," not be "flannel mouth," and prove my critics wrong. Even with a Cockney accent, the audience needed to understand every lyric in Steve's brilliant score.

Steve gave me great insight into the character of Mrs. Lovett. He explained that she's the real villain of the piece because she's a pragmatist. She has all the facts: Lucy, Benjamin Barker's wife, is deranged but alive, and Johanna, their daughter, is living down the road as the ward of the dreaded Judge Turpin. Sweeney knows none of this and dear Mrs. Lovett does not tell him. Sweeney has one sole purpose, to kill the judge. Mrs. Lovett's sole purpose is to hold on to her love. It's a masterpiece of tragic proportions.

When the Tony nominations were announced in May, we

received several nods, including Michael, Mano, and me. It was the second time I was predicted to win in every newspaper across the country. Win hands down. Can't possibly lose. (You see where this is going.) The night arrived again. I sat and waited. None of the actors won. I saw the writing on the wall when *Pajama Game* won Best Revival. No, I saw the writing on the wall when I clocked where they had seated the *Sweeney* nominees. It was a flashing instinct. It was an accurate instinct. The show did win two Tonys: John Doyle for Best Direction of a Musical, and Sarah Travis for musical arrangements. Both were richly deserved. For me, it was hard not to be disappointed again, but I did get some great consolation notes.

Sadly, our audiences began to taper off. When that happens, it's the beginning of the end in my mind. Sometimes hit shows fall apart when the closing notice is looming. Not this show or these hardworking, very talented actors. *Sweeney* stayed tight and it worked every night.

The show also gave me memories and moments I've only had a few times in the theatre. They are rare moments when you lose yourself and you transcend the reality of being onstage. The person playing opposite you has become real, not a character. It sounds so cliché, but there are moments where you're so lost in the setting that you stop acting and you're living. It's a heightened reality, an amazing, almost out-of-body experience. It's why I'm onstage.

The moment in *Sweeney* happened mainly when Mano Felciano was singing "Not While I'm Around" to me. It was in that moment and in that entire scene that I was transported to the London slum we were living in—for real. It was transcendent.

In the late summer, I was slated to take a three-week hiatus from *Sweeney Todd* to play Mama Rose for the first time in *Gypsy* at Ravinia. This was to be the last show in Welz Kauffman's five-year Sondheim celebration. The *Sweeney* audiences were already diminishing and I knew we were coming to the end of the run. I was not surprised to learn just before opening in Ravinia that *Sweeney* would be closing in early September. After *Gypsy* I returned to the Eugene O'Neill for a handful of performances and to close *Sweeney Todd* on September 3.

We ran 384 performances. Experienced actors who have been through many closings simply say their farewells, but when you're younger, there are always tears, and for the performers making their Broadway debuts, this was a tough farewell.

Closing night was especially sad, because this experience had been so good and so intense for all of us. On most closing nights the audience is made up of family, friends, and fans who have seen the show several times. On this occasion fans in both the orchestra seats and the mezzanine bombarded us with roses. By the end of the curtain call, the stage was covered with flowers. Steve was in the tenth row, on his feet cheering like everyone else.

Sweeney was an extraordinary experience in so many ways—what a way to come back to Broadway in a musical. It had been a long seventeen years since I'd last performed there. Hard to believe, isn't it? Now, on September 4, I was back to being a working actor again—wondering what was next and waiting for that telephone to ring. I thought *Sweeney* was as good as it got. Little did I know that yet another twist of fate was going to bring me the best theatrical experience of my life.

Gypsy

RAVINIA, AUGUST 2006–
ENCORES!, JULY 2007

"Everything's Coming Up Roses."
RUSSELL JENKINS/RAVINIA FESTIVAL

*S*ing out, Louise! is Madame Rose's opening line from *Gypsy,* spoken as she walks up the aisle to the stage.

Rose Hovick—Madame Rose—is commonly stigmatized as the mother of all stage mothers, but that's not the woman I see. Reading Arthur Laurents's brilliant script, I don't see a monster. I don't hear it in Stephen Sondheim's lyrics. She may do monstrous things, but that doesn't make her a monster. I see a misguided woman, a misguided mother, as my mother was misguided, as my grandmother was misguided, as I pray to God every day I am not misguiding my son but probably am. God help the kid.

I see a woman who loves her daughters. She's ferociously driven, but she loves her kids. The real Rose Hovick obviously saw talent in them because they both became stars. The stage Rose and the real Rose tried to showcase their talents as best she could, even though she did it in a crude and ultimately destructive way.

I'd played Louise (Gypsy) with the Patio Players in Northport when I was fifteen years old, but at the time I didn't pay any attention to the character of Rose. I was a kid—Rose was beyond me. There was no way for me to wrap my brain around the idea of a mother wanting something so desperately for her children, and going to such extremes to get it.

The first time I played Rose was at the Ravinia Festival in August of 2006. Welz Kauffman and Lonny Price, the director, wanted to do *Gypsy*.

But there was one small problem, and that problem was me. "You know that I'm banned from Arthur's work," I said to them. "At least as far as I know."

About five years earlier, Arthur himself had offered me the lead in his play *Jolson Sings Again,* and I had agreed to do it. Arthur and I first met in London when I was doing *Sunset Boulevard*. He and his partner, Tom Hatcher, came backstage and Arthur was very complimentary. We sat and talked for about fifteen minutes. I was thrilled to meet this legendary man and even more thrilled that he took the time to come backstage.

Almost a month after Arthur and I talked about *Jolson Sings Again* at his town house in Manhattan, the producer called and made what I considered to be a very insulting offer. I don't know why he thought I would be willing to work for that amount of money. He said take it or leave it.

I left it. I soon found out that my doing so caused the project to collapse. I was in Montreal when I received a phone call from a very angry Arthur Laurents. He held me directly and personally responsible for torpedoing *Jolson Sings Again*. No amount of explanation on my part would calm him down. By the time he hung up on me, I was in tears, shaking.

Arthur never said so explicitly, but after that blow-up, I'd been told many times by others that he had banned me from all of his work. To be personally blacklisted by this towering figure of the American theatre was heartbreaking, but Lonny and Welz assured me that in terms of doing *Gypsy* at Ravinia, it was not an issue. Arthur had control over who appeared in full productions of his work, but not over concert productions.

I took a hiatus from *Sweeney Todd* to play Rose at Ravinia. We were actually given a longer rehearsal period than usual—three weeks, including the technical—which is still not a lot of time. I remember the night I arrived there. I agreed to start work as soon as I got off the plane. I didn't even check into the hotel. I was driven straight to the rehearsal room. Lonny was there with Paul Ford, the pianist, and Paul Gemignani, our conductor. We began working on a scene, and Lonny starting asking for immediate acting results.

There was a lot of pressure on me to deliver this role. Pretty much since *Evita,* and even more so since *Anything Goes,* people had been telling me that Madame Rose was the role I was born to play. I was putting pressure on myself, but I was unwilling to let Lonny put any added pressure on me—Lonny or anyone else, for that matter, living or dead. The ghost of Ethel Merman was surely hovering. Ethel was the original Rose. Even though I'd never seen her in the role, and even though other actresses had played the character in subsequent revivals, it was inevitable that many would compare my performance with hers.

Which was all the more reason I had to make Rose my own. I'd worked with Lonny many times before, and I knew that his job was to get this show on its feet in a very short period of time. Nevertheless, what he was doing was not helpful. As we began rehearsal that night, I thought he was pressing me for way too much, way too soon. As he continued to push, I built into a rage that culminated in a volcanic eruption. "What are you doing? I just got off the plane, I just opened my mouth, and already you want results? I will figure this out in time, but you cannot ask me to deliver results this minute."

During the rehearsal period it took my Herbie, Jack Willis, and me together to convince Lonny to ease up a little. "We're not stupid actors," we told him. "We know there's not a lot of time, but we've got to discover this organically. We'll figure it out." Lonny slowed down because he's an actor himself and trusted we would.

It all paid off. Audiences were ecstatic. The place was sold out. We had the Chicago Symphony Orchestra behind us. You rarely hear symphonic orchestras able to play a Broadway score, but under Paul Gemignani's baton, the orchestra came alive. I took my time and delivered a performance during which my heart was in my throat every minute. A lot of it I didn't fully understand yet—especially "Rose's Turn." I struggled with the choreography. We were handed the "approved" choreography from the Jerome Robbins estate, but I couldn't figure out how it came about, because on my body it made no sense. On Ethel's body, it did. Lonny helped me through it as best he could.

The buzz in the media and within the theatrical community was extremely positive. There was enough excitement generated around the possibility of seeing me continue to play Rose that several major producers bought tickets to fly to Chicago. Only one actually made it. Everybody else canceled because they were too scared to fly. The day before we opened, a terrorist plot to blow up ten commercial aircraft flying between London and New York had been uncovered. The one man who made it to see *Gypsy* at Ravinia was Jack Viertel, who wanted to mount a full production of the show as part of the Encores! series at City Center.

And that brought me full circle back to my problem with Arthur Laurents. If Arthur had barred me from performing his work, how could I appear in a full production as Rose at City Center, or indeed anywhere else? I called Philip Rinaldi, my press agent, who suggested I call Scott Rudin, Arthur's closest friend. I did. "Call Arthur," Scott said to me.

The last time I'd spoken with Arthur it had ended so badly that at first I was afraid to make the call. Having been yelled at like that, I didn't really want to go through it again. On the other hand, I knew what it felt like, so the element of surprise would be eliminated. The last time it had been a shock, but this time I'd be prepared for it, in case it happened again. I was already barred from his work—how much worse could it get? I had nothing to lose, and if I wanted to play Rose, it was a call I would have to make.

I summoned up all my courage, took a deep breath, and picked up the phone. When Arthur answered, he was gentle and soft-spoken. He complimented my performance as Mrs. Lovett in *Sweeney Todd*. Then he told me he wanted to talk about the future.

"Patti, I want you to come to New York, and you and I are going to sit down and have a nice, long talk," he said. "We're going to do *Gypsy*. I'm going to direct it myself, and I'm going to cast it with actors." There was no anger, no rancor. Just a loud thump when I fell to my knees in gratitude.

Holy shit! I said to myself. The phone had felt like it weighed a ton when I started to call him; I aged twenty-five years just picking it up. Now, with just a few kind words from Arthur, it was a feather, and that dark cloud of banishment that had been following me for several years just evaporated. What a gigantic relief! The phone call that I had dreaded so much turned out to be the beginning of a wonderful new chapter in my career, and in my relationship with Arthur Laurents.

When I got to New York, I was anxious. I was so vulnerable to the man. I really didn't know him, just his reputation. Walking into

Arthur's house, I fought off the memories of the last time I'd been there, when I agreed to do *Jolson*. But as Arthur spoke about what he wanted to accomplish with *Gypsy*, my fear dissolved.

I had to tell Lonny Price that he would not be directing *Gypsy*. "Is this about me?" he asked.

"No," I said. "It's about Arthur."

That was the absolute truth. During that first conversation in his home, Arthur told me why he had decided to do this. When I went to see him, Tom Hatcher, his life partner of more than fifty years, was already gravely ill. He passed away not long afterward. From his deathbed, Tom had told Arthur, "You have to direct *Gypsy*, and you have to do it with Patti." That was one of his dying wishes, but it was less about me than it was about Tom's desire to keep Arthur alive and creatively productive after he was gone.

Arthur decided to do the show out of the love that Tom had imparted to him over half a century. This is the love that Arthur then took and gave to all of us, an entire company of actors, around a table. It was a master class in storytelling, and a master class in respect.

Our rehearsal period started three weeks before opening night. Because of the expense, City Center would not give Arthur the entire cast for that length of time. Arthur asked instead for the eleven principals around a table for the first week and Jack Viertel agreed.

It was dicey at first. Arthur arrived at the initial read-through with his prompt book and his stage managers from the 1989 production of *Gypsy*, when Tyne Daly had played Rose. Using that prompt book as a blueprint, he began working with us. He gave us specific line readings and blocking: *This is how you get the joke; this is where you move; and no, that's not the line reading.* He was virtually replicating the 1989 show.

Why? Because you don't mess with success. I think that in Arthur's mind, the Tyne Daly *Gypsy* had been the last successful production. He pretty much disowned the Sam Mendes *Gypsy* from 2003. It was something of a risk to mount a *Gypsy* revival less than five years after the last one, and he wanted to stick with what worked. Arthur was almost ninety years old, and his age was a risk of its own. He wanted to make this *Gypsy* one he could be proud of, not just for his own legacy and sense of accomplishment, but as a way to honor Tom's dying wish as well.

That may explain why we started out handcuffed to the 1989 prompt book. As we continued to work from it, the actors started to mentally turn in and collapse. It is almost impossible to replicate another actor's performance. And we were all actors enough to put our own individual stamp on these timeless characters. Even though we were thwarted at practically every turn, Boyd Gaines (Herbie), Laura Benanti (Louise), and I continued to question Arthur relentlessly about our scenes. Our probing ignited Arthur the playwright to reinvestigate his script, which in turn ignited Arthur the director to redirect his play. As this process took hold, he tossed the old prompt book out and freed us up to explore. With Arthur's encouragement and guidance, we discovered our own line readings, and in the process he rediscovered the play he wrote.

Arthur's transformation was as speedy as it was remarkable. "This is already one of the best times I've ever had in the theatre," he told a reporter at the time. "I don't care what happens. It's worth it for this."

He grew younger by the day. I could see the light in his eyes. He went from trying to re-create *Gypsy* to "Let's see what happens."

And what happened was this miracle.

A whole new play emerged in Arthur's eyes. He kept saying it was coming out of love. And he stopped us from "acting." "You're acting," he'd say. "Stop acting. Just say it!"

You can imagine our surprise when in the middle of one of our readings he announced that *Gypsy* had never been rehearsed this way before. All eleven of our jaws dropped. "Excuse us?" we exclaimed, pretty much in unison. "What do you mean?"

We were shocked, but as we thought about it, we realized that's the way musicals are usually brought to the stage. Rehearsal time is precious, so only rarely does the company ever sit around a table and read the play.

And only rarely is the script from a musical worth the time. *Gypsy* was and is worth reading again and again. There is so much to discover. The scenes are layered and nuanced. The characters are complex and conflicted, Rose most of all. Many have called it the greatest American musical. Certainly it's got the greatest book of any American musical.

The eleven of us around the table dove joyously into those layers and nuances, and into the complexities of our characters. Not a note was sung. We spoke the lyrics. We gelled as an ensemble. We played off one another. We supported one another, so that everybody was allowed to fly. By the time the rest of the company joined in, *Gypsy* was a living, breathing thing, blooming and vibrant in each and every one of us.

Including Arthur. The more we rehearsed, the more Arthur would engage, the more he fell in love with theatre again. The more he fell in love with us as a company, the more he felt renewed as a human being. And he turned around and gave that all to us as we sat around the table.

There was so much love and laughter around that table. That single week of table reads was such an extraordinary time that I never wanted to go into performance. I didn't care if we were in rehearsal for the rest of my life. I did not want to leave this environment, where I was learning and laughing every single day.

This kind of experience is why I love the stage. For an actor it is exhilarating—and extremely rare—and to have had it twice in a row, first with *Sweeney* and now with *Gypsy,* was nothing short of phenomenal. Arthur and I formed a new and meaningful friendship. And, of course, he helped me deepen my portrayal of Rose.

If it ain't broke, don't fix it. I think the problem with characters that become iconic, the way Rose has, is that the portrayals can become petrified. Ethel Merman remains an incredibly powerful presence long after her passing, and her Rose has always been the gold standard. The temptation is to get out the cookie cutter and try to make every Rose thereafter do exactly what she did. For an actor, however, that quickly becomes stifling. It does a disservice to the show, because the performance seems rote—you may be in Rose's clothes, but you're not in her skin.

Actors' interpretations are highly subjective. You read the script; you're guided by the playwright's intentions, but then the development of the character is up to you. That's why so many great characters are universal: As long as they are fulfilling the needs of the story, most can be played in different ways. That's why we still love Shakespeare: His heroes and villains are truly timeless. Moreover, Shakespeare's characters give actors lots of choices in how they portray them.

Rose is that way as well. Arthur and I talked about her, and I was straightforward with him from the beginning. I told him that very first day that I would interpret her differently from how she had been in the past. It's not that I intentionally chose to play her in another way; it was far more than simply change for change sake. I actually read her differently within the context of the play. What I saw in Rose was not the "child-flattening maternal steamroller," as *New York Times* reviewer Ben Brantley described her. Reading the script, I kept seeing vulnerability and humanity—not that she wouldn't turn into a tigress at the drop of a hat, but I saw her humanity.

At one point Herbie calls her "a pioneer woman without a frontier." I suspect that what Rose Hovick herself faced in real life was close to the same thing. She was an independent woman with large dreams at a time when women were not independent or allowed to dream such inconceivable things. The tragedy of the play culminates in the ultimate scene with her daughter Gypsy, when she realizes and admits that this desperate attempt to make one of her girls a star was primarily coming from her own desire.

Opening night was July 9. We opened to a wildly enthusiastic full house. We were sold out for our entire three-week run. It took pride, respect, freedom, and bravery—and yes, a lot of love—to put this show together. It was an extraordinary experience. We were so well rehearsed, and Arthur had given us such freedom, such loving freedom. He was so proud of his actors. And we were proud of ourselves—we thought we'd done well. The producers had assured us that the production would be moving to Broadway.

Or not. Ben Brantley was less than enthusiastic, and my performance was in his crosshairs. Worse yet, the very thing I wanted most to project as Rose—her humanity—seemed to be what he disliked the most:

> *Ms. LuPone has endowed the thwarted Rose with charm, sensuality, a sense of humor, a startling lack of diva vanity and even a spark of bona fide mother love. She has given*

us a human Rose, with doubts and a nagging tug of self-awareness. But once you introduce such traits into Mama Rose, the air starts to leak out of her. Ms. LuPone is less a Rose of billboard-size flair and ego than the sort of pushy but likable woman you might compete with at the supermarket for that last perfect sole fillet.

Clearly, that was not what I was going for.

Gypsy

"Together, Wherever We Go." Kindred spirits, Laura Benanti and Boyd Gaines. PHOTO BY © PAUL KOLNIK

ypsy almost choked to death on that sole fillet.

Backstage in July 2007 on that City Center opening night, the producers for the Broadway production had been so excited. The show felt right on stage. It felt right out front, too. The audience gave us a standing ovation, not just on opening night, but on every night of our brief three-week run. All of us were so sure we were going to Broadway.

Then came the Ben Brantley "sole fillet" review.

It's a sad reality in my business that one review matters so much, but that's the way it is. From Brooks Atkinson to Clive Barnes to Walter Kerr to Frank Rich to Ben Brantley, the *New York Times* critics and their reviews have been make-or-break for Broadway shows and actors for decades. No other publication carries as much weight.

After the Brantley review came out it looked like there would be no move to Broadway. The Encores! production at City Center would be the end of the road for *Gypsy* and this magnificent company. Arthur and I made a personal plea to producer Roger Berlind, who said to us, "You would have to be crazy to bring *Gypsy* to Broadway after a review like that." The second time he said that to me over the phone, I said, "Roger, you give the critics the power. If you don't want to do it, that's one thing, but if you don't want to do it because of a critic, then why bother producing anything? I can't guarantee you a good review," I said. "If you look at my history with the *New York Times,* this is nothing new. I can only do what I do and you've seen that. You've seen this extraordinary production and cast, and you've seen how the audience reacts. Trust your instincts and don't give critics the power." I felt like I was speaking for every actor who had ever been in a good show that closed because of one bad *New York Times* review.

The producers truly loved Arthur's production. Ultimately they had more confidence in what they had seen with their own eyes than they had in Mr. Brantley's critique. *Gypsy* would be moving to the St. James Theatre on West Forty-fourth Street. Opening night was set for March 27, 2008. Previews began March 3.

Rehearsals began February 4. The first day back, we had a meet-and-greet before we had a read-through around the table. We stood in a circle, said our names and what part we were playing—except Arthur, who just said, "Hello, everybody!" as Baby June. He was in great spirits. We read through the play, and by the end of the day Arthur was energized. It was great to see and a powerful lesson to us all.

The cast that gathered around the table was virtually identical to the Encores! production. The only change was Lenora Nemetz, who took over the roles of Miss Cratchit and Mazeppa from Nancy Opel, who'd chosen to go out on the road with *The Drowsy Chaperone.* Lenora was a great addition. We'd been friends for thirty years, since we were both in Stephen Schwartz's

Working and Bill Finn's *America Kicks Up Its Heels,* two bombs straight from hell.

There was a gap of six months between the closing of the En-cores! production and the beginning of rehearsals for Broadway. There's something to be said for letting a role rest. When we re-sumed rehearsals, I was deeper into Rose—or she was deeper into me. It must have something to do with reflection and confidence.

I still struggled with "Rose's Turn." Arthur and I spent a lot of intense time on it. We'd work on it for an hour before the company was called. In that hour I would do it six times at least. I knew what it was saying, but I didn't understand the choreography. I didn't understand the striptease in the middle of it. I thought if Rose was trying to prove she was equal to or better than Gypsy, then why wasn't she doing June's number? It was her creation. Granted, a striptease is sexier than a cartwheel, but Rose says to Gypsy in the penultimate scene, "You need something to remind you that your goal was to be a great actress, not a cheap stripper." Why then does she imitate Gypsy's strip in the song? She had just denigrated Gypsy. The "Rose's Turn" lyrics and the choreography were contradicting each other, I thought. The song is a massive breakdown and reckoning. This end-of-play monumental actor's turn was my monumental actor's block.

In rehearsal, Arthur was totally flexible in allowing me to take it out as far as I could in order to find my way back to the center and make it my own, to use my own understanding of this break-down, this angry collapse and resurgence. Our choreographer, be-loved Bonnie Walker, was the one who really allowed me to break free from the Robbins choreography. Bonnie and I were together for all three productions, from Ravinia to City Center to Broad-way. She saw me struggle at Ravinia. She knew I would eventu-ally get it, but she freed me by throwing out the dance steps that blocked me. She was so generous with me, for which I will always be grateful.

When Arthur started directing me, he supplied insight into Rose's thought process because he wrote it! Thank God for that information. Once it was established that the dance steps could be reinvented within the guidelines of the approved choreography, the number started to evolve and make sense to me. It took me as long as I played Rose to understand this great—and I mean great—theatrical moment in American musical history. I started to understand the strip . . . but understand it my way. It has to be said again: It's almost impossible to "re-create" a role if it doesn't come from one's own gut and heart and brain.

I was stuck in the telling of the story and telling the story is my primary responsibility. I have to start at the beginning: What is the playwright saying? What is the journey? Why is my character there? Once I have all that information, then generally the lines start to make sense and the character becomes apparent and I'm free. It's a sticky feeling to be onstage confused, not knowing what you're playing. *Gypsy* is so well written but it's a very tricky play. With probing came the knowledge and with the knowledge came the freedom.

Our freedom came straight from Arthur Laurents. He attacked his direction of this piece once he trusted us. I'll never forget the day Arthur let me cut the reprise of "Small World" in the second-act dressing room scene. This was in the Encores! rehearsal period. He trusted me enough to know that my lack of understanding wasn't just a dense actress (although I've been known to be that), but that something was getting in my way and impeding the story. I knew what it was but I couldn't say what I was thinking. The playwright was in the room. He saw me continually stumble in the same spot.

"Is the song getting in the way?" he asked.

"Yes," I told him. "I don't know why it's there."

"Do you want to cut it?"

"Can we at least try it?"

He said yes. *Holy shit!* I thought. *I'm cutting the reprise.* Arthur was allowing it to be cut because he, too, saw that it slowed down the impetus of the play. We were nearing the end of the story. Why were we breaking the action to sing a ballad? Sure enough, the minute it was cut, the scene flew seamlessly into the next scene and I got to the line "And you are going to be a star!" faster and with more urgency.

So why was it there in the first place? Arthur explained that Ethel needed something to sing in the second act. That made sense, and it probably worked well for her, but to keep things alive in the theatre, especially a revival of an almost fifty-year-old musical, it has to be imbued with life. It can't be revered to the point that it becomes a mausoleum.

The casting of Boyd Gaines as Herbie was a kiss from the gods. Besides being a great actor, Boyd is a sage. A lot of our company was young. This company rarely missed a performance or took the notorious "personal day." Every night on the stage all of the players were alive and performing at a hundred percent. Boyd said that Arthur gave everybody ownership of their roles, however large or small. Boyd is another Juilliard graduate, a generous human being, and a consummate gentleman. He is also an intelligent actor. Boyd was praised for portraying Herbie as a man, not just a cardboard backdrop for Rose. It's all true and so much more. Boyd was a true acting partner. We worked together like a dream. In rehearsals, he also had some sort of sixth sense about what I was trying to ask for or explain. When I fumbled, got emotional, and couldn't talk or couldn't explain, I'd turn to him and he would succinctly put into words what I was trying to say. He did so effortlessly. He just knew my mind. He is the most diplomatic person I've ever encountered in this business. He was our leader onstage and off. I cannot wait for the next time I'm onstage with Boyd Gaines.

And then there was Laura Benanti—Louise. I didn't know Laura before this, but we became sisters and friends. Laura is beautiful, very funny, too smart for show business, and a talent to be reckoned with. Boyd, Laura, and I took the freedom that Arthur gave us, and then gave one another permission to be free with each other. That is a big and very brave step for actors: to give permission to be free, without fear. It's a generosity that is rare.

Celebrated Broadway director Jack O'Brien said to The Acting Company ensemble when he was rehearsing *The Time of Your Life*, "Fly, I'll catch you." It refers to danger and taking risks onstage. That's what Boyd, Laura, and I were doing. I was flying, they were catching; they were flying, I was catching. The farther I had to reach for them, the more fun I had. Freedom and danger onstage—there's nothing better. Why act otherwise?

That's what we had, and that's what helped create what was undoubtedly the happiest company I've ever been a part of. I've never seen a crew and a cast comingle and care for one another the way this company and crew did. There was just a lot of love, and a lot of fun backstage. You saw people laughing with one another before they went on. And it was not out of disrespect; it was out of this wonderful working environment. It's so rare to see that kind of thing happen. That's the way it's supposed to be. And the Sunday brunches, headed by Robert Guy, that our wardrobe department would lay on! It was a Sunday gathering at the altar of food for the last show of the week. Everybody brought something in and we ate like piglets, socialized, and wished one another a good show and good day off. Those little Broadway traditions—Sunday brunches, notes passed back and forth from theatre to theatre, the dimming of the Broadway lights when a colleague has died, the theatre ghosts, the Gypsy robe, the Broadway softball league—I love Broadway.

At one point during the Broadway rehearsal period, Lenora Nemetz grabbed Arthur and me and took us to another floor at the New 42nd Street Studios. The three of us walked into a rehearsal room where two actors were working, but these weren't just any two actors: Chita Rivera and George Hearn were rehearsing *The Visit* in preparation for an opening in D.C. in May.

Everyone in the room was happily connected to everyone else via theatre experiences and bonds of affection that stretched over decades. George, of course, was my beloved first Sweeney and my Frederik in *A Little Night Music* at Ravinia. When Arthur directed *La Cage aux Folles*, George portrayed Albin. Chita Rivera was Arthur's original Anita in *West Side Story*. Lenora was Chita's cover in the original production of *Chicago*. It was a heartfelt reunion filled with genuine affection, camaraderie, and Broadway history.

Rehearsal flew by, and as the technical week was approaching, we ran the show for the St. James Theatre department heads. After Tony Yazbeck, who played Tulsa, did "All I Need Is the Girl," Arthur said to me, "Now I know why I cry every time I watch this number. Jerry Robbins didn't much like the song and delayed in choreographing it. I made Jerry work on it one day, so he and I rehearsed it on the roof of the New Amsterdam. Jerry made me play Louise. It was the first time in my life that I danced. It took me forty years to realize why I cry every time I see it. I don't dance and Jerry made me dance. To me, it's the greatest dance number choreographed in the musical theatre."

We moved into the St. James, where the production fit like a jewel on the stage. The St. James is a blessed little place, supposedly haunted with its own ghost. The St. James is also where Arthur directed Tyne Daly in *Gypsy*—a very good omen.

We were well into previews when Arthur said out loud what must never be said inside a theatre: He uttered the actual title of the Shakespearean tragedy we call "the Scottish Play."

Theatre people are notoriously superstitious, and saying the name *Macbeth* backstage or in a dressing room is the biggest, darkest superstition of them all. It's taken seriously with good reason. Actors can tell tales of accidents and close calls after someone uttered the word. Soon it began happening to us, too. Things started to go wrong. The curtains got snarled in the "Rose" light at the end of "Rose's Turn." Sami Gayle, our Baby June, fractured her pelvis warming up and missed the Broadway opening. This was serious stuff, and something had to be done before there were any more mishaps. Lenora pulled me aside and was adamant that Arthur break the curse. She had a deep look of concern on her face, as if she'd be next in the line of injuries.

The ritual to break the curse of the Scottish Play is very specific, and more than a little peculiar. In accordance with the time-honored procedure, I made Arthur go outside onto West Forty-fourth Street, only because that's where I found him backstage—right next to the door. It was almost thirty minutes before we were due to go on. He was baffled at my insistence that he go through this ritual. He was outside on the street and I told him through the closed door to turn around counterclockwise three times, spit over his left shoulder, curse, then knock on the door and ask to come back in. Well, we heard him swear like a drunken sailor, even though there was a line of ticket holders standing next to the door, intrigued or horrified by the sight of Arthur Laurents spinning, spitting, and swearing. But it had the desired effect, and the spell was broken.

We never did see the blue lady in the mezzanine—the ghost of the St. James, that is. It may be one of Broadway's most haunted houses, but it's now my favorite theatre.

One night after the show, Bernie Gersten and his wife, Cora Cahan, took Stephen Daldry and me to Orso for supper. As he was leaving, Joel Schumacher came to our table and complimented me. He'd seen the show that night. He then told us a story about the making of the movie *Phantom of the Opera*. According to Joel, at one point during the casting process Andrew Lloyd Webber suggested that I should play Carlotta.

"But Andrew," Joel explained patiently, "she doesn't talk to you."

"Oh yes," Andrew replied. "There *is* that."

We opened the show again to near-hysterical audiences. I got through it as best I could, just really grateful that we were now open and hoping we'd settle into a run. All my dearest friends who always show up on my openings were there. I love them for putting up with the utter chaos of openings and the after-party, which I abhor.

Ben Brantley's review for *Gypsy* at the St. James was as much of a rave as one could ask for:

> Watch out, New York. Patti LuPone has found her focus. And when Ms. LuPone is truly focused, she's a laser, she incinerates. Especially when she's playing someone as dangerously obsessed as Mama Rose in the wallop-packing revival of the musical Gypsy, *which opened Thursday night at the St. James Theater. . . . And yes, that quiet crunching sound you hear is me eating my hat. . . .*
>
> When Ms. LuPone delivers "Rose's Turn," she's building a bridge for an audience to walk right into one woman's nervous breakdown. There is no separation at all between song and character, which is what happens in those uncommon

moments when musicals reach upward to achieve their ideal reasons to be.

Once in a while you get a review worth reading yourself.

Scott Wittman told me to send Mr. Brantley a hat after the review came out. It was a chocolate cowboy hat in a very pretty hatbox. I wanted to eat it myself and keep the hatbox.

With our great reviews, ticket sales skyrocketed. We played this great musical joyously.

When the Tony nominations were announced in May, I was not surprised to be nominated, but I was afraid to hope for anything more. I'd been disappointed twice before. Everyone had told me I was "a cinch" as Reno Sweeney, and "a lock" for Mrs. Lovett. Well, this turned out to be my year, and on June 17, 2008, David Hyde Pierce opened the envelope and read my name.

During the weeks leading up to this moment, Pat White and I had started writing acceptance speeches for a laugh. They were pretty funny, but it was Jeff Richman who wrote the first line: "It's such a wonderful gift to be an actor who makes her living working on the Broadway stage—and then every thirty years or so, pick up one of these!"

The long time between speeches left me with three decades of people to thank, and very little time to do it. Toward the end of what they thought should have been my allotted time onstage, the orchestra started to play me off.

I couldn't stop where the director of the TV show wanted me to stop. I still had very important people to acknowledge, including Boyd and Laura, both of whom also won Tonys that night, and the real Rose Hovick, without whom none of this would have happened. I did forget to thank my terrific musical director,

Patrick Vaccariello, so I'll thank him here. It could be another twenty-eight years before I stand on that stage again, and I'll be drooling by then.

Playing Rose eight times a week demanded stamina, both physical and emotional. I could handle the singing, but it was emotionally draining and physically exhausting. If I wasn't running, I was singing; if I wasn't singing, I was shouting. I was expected to deliver this role, and if truth be told, I was already at least fifteen years too old for it. It took every ounce of energy and strength this little Sicilian engine could muster . . . and then some.

But this was the time I was given to play it. I knew I wouldn't fail in the delivery of it, but I was worried about failing in the physicality of it.

I didn't want to admit the frailty, but about six months into the run, I hit the wall. I went to a nutritionist, Oz Garcia, to sort out my health, because I didn't think I was going to make it. Oz changed my eating habits and put me on a lot of supplements. I don't know what I would've done if the choreographer, Gillian Lynne, hadn't sent me to Oz. My body energy changed radically and I ended the run physically stronger than when I started it.

It still took every ounce of energy. Boyd and I would come offstage during the Grantziger scene in the first act gasping for air. It was our age, but it was also the intense emotional outpouring of both of these characters. We had a sweet ritual before the show. I'd come down the stairs at the places call and he'd be waiting for me outside of his dressing room. We kissed each other, and then came the inevitable question, followed by the equally inevitable answer:

"Did you sleep last night?"

"No."

"Neither did I."

I was wired to beat the band. I'm high energy, but I needed

*Arthur told me not to
cry in this scene. It was
so hard to do. He was
so right.*

© JOAN MARCUS

double my energy to play Rose, and the energy that wasn't burned
off onstage kept me going till at least 3:30 A.M. But nervous energy
or not, lack of sleep or not, when I met Boyd for the traditional
hug and kiss, I knew that when I saw him onstage in our first
meeting, he would infuse me with all the strength, energy, laughter, challenge, and love I needed because we had so much fun out
there. It was a great game we played every night and everything
informed our performances, as it should be. The show was never
the same, which was fine by Arthur. At one note session he said to
us, "It's never the same but it's always right."

At the end of September 2008, it suddenly began to look
like the world, at least the financial world, was coming to an end.
The stock market was in free fall and it wasn't long before the
economic meltdown turned into blood on all the streets in the

Theatre District. Because times had become uncertain, people stopped buying theatre tickets in the same way that they stopped buying everything else that wasn't absolutely necessary.

Virtually every production on Broadway started hemorrhaging red ink—the biggest hits, the best shows, including *Gypsy*. We had been playing to sold-out houses. When I started seeing empty seats, then lots of empty seats, I knew the handwriting was on the wall. We were one of eleven shows that closed in the first two months of the year. Instead of closing in March, as planned, it was announced that we would close on January 11, 2009, seven weeks ahead of schedule. Even though it was hardly unexpected, it was painful to think that this extraordinary company would be disbanding. We played the rest of the month in a kind of denial. There were tears and then there was laughter. There were long faces and mournful sighs and then out on the stage these troupers went with their biggest smiles. As they say in the song:

> *There may be streets that have their sorrow*
> *A smile today a tear tomorrow*
> *But there's a street that lives in glory*
> *It always tells the same old story*
>
> *Don't bring a frown to old Broadway*
> *You've got to clown on Broadway*
> *Your troubles there are out of style*
> *'Cause Broadway always wears a smile*
> *A million lights they flicker there*
> *A million hearts beat quicker there*
> *No skies of grey on the Great White Way*
> *That's the Broadway Melody*

January 11, 2009: It was an unforgettable closing night.

Epilogue

Closing Night, *Gypsy*

BROADWAY, JANUARY 2009

O pening nights are like a little death because the nerves can literally take minutes off your life.

Closing nights *are* a little death. It is the end of a theatrical experience, of the atmosphere onstage and off, of the interaction with the audience, the interaction with the characters, of the camaraderie among the players, the Sunday brunches, the practical jokes, the corpsing onstage, the missed lines—the life in the theatre.

My closing nights for *Gypsy* were extraordinary events. I don't remember the Patio Players closing night, just that damn sheep. I do remember Ravinia, City Center, and the St. James closing nights. Ravinia's was frenzied because there were only three performances. Friends and strangers alike covered the lawn and filled every seat of the Pavilion Theatre to see the show. I remember hearing the applause but it's a vast theatre—more like an amphitheatre. You can see the first couple of rows—then you *feel* everyone else. There were thousands of people on closing night. Three performances of any show are more exhausting than an eight-show week, and I left Ravinia wrung out and needing a month's vacation.

City Center's closing night was the same kind of madness. I'm a New Yorker, and fellow New Yorkers showed up to say farewell to my Rose. After that Brantley review, I'm sure they thought it was farewell for good.

The City Center Theatre, which is in excess of two thousand seats, was packed to the rafters. Each song delivered by each character was met with thunderous applause. The curtain call was deafening. People were standing and cheering. When I came out for my call—well, let's just say I was grateful to be alive. It had been arranged that Arthur and Stephen would take a bow. They left their seats in the house, made their way onto the stage, and turned to face the audience. The roof blew off. The company surrounded them, we all took our final bow, and then another bow, and then another bow. The audience would not let us leave the stage. Craig Jacobs, our stage manager, did something so inherently theatrical. I just love it when people maintain tradition in the theatre. He did not bring the curtain in. The curtain never closed on City Center's *Gypsy*.

We all walked off the stage amidst the still-cheering crowd. I said my farewells and went with my husband and son back home to Connecticut, exhausted, elated, and wondering what the future had in store. *Gypsy* was done. . . . but not really.

The closing night of *Gypsy* at the St. James Theatre on January 11, 2009, was perhaps the most extraordinary closing night I have ever been a part of. I had prepared for this day for a month. I'd moved pretty much everything out of the apartment that the company had rented for me. There were just bits and pieces left. A couple of days earlier, I cried myself to sleep and then slept like a baby, which I hadn't done in months.

I'd moved everything out of my dressing room as well—the opening night gifts and the accumulation of ten months of *Gypsy* souvenirs. The rooms were barren but not the walls because wherever a picture had hung I drew a replica in Magic Marker with little quotes underneath, such as "Here was Ethel Merman" or "My Orpheum stock runneth out." People coming into my dressing room during those final performances could literally see the writing on the walls.

I went to the theatre in preparation for the same onslaught I experienced opening night. Closing nights are equally as busy as opening nights. There are flowers, champagne, cards, and tears. I got there in plenty of time to get made up and costumed so that I could hug and kiss my beloved company and the St. James backstage crew farewell. My son, Josh, who had spent the summer with me, engulfed in the backstage life, was visibly upset. According to Josh, it was the best summer he'd ever had and now it was over. He had tasted the magic and the heartbreak of Broadway.

Steve came to my dressing room and chatted with everybody there. He found a cute hat on my couch, put it on, and left with it. Choreographer Joey Pizzi has been too scared to ask for it back ever since. Matt and Josh stayed as long as they could, then Matt took his seat and Josh stayed backstage for one last poker game in the men's dressing room. My friends hugged and kissed me and took their seats. Arthur came in and vowed we'd do this again. We had weary tears in our eyes. Places was called. Laura, Boyd, and I refused to say good-bye. We just silently hugged each other. I took my position, as I had done for ten months, at the back of the house, house right, with my dresser standing next to me, and Margaret the usher making sure the path was clear for my entrance down the aisle.

When my cue came, I said my line, "Sing out, Louise," and started down the aisle. The theatre erupted. Baby June (Sami Gayle) and Baby Louise (Katie Micha) were facing the audience and I could see Katie crying uncontrollably. When I reached the stage, I shielded my two little friends. As the ovation continued, with my back to the audience, I cupped their chins and said, "No tears, no tears, no tears." When we were able to begin the play, it took every ounce of energy I had to keep the play onstage. It was turning into a grand and glorious free-for-all in that theatre. But we played our play as we had rehearsed it around that table with Arthur at the helm, with one small difference: In each scene, if it was the last scene we played with a particular character, we said our farewells to each other. My last scene with Boyd broke my heart. My last scene with Laura broke it again. I was a bloody mess by the time I got to "Rose's Turn" and drew on the very last ounce of energy I had to turn it out, knowing it was the last time I would be doing this monumental actor's turn, now unblocked and wildly free. The release on a closing night is extraordinary. Every acting dilemma, every confusing plot point, every bad staging issue is resolved, and the liberation one has in a final performance informs a character more than eight times a week for ten months does. The irony.

*Onstage at the
St. James with
Arthur Laurents.*

Our curtain call was festooned with roses upon roses upon roses. I picked up as many as I could and gave each company member a flower. Boyd, Laura, and I were holding hands for moral support, but each of us was hanging by a thread, barely keeping it together. Then Arthur and Steve came onstage. Again, it was an overwhelming moment, a truly historic moment, one that would never be repeated. *Gypsy* is unlikely to be revived anytime soon.

The ovation lasted more than twenty minutes. We remained onstage well into our stagehands' golden overtime. This was an event nobody in that building ever wanted to forget—the audience, ushers, stagehands, and cast. The curtain rang down on this *Gypsy.*

Behind the main drape, we all remained onstage. There were bittersweet hugs and kisses, a champagne toast to Arthur, then tears and bowed heads as people disappeared into the woodwork.

I miss this company more than I can say. I have never experienced such talent, dedication, goodwill, and generosity. I treasure the memory of our table reads, of watching the actors, from character men to children to young adults, listening to Arthur, absorbing every single word he said, then watching scenes being investigated, watching us fail, watching us succeed. I will never forget the actors making their Broadway debuts with starstruck awe in their eyes. Their gratitude and desire came onstage every single night. Nobody ever phoned it in, ever.

I know that *Gypsy* will remain one of if not *the* best experiences I've ever had in my career.

I don't normally finish a run. I usually leave it before the show closes because of how emotionally painful a closing can be. (Of course, that's still no guarantee it won't be painful—again, see the *Sunset Boulevard* chapters.) But I was proud and thrilled to have been on that St. James stage closing night. Theatre memories are precious to me—the only thing a stage actor has, really (besides stolen bits of the producer's property)—and this one was a big one.

How ironic that this show, one that initially generated the most theatrical controversy for me, turned out to be the most blissful production, the kind everybody lives for. And if you choose a life on the stage, my wish for you is the kind of experience I had—the kind of experience we all had—in this show.

Coda

I have been incredibly fortunate over the course of my career to have been associated with some extraordinary dramatic and musical productions, and also some rather spectacular disasters. Looking back, I can find gifts and life lessons in every one—even the flops.

From Esther Scott and the Northport music department, I got the nurturing I needed, and the confidence in my talent to make it my lifework. From Juilliard and John Houseman, I got perseverance, versatility, resourcefulness, and the ultimate actor's training. From The Acting Company, I learned about life on the road, gaining years of technique that would serve me the rest of my career, life with my first love, and eventually, *The Robber Bridegroom.*

From *The Baker's Wife,* I learned the true meaning of the phrase "The show must go on," and on and on and on. As dysfunctional and emotionally debilitating as *The Baker's Wife* was, I would not have had the gift of "Meadowlark," one of my signature songs, without it.

Encouraging me to abandon the idea of "acting" and to trust the script to do the work, David Mamet's sage advice to live your life and ply your craft and keep the separation clean, has truly been a touchstone.

Evita made me a star, but it took its toll on every part of my being. Its lessons were often hurtful, but ultimately rewarding and highly valuable. With Mandy Patinkin I perfected the art of roping in skeptical audiences who dared us to be worth the money. I learned what happens when one is sucked into the Andrew Lloyd Webber musical machinery . . . and eventually I learned how not to be ground to bits by its relentlessly turning gears. But I was also given the gift of another signature song—"Don't Cry for Me, Argentina."

With *Les Misérables,* I was linked to the priceless connection between the long and revered history of the acting profession in England and my training at Juilliard. I also learned not to lose track of time in the dressing room between appearances onstage. With *LBJ,* I was given one of the greatest gifts of my life—my husband, Matt.

From *Anything Goes,* I learned how universally healing laughter can be when it rings in a theatre. (And Matt and I learned to always build the house *before* you get married.) From *Life Goes On,* I learned that even in unpleasant circumstances quality work can still be done and great friendships can be formed. On

LGO the other greatest gift of my life was given to me—my son, Joshua.

With *Sunset Boulevard*, the lesson was reinforced that whatever doesn't kill you makes you stronger—but not until it almost kills you first. Almost. In the midst of huge emotional pain, I was rescued by the outpouring of love from the audience, my cast mates, and my friends who flew to London just to put their arms around me.

I learned that when you're hurting, it's all too easy to lash out at those who love you—and that it's not easy to stop, even when you finally realize that's what you're doing. I learned that the people who love you will continue to love you, stand by you, and help you get through it.

There is a silver lining, and sometimes its name is Welz Kauffman. Welz gave me not only the chance to play Nellie Lovett in *Sweeney Todd*, but also the gift of a string of fantastic opportunities to perform the works of Stephen Sondheim.

Welz brought me to Chicago to play Rose several summers ago, which eventually led to a happy and heartfelt reconciliation between Arthur Laurents and me. A magnificent gift if ever there was one.

From there, *Gypsy* became the gift that kept on giving—in the relationships with other actors in the company, with Stephen Sondheim, and with Arthur himself.

And after all these years and all those experiences, I've never wavered from my love and dedication to the craft of acting and the belief in the value theatre holds in our culture. Whether you're in the audience or on the stage, theatre is eternally transportive and transformational, allowing the soul to breathe and the spirit to rejuvenate.

The wonderful actress Patricia Elliott sent me a William Butler Yeats quote that says it about as well as anything:

What is there left for us, that have seen the newly discovered stability of things changed from an enthusiasm to a weariness, but . . . to rediscover an art of the theatre that shall be

> *joyful,*
> *fantastic,*
> *extravagant,*
> *whimsical,*
> *beautiful,*
> *resonant,*
> *and altogether RECKLESS.*

Acknowledgments

AMY RENNERT, my literary agent and the reason this book exists.

SHAYE AREHEART, my editor and publisher, the reason this *actual* book exists with pages and a cover, and SUZANNE O'NEILL, for the finishing touches.

DIGBY DIEHL, for the blueprint and the way forward—a true gentleman.

JEFFREY RICHMAN, for so many words, so much laughter, so much love.

PHILIP RINALDI, my friend and beloved press agent, whose job protecting and defending my reputation would've killed a lesser man.

PHILIP CAGGIANO, my oldest pal and source of many recovered memories.

KATRIN HALL, the last stop before turning this book in, for her invaluable input.

TIMOTHY JEROME and KURT PETERSON, my *Baker's Wife* cast mates and fellow survivors who bore witness to the insanity of that time and helped me laugh about it.

KIMBERLY RIMBOLD of Actors' Equity, who patiently explained David Merrick's proposed A, B, C, D.

PETER MARINOS, my *Evita descamisado* who remembered the Casa Rosada better than I did.

ESTHER SCOTT, my teacher and inspiration.

Joan Lader, the angel who saved my voice and taught me how to sing.

My teachers from the Juilliard Drama Division, who shared their knowledge and gave me the foundation for a life in the theatre.

The genius Ethan Hill for the cover photograph.

Sylvia Grieser, stylist; Angelina Avallone, makeup artist; Clariss Morgan, hairdresser; and Laura Duffy, jacket designer, for making me look so great on the cover.

Barbara Sturman, for her exquisite design of this book.

All the wonderful theatre photographers who have documented my career:

Stephanie Berger

Donald Cooper

Fritz Curzon

Joseph Giannetti

Diane Gorodnitzki

Russell Jenkins

Paul Kolnik

Brigitte Lacombe

David J. Lans

Michael Le Poer Trench

Joan Marcus

Robert Millard

Jack Mitchell

Jim Steere

Martha Swope

Richard Termine

Gary Gersh, my theatrical agent.

Daisy DeCoster, my archivist.

Bruce Glikas, for recording the celebrations.

Index

Page numbers in *italics* refer to photographs.